Elephants
and the
Business Laws
of Nature

and how to manage them to help you and
your business realise full potential

John Vamos
Karen McCreadie

First published in 2010

Copyright © 2000–2010 John Vamos and Karen McCreadie

All rights reserved. This publication is copyright and may not be reproduced or transmitted in any form or by any means, electronic or mechanical (except excerpted for *bona fide* study purposes in accordance with the *Copyright Act 1968*) without the prior written consent of the Publisher.

Every effort has been made to ensure that this book is free from error or omissions. However, the Publisher, the Authors, the Editor, or their respective employees or agents, shall not accept responsibility for injury, loss or damage occasioned to any person acting or refraining from action as a result of material in this book whether or not such injury, loss or damage is in any way due to any negligent act or omission, breach of duty or default on the part of the Publisher, the Authors, the Editor, or their respective employees or agents.

Publisher
Institute of Organisational Coaching Pty Limited
ABN 60125 207 383

National Library of Australia
Cataloguing-in-Publications entry: (Submission pending)

>   Vamos, John
>   Elephants and the Business Laws of Nature
>   ... *and how to manage them to help you and your business realise full potential*

ISBN 978–0–9808071–0–3

1. Thinking System. 2. Performance improvement. 3. Organisational coaching.
4. The elephant metaphor. 5. Workgroup methodologies. 6. Business planning

I. McCreadie, Karen, II. Title.
Cover Design: XOUCREATIVE

Illustrations by Lesley Vamos
Set in 11.25/16 pt Adobe Caslon Pro by Bookhouse, Sydney
Printed by Griffin Press

Acknowledgement

We would like to thank:
- All the clients of BCS and the 30,000-plus people who have been the beneficiaries of our processes. Their contribution helped make the conclusions in this book possible.
- The BCS Coaches who supported the evolution and showed respect for the methods that *Thinking Systems* unlock in all of us.

Contents

Acknowledgement   iii
Foreword   vii
Author's Foreword   ix
Preface   xiii

Introduction   1

Part One   The Elephant Metaphor

1. The Performance Gap   18
2. Enter the Elephant   27
3. A Very Expensive Elephant   36

Part Two   The Elephant Deconstructed

4. Default Settings or Your Elephant Is Lazy   47
5. The Greatest Default of All or Your Elephant Is Pessimistic   59
6. Emotion and Reality Are Mutually Exclusive or Your Elephant Is Moody!   65
7. Language Has No Unambiguous Dictionary or Your Elephant Isn't Verbal   80
8. Your Elephant is Unqualified for Business   99
9. It's Not All About the Elephant   104

Part Three   Managing Your Elephant Through Smart Thinking

10. Binary Thinking   122
11. The Thinking System   132
12. The Thinking System in Action   150
13. Questions – The Essence of the Thinking System   160
14. Three Examples of Business Thinking Systems   178

Part Four   Managing Other People's Elephants Through Smart Working Dynamics

15	Setting the Scene for Taking on the Task	194
16	Business Law of Nature 1: Design = Ownership = Motivation	203
17	Business Law of Nature 2: Know Every Other Player's Position	213
18	Business Law of Nature 3: In Time Right Becomes Wrong	221
19	Business Law of Nature 4: Everybody Has a Right to Know the Score	228
20	Business Laws of Nature 5: Business Is a Shortcut to an Outcome	237
21	Business Law of Nature 6: Only Do What Only You Should Do – *Lead*	244
22	Overcoming the Elephant by Engineering Virtuous Circles	258

About the Authors	263
Bibliography and Notes	266
Index	269

Foreword

Professor Stewart Clegg
School of Management, University of Technology, Sydney

I am a sociologist. That's my discipline. I am also a Business School professor in a School of Management. That's my job. Many times I have wondered why so much management theory is bad sociology (because it fails to connect with what people actually do when they do management) and why so few sociologists seem interested in what it is that managers ordinarily do. When they do get interested, they often seem to do it for all the wrong reasons, to apply some or other grand theory, some prescriptive viewpoint, to what people do.

There is one brand of sociology I have always had a soft spot for, more than any other, that has always eschewed grand theory, and that is one known as *ethnomethodology*. Horrible name, isn't it? But it is quite descriptive. It means, literally, 'folk methods' – the methods that people ordinarily use to make sense in their everyday lives. Its progenitor, Harold Garfinkel, was deeply immersed in studying what he saw as the methods of everyday life; the myriad ordinary ways in which, through which, by which, people make sense of each other and their doings.

John Vamos shares one profound insight with this branch of social science: that there is no need to step outside of everyday knowledge to tell people how to do what they do – otherwise they wouldn't be able to do it. Sometimes, however, one needs to be able to bring how it is that people are able to do what they do to their attention, consciously, so they can do it better.

People always know a lot more than they can say and they always have great depths of knowledge about what they do. And sometimes they don't know what it is that they do know: their knowledge is too tacit, too taken-for-granted, such that they are unable to easily explicate the grounds that make possible all they do and all they *could* do. The gap between what they do and what they could do is not one that is best plugged by what they don't know and that someone else – a management consultant, guru, or a lecturer – does know. It is best plugged by making explicit all they do know and draw on, in doing what they usually do. Nobody knows their business better than they do. This is the fundamental insight of this book.

Over a number of years, together with colleagues at the Centre for Management and Organisation Studies at the University of Technology, Sydney, I have been researching the field of Business Coaching (see Clegg *et al* 2005; 2007)[1,2]. While there are many offers in the marketplace, our findings are that none is as distinctive as, nor more useful in terms of business improvement, than the methodology of organisational coaching that John Vamos has pioneered. Having watched his coaching in action, we can see the sequences of questions that have been devised act as prompts to unlock potentials that were already there but otherwise lying dormant.

What the book provides is a way of unlocking all the taken-for-granted and tacit knowledge, the constitutive grounds that we all already have but either don't recognise or know about, yet implicitly trade off in our everyday business life. This book will help you devise those Thinking Systems through techniques that anyone can learn and apply and profit from.

Think of this book as an *ethnomethodology* for everyday business life. Apply it to your business life. And profit from what you already know but did not know you knew, which this book will help you discover.

Author's Foreword

To illustrate the fundamental thrusts and purposes of this book, we begin with a reminder: Nobody thinks driving while drunk is clever. In fact it's stupid and downright irresponsible. Yet most of us have probably done it. If we haven't, we may have at least been somewhat intoxicated at times.

Why we drink and drive is easy to explain: we make the decision to drive when we are in no condition to decide anything at all – often late at night. And, as any sports coach will tell their young team: nothing good happens after midnight.

The part of the brain that thinks drink driving is dumb is your *frontal lobe* – a part of the *neo-cortex* with all its complicated rules and a generally rational approach. In contrast, the chemical factory of the *midbrain* can then run amok: assault strangers, take offence easily, protect a mate, and even jump behind a steering wheel. Drink driving is an example of the *midbrain* in charge at its worst.

With or without alcohol, the contest between the two brain structures is biologically fundamental, is raging constantly and, if unchecked, can be hugely detrimental to your endeavours.

In this book we pursue three themes. First, we detail the ongoing battles between those two warring factions, about how their battles affect us at work and outside work. Second, we show the basic principles we need to be conscious of in recognising and dealing with those battles. And third, we offer effective and practical techniques and behaviour templates that we have developed and applied over decades.

We found that wherever those templates were utilised, they were very helpful in meeting the challenges arising from our bio-fundamentals – those inherent in the cards we humans have been dealt. We believe they will be helpful in overcoming obstacles to realising your full potential in managing and leading – in and outside business.

Terminology

This book is designed for Business Owners, Managers, Team Leaders, Workgroup Leaders and Department Heads – basically anyone whose job is to manage people. Rather than repeat this list throughout the book, we use one of the terms with the intention to describe all these stakeholders.

Another point that needs mentioning is that most of the ideas expressed in the book are those of John Vamos and, when the text refers to 'I', then it is John talking in the pages. You may have noticed, however, there are two names on the cover of this book. The reason for this is simply that, without Karen McCreadie, this book would never have made its way out of John's head and onto paper. To learn more about other books Karen has written, visit her website at www.wordarchitect.com.

About the Source

Business Coaching Systems (BCS) is a business coaching company that delivers strategic, operational, and personal performance improvement programs across a wide variety of industries and sizes of business.

Founded in 1995 by John Vamos, the company has formulated unique business improvement processes and now has trained practitioners in Australia, New Zealand and Singapore.

Applying the Thinking System tools described in this book, BCS Coaches have assisted more than 4000 workgroups in more than 2000 businesses in four countries. The size and scope of those operations ranged from small businesses, to multi-million dollar organisations. Today, BCS specialises in assisting family-owned businesses of all sizes and works with many of Australia's most respected family-owned corporations.

The statistics noted on these pages are supported by data collected over the past 15 years. They reflect verifiable outcomes facilitated by BCS business coaches during this period.

The Business Coaching Systems database continues to grow through the collection of information gathered since 1995. Secured databases of operational plans and/or strategic plans are authored by the workgroups in partnership with their BCS Coach and are developed in accordance with BCS-proprietary techniques. The plans include, in more than 75 per cent of cases:

- Complete task lists
- Workgroup self assessments
- Benchmarks and performance indicators
- Action plans and commitments

On our website you will find information about our IP and the scope of our IP library. A quick review will help put into perspective some of the principles we discuss in this book. You are invited to visit *bcscoach.com.au* or *organisationalcoaching.com.au* and download documentation.

In total, more than 1.2 million discrete responses to specific performance-related questions or related data elements have been gathered. In relation to workgroup performance and executive coaching, BCS believes this to be the most comprehensive single repository of source data compiled by a single organisation. The findings and claims in this book are our express conclusions after participating in, collecting, observing and responding to the information contained in our database.

With such unique foundations, we have intentionally presented the solutions and advice in a somewhat prescriptive tone, as if it were easy to give advice derived from the experience. We leave you, the reader, to decide whether or not such tone is suitable.

Preface
Rules for the Road

Before we start in earnest, I want to suggest that you approach this book a little differently. I want you to consider for a moment that there are ideas everywhere. Everyone you meet seems to have the greatest new idea. Great ideas are all around us. But despite the abundance of creativity, the fact remains that ideas are useless without action.

Unless you are going to take action, buying this book will have been a waste of money.

Just as people write books for a number of reasons, people read them for a number of reasons too – to gather information, to acquire knowledge, for fun, or just to pass the time at the airport.

I don't know why *you* are reading this book but I can hazard a guess that you are seeking ways to improve the productivity not only of your own performance but that of your workgroup or team. Perhaps you are perplexed at why, despite all your good intentions, you are still not the expression of your true potential. I can guarantee you one thing – this book will provide solutions to that challenge. Not only that, it will shed light on why we so rarely produce to our potential. (In fact, we are 'designed' to underperform!)

Knowing the answers and applying them are, as we will discover, two *very* different things. I promise you that reading this book will provide you with new ideas and possibly the odd paradigm shift.

But you need to be actively engaged with the pages and that means reading it mindfully.

There was a great article by Nicholas Carr printed in *The Australian* in June 2008[3] that asked, "Is Google making us stupid?" In it, Carr suggests that we have become so used to the speed of access to information that our ability to really immerse ourselves in knowledge has been negatively affected. In relation to reading, he states, "Once I was a scuba diver in the sea of words. Now I zip along the surface like a guy on a jet ski."

I urge you not to zip along the surface of this book like a guy on a jet ski for the simple reason that it will not alter your results. If you sit and read this and nod occasionally, perhaps even enthusiastically – that's great for me. If you discuss the validity of some of the arguments over coffee with friends – that's great for me. But neither is necessarily great for you because they don't take you anywhere different.

Rather than just give you new ideas, I genuinely want this book to take you somewhere different. And if you truly engage in the sea of words, then they genuinely will take you somewhere different, liberating your thinking in all areas of your life in the process.

People usually read passively – simply moving their eyes over the words. And they rarely do anything different as a result. Even the environment where you choose to read something indicates how serious you are about implementation ...

Time is precious, so don't waste your time reading this book unless you expect to be doing something different as a result and that you will derive something of lasting value.

So may I suggest that you:

- Decide when you're going to read it.
- Book in those hours in your diary.
- Buy a notebook and dedicate its use to recording the ideas you have as you are reading this book. Or, if you prefer, simply write in the margins of the book as you read. Some people can't bring

themselves to deface a book in this way but I highly recommend it! Or, if you're particular – jot down your thoughts on coloured post-it notes and stick them in the appropriate section of the book.
- Sit somewhere that supports your intention.

Engage in what is being written and watch what appears on the movie screen in your mind. Record what appears there because those sparks of thought will merge with the thinking in this book to create your own unique applications of *The Thinking System* and its related methods.

What you read is important to the author. What you think, as a result of what you read, is important to you. Write that stuff down.

If you are pressed for time and need first to assess how important or relevant you might find this book, then skimming would seem unavoidable. In that case what you should read are the *Introduction*, the introductory pages of each of the four *Parts*, and the *Chapter Summaries* or *Comprehension Checks* found at the end of most chapters.

Read with intent to act. Don't stop and debate your thoughts. Just record them. Then go back at the end of each chapter and flesh out your own thinking. Test the ideas that come to you and see if they work. Implement those that do and discard or modify those that don't. Make the ideas in this book come alive in your organisation and you will be astonished by the results.

INTRODUCTION

This book is one hundred per cent occupied with the gap between performance and potential: why it is that, more often than not, we and the people in our businesses are not a living expression of all that we know. There are books that explain the 'gap problem' and there are books that explain a plethora of potential solutions. But rarely are there books that connect the two. This is a book that does.

When I first considered writing this book, I shared the industry-wide illusion that 'business solutions fix business problems'. I genuinely wanted to help and spent hours with my clients wrestling with *their* particular challenges. Initially, I even accepted the view that *their* problems *were* unique and that particular situations demanded a very particular tailor-made solution. So off I'd go in search of that unique solution and, invariably, I would arrive at the logical conclusion that things would be improved with some new information or some skills training.

This seemed valid and certainly the amount of training programs available today would support such a conclusion. Yet time and again we would find that even the best training in the world had little impact on the problem. The problem remained.

So lack of knowledge was obviously *not* the problem. I was forced to look elsewhere for the solution. If it wasn't knowledge, then what *was* stopping businesses from reaching their highest potential? Perhaps it was motivation. Maybe the business owners and managers just weren't that passionate and committed to the outcomes of the business. Yet when I looked around at my clients to test that hypothesis, there was absolutely no evidence for such an explanation. These were extremely motivated, hard-working and committed people. Yet the problems remained.

So the problem was not knowledge based, it was all down to application.

I discovered that the people 'in difficulty' invariably already *knew* what was wrong. They even knew the solutions. But they couldn't or wouldn't apply them.

So it wasn't lack of knowledge and it wasn't lack of motivation. It was a problem with application. People were not doing what they *knew* they should do. This is hardly a revelation when you consider the global diet industry or the mountains of unused gym memberships.

But what really puzzled me was *why?* Why would someone *continue to do* something that was causing them difficulties, or *not do* something that would solve their problem, even though they knew what they needed to do?

Why would someone spend thousands of dollars going to seminars and training courses and not implement a single idea from those events . . . then go and repeat the same charade a few months later?

Why? *Because we are not in charge of our thinking.*

We are not in charge of our thinking

This is the reason there is such a massive gap between performance and potential. The explanation and, more importantly, the solution to this challenge is the focus of this book.

As a business coach, it was natural for me to be preoccupied with this performance gap. Over the years I realised that whilst most people knew as much, if not more, than I did about business, the problem, the cause of the gap, was not knowledge based. It was all down to *application*. In other words, it didn't really matter what someone knew or didn't know. What mattered was what they did with what they knew.

In trying to understand why we didn't do a great deal with what we knew, I came to the inevitable conclusion that the reason seemed to be down to distraction. I started to notice how easily people were distracted, how easily they were pulled off task by competing priorities or petty challenges. For a while I was quite excited by this simple yet powerful observation. I must confess I found it highly amusing demonstrating its accuracy.

You don't think as smart as you are[4] is a statement often met with howls of derision when I announce it at presentations. No amount of explanation seems to convince the audience of its validity, so I engage them in a simple demonstration.

I ask the audience, "Who's in charge of what you think?"

The answer is always a somewhat indignant chorus of, "I am" and "We are".

I then pretend to look distracted, as though I've just remembered something. And, depending on the time of year and what events are coming up, I turn to the audience and ask, "Oh by the way, who's going to win the Grand Final?" Or, if it's election time, I may ask, "Who do you think is going to win the next election?" Or, I might throw in a real curve ball and ask, "Which religion do you think makes the most sense?"

What usually follows is a vigorous debate as they engage each other with their various points of view. I usually allow this to continue for three to five minutes. I then ask them if they intended or expected to spend time at this gathering debating politics, religion or sport. The answer, of course, is 'No'.

So I ask, "Then *why* did you?" They respond as one, "Because *you* asked us the question".

Someone in the audience always protests at this point. They are adamant about not engaging in the debate about the relative merits of Taoism; that they were, in fact, wondering what I was doing. The commotion was triggered by *me,* the speaker, regardless of what anyone was thinking. It was all around one thing.... *my* questions.

The audience members were all thinking something that was, in every sense, triggered by me, even that protester's dissenting thoughts.

For some, the penny drops... We are *not* in charge of what we think *about!*

Your thoughts are reactions to what you see, what you hear, and much more. A car that pulls out in front of you without indicating could steal your thoughts for a month! Your family, your staff, your colleagues, even complete strangers, are often more in charge of what you think about than you are.

After several hours sitting on a deserted beach, or late at night while everyone else in the house is asleep and you haven't spoken to anyone or watched TV for at least two hours... then perhaps you may be in charge of your thoughts. Or, first thing in the morning, as you muster the energy to get out of bed, you may be in control of what you think. The rest of the time you're not. You are almost permanently distracted. You are a walking *reaction* to the environment around you. Exactly what you evolved to be!

I felt sure this was a crucial piece of the puzzle. And certainly it is. But soon the real culprit emerged from behind the veil of symptoms and excuses for poor performance...

The reason that you do not live up to your enormous potential is not lack of knowledge, training, skill, motivation, or even because you are constantly distracted. There is a bigger, much more powerful force at work. Lack of knowledge is not the problem. It's a symptom. Lack of training isn't the problem. It's just a symptom. Lack of skill or motivation isn't the real problem. Nor is the level of distraction we deal with on a daily basis. All of these – and a bucket load besides – are merely symptoms.

The real problem is *the way our brain works*. You *really don't think as smart as you are* because ninety-nine per cent of the time you don't actually think at all. Instead, a much more powerful force, that you're probably not even aware of, is at work. Let me take a moment to step back and explain...

The bridge towards this book

Those presentations about smart thinking were well received. The material resonated with the audience. But something was missing from the explanation of both the source of the problem and the reasons why the proposed solutions solved them.

In an attempt to resolve this flaw, I re-drafted the presentation around the importance and contribution of coaches in guiding people towards solutions to their problems. That didn't quite do it either.

How do you get someone to understand the challenges they face when those challenges are so pervasive they affect every aspect of an individual's life – from the relationships they have with their kids, to arguments in the boardroom, to deciding on a new product line, or where to take the family on holiday?

It's like trying to explain water to a fish! A fish has no concept of water. Water is such an integral part of being a fish that the fish is completely oblivious to its importance or even existence. (If by some unlucky circumstance, the fish does discover its reliance on water, then it's invariably a short-lived revelation!)

What I struggled with was how best to make the ideas about the real problems, their solutions, and the dots between them more accessible and useable.

The world has since moved on and, in many ways, we've gained additional understanding. The ideas I've been so committed to for the past 20 years, which have been conclusively proved over and over again with my clients have, in that time, also found external validation through a diverse source of new, supporting knowledge and scientific understanding.

It is clear that to explain the source of the difficulties, the effective solutions to the challenges, and the reasons why the solutions work, go beyond the scope of a normal business book. It is not enough to simply analyse the symptoms of the challenges. We need to go beyond explaining their effects and get to their true biological cause. We need to fully appreciate that the very thing that makes us human is also the thing that is holding us back from *thinking as smart as we are*. And that's what this book is all about.

The first step in tackling the tasks is to remember that the best way to explain something new is to link the new – the 'unknown' – to a 'known'. This is called Hebb's Model. In 1949, Donald Hebb[5], a Canadian neuropsychologist, presented a theory of learning. His model essentially suggests that we learn new information when our brain forms new synaptic connections between neurons, thus increasing our capacity to remember – "neurons that fire together, will wire together". This means we can quickly learn new skills by searching through past experiences and abilities stored in memory, find a close match, and use that 'known' to connect to an 'unknown' to accelerate learning.

For example we might use our experience of skateboarding to help us water ski. Because of the similarity between the two experiences, the part of the brain that fired up when you learned how to balance will re-fire. Surrounding neurons will start firing and new connections can be made for the specific differences between the two skills. This is possible because the brain kick-starts the learning by attaching an 'unknown' to a previously experienced 'known'. This process is also known as the 'Law of Association'. We'll explore it further in Chapter Four where we discuss the role of associative memories.

This known/unknown connection is also why simile, analogy, and metaphor are so powerful. They allow the recipient to have an 'a-ha moment' – an almost holographic insight into the true meaning and implication of the new knowledge.

Simile, analogy, and metaphor allow people to instantly perceive multiple layers of information at once, thereby leaving them much more likely to really 'get it'.

> This 'Law of Association' states that what allows us to quickly learn new skills is searching through past experiences and abilities stored in memory to find a close match, connecting with which will accelerate our learning.

So when I read about the work done by social psychologist Jonathan Haidt[6], who also argues that human thinking depends on metaphor, I was inspired to put the ideas across through the use of a suitable metaphor.

Added perspective on the real problem

In an effort to facilitate your own personal 'a-ha moment' so you can transform your results as quickly as possible, I've adopted Jonathan Haidt's metaphor concept in relation to *thinking*.

Metaphor will help you appreciate the source of the obstacles to *smart thinking*. You will also appreciate the solutions for overcoming those obstacles and see how those solutions will have a beneficial impact on your performance. That way, you can stop berating yourself for perceived inadequacies and get on with the task of creating and building the business you really want.

Haidt suggests that the best metaphor for understanding how your mind works is to imagine yourself riding an elephant! That elephant is also the powerful force causing havoc with your performance.

Just think for a moment about riding an elephant[7]. Regardless of how big you are, or how strong you are, or how clever you are, you're pretty insignificant against an elephant's intent. Sitting astride your placid pachyderm, you can control which direction he travels in. You can turn him right and left, and you can probably even stop him when you want. But, let's face it, you only have control when your elephant is happy to go along with your direction. If, for whatever reason, he decides to stop, there is bugger-all you can do about it. You could kick him till your legs were black and blue and all he'd feel would be an irritating tickle. If he wanted to

> The best metaphor for understanding how your mind works is to imagine yourself riding an elephant! And it is that elephant that is the powerful force that is causing havoc with your performance.

change direction, you'd have absolutely no influence on the outcome.

The same is true with your mind. You think you are in control of your own mind because occasionally it does what you want it to. Occasionally, you do see things through and take action on that good idea you heard. Occasionally, you might plan a course of action and take it to fruition to experience the success you crave. Occasionally, you may even surprise yourself at just how brilliant your thinking really is. But the truth is, these moments of success only happen when your elephant happens to be going in the same direction at the same time you are. When, whether through luck or synchronicity, the elephant and its rider[8] are in alignment.

> The conscious mind, the one we believe is in charge is, nothing more than 2IC to the elephant. The rider may look like he's the boss but think what happens when there is a disagreement about the objective . . . Who wins the argument?

We are reluctant, at this stage, to mention conscious and subconscious mind because of confusion that may arise at the mention of these terms. Suffice to say, for the sake of this introductory exploration, that if you think of the elephant as your *subconscious mind*[9] and the thing you call 'you' as your *conscious mind*[10], you'll start to see what you're up against – especially when you consider the division between what we are aware of and what we are oblivious to.

According to recent research discussed in the book *The Physics Of Consciousness* by E. H. Walker[11], scientists have shown that the brain processes about 400 billion bits of information per second. Out of that vast sea of information, we are aware of only 2000 of those bits. It would be extremely foolish to assume that the information we are not aware of is therefore unimportant. Far from it. That sea of information is making a huge impact on how we live our lives – we just might not realise it!

The conscious mind versus subconscious mind issue is something we'll clear up later. For now, we will assume that our conscious mind

– the one that's reading these words – is in control. In reality, our *frontal lobe* is reading; our *midbrain* is checking our temperature, assessing our safety, digesting our lunch, and temporarily suppressing emotion (this is, after all, a business book, not a novel!).

If we say we want something, and we are passionate about attaining that outcome, then surely we are able to muster our resources, exercise control, and achieve it?

The answer is 'yes that's true'... *provided* that what *you* want and what *your elephant* wants happen to be the same thing. The conscious mind – the one we believe is in charge – is, in this view, nothing more than second-in-charge to the elephant. The rider may look like s/he is the boss but think what happens when there is a disagreement about the objective... Who wins the argument? Just ask Tiger Woods.

If you were to visit parts of the world where people ride elephants, you would be struck by one of two things:

a) The scale of destruction an unruly elephant is capable of when it dislodges or ignores its rider.
b) The unique capacity for productivity and effectiveness that a happy elephant demonstrates when put to work by a skilful rider.

Your subconscious mind is that elephant and, if you genuinely want to achieve those things you say you want to achieve, you need to learn how to become a skilful elephant rider. Like it or not, the subconscious mind is the *real* powerhouse that is directing and influencing your results.

> "When it comes to sheer neurological processing abilities, the subconscious mind is millions of times more powerful than the conscious mind"
> – Lipton

Bruce H. Lipton[12] puts it well in his book *Biology Of Belief: Unleashing The Power Of Consciousness, Matter and Miracles*, "The conscious mind is the creative one, the one that can conjure up 'positive thoughts'. In contrast, the subconscious mind is a repository of stimulus-response tapes derived from instincts and learned experiences. The subconscious mind is strictly habitual; it will play the same behavioural responses to life's signals over and over again, much to our chagrin ... When it comes to sheer neurological processing abilities, the subconscious mind is millions of times more powerful than the conscious mind. If the desires of the conscious mind conflict with the routines in the subconscious mind, which 'mind' do you think will win out?" Lipton goes on to assure us that "your subconscious mind will undermine your best conscious efforts to change your life".

The subconscious mind is like a chemical factory. It is not a discerning beast. No decisions are made by the subconscious mind. Using a 'language' of emotion, its function is not what we call thinking. It doesn't 'think', it just does. On the other hand, the rider of the unruly elephant – the conscious mind – *does* think. But it doesn't have the muscle to compete with such a powerful force. In the face of conflicting objectives, the elephant will always win ... unless you utilise solutions like those contained in this book! Solutions that are based on the Business Laws of Nature. Like all Laws of Nature, you can choose to work with them and get results, or ignore them and get annihilated.

Psychologists, such as Haidt, tell us the brains and the brawn of your mind have been cruelly separated through evolutionary circumstances. Nevertheless, your elephant has done a remarkable job taking care of your existence and making sure you survive. These achievements may not necessarily fall in line with your business or commercial goals. To be candid, your elephant doesn't really care about your business unless he suspects it might affect your physical survival!

You can harness the best of both your conscious and subconscious minds by learning to ride your elephant. If you don't learn, then you will continue to sabotage your best efforts and cause chronic underperformance in your life. You will be confused by your own behaviour and continue to ask yourself, "Why on earth did I just do that?" And you will continue to make plans for the future and set business and personal goals without ever seeing them come to fruition. It is this misunderstanding of who or what is really in charge that causes so many of life's difficulties.

With the help of the elephant metaphor...

That you are an unwitting passenger on a large wrinkly grey lump is a detail no one actually tells you. The school system doesn't tell you... Business consultants won't tell you, nor will motivational speakers – perhaps because *they* don't often realise it themselves – as their own stories often prove it.

The elephant metaphor provides a vivid picture of the nature of the biological challenges we face – how the mind works; the way we think and, ultimately, *the way we behave.*

Our *behaviour* is what we do to pursue our aims, including what we do to minimise the performance gap, in and outside business. As it is our *thinking* that governs our *behaviour* it is vital that we understand more about it.

Thinking is a composite of conscious and subconscious processes. Of the two the subconscious (the elephant) has far more clout and yet ironically we remain largely oblivious to its effects.

The reason is because we don't know any different. It is the same with many of the *laws of nature*. We don't for example appreciate gravity and its impact on us because the vast majority of us have never experienced an alternative. None of us can beat the *laws of nature*, we can only accommodate them and work with them toward our goals.

The *business-related laws of nature* are similar such realities that affect behaviour in a work place. We can't beat them but we can accommodate them, navigate them, work with them and massively dilute their negative influence in a business setting.

...It becomes possible to fix the real problem

To accommodate them we need to understand the *business laws of nature* and, if possible, need effective methods and special tools to harness them and that's what this book is all about. In contrast, equipped with understanding and special business tools we can adjust our behaviour and we can *overcome the gap*.

Thus our title is shorthand for ... ***the elephant metaphor and its lessons about human nature for learning and adopting effective behaviour towards managing the performance gap, in and beyond business***. This, admittedly, would have been too long even for a subtitle ...

Consultants, motivational speakers look at the individual challenges we face, either in our home life or business life, and offer a plethora of novel ways to diagnose and treat those problems. Where their solutions happen to allow the rider to more effectively control his or her elephant, then their methods succeed. However, where the solutions make no impression on the elephant, or impose no framework for removal and don't align behaviour with the Business Laws of Nature, they do not work ... at least not in the long term.

Typically, the connection between the elephant and the solutions offered is not made. So, frustrated recipients of those 'solutions' are unable to make the lasting changes needed to produce consistent results. And they are certainly in no position to apply the knowledge widely across other challenging areas of their lives.

It's time to stop beating ourselves up over our inability to solve a myriad of business or personal challenges and go to the heart of the problem – that your life is currently directed by an out-of-control elephant you didn't even know you had! And take comfort ... as the rider of that elephant, you have more power than you think. The first step is to realise you are actually riding an elephant.

We've all repeatedly done things that actively compromised our own potential. We've also been guilty of deliberately avoiding things that would have facilitated success. But if you feel despondent or confused about your inability to translate into reality what you so passionately want, take heart: understanding those reasons is at hand.

It's obviously not because you're lazy or stupid or unmotivated. It's not because you have a short attention span, or that you prefer to watch TV in the evenings. The real reason is that you have failed to realise there is a bigger, much more powerful force influencing your behaviour. And if you've failed to even realise you are riding an elephant, what chance do you have of controlling him and harnessing his enormous potential to contribute to attaining your objectives – objectives as a person and, especially, as a leader in your work?

In *Part One*, we will focus on your 'virtual boss' – or elephant – in more detail. We'll spend some time investigating just how easily and often the symptoms of poor performance are misunderstood by professionals. And to ensure that you are sufficiently motivated to read on, we'll look at what your elephant costs you in business.

In *Part Two*, we'll deconstruct the size and shape of your elephant so you can appreciate the havoc he can cause if left unchecked. There are additional challenges you may not be aware of, so we'll explore each characteristic individually to reveal those challenges.

In *Part Three*, we'll explain how to turn the situation around so you can learn how to manage your own elephant. This section will show you how to adopt the new tools of *binary thinking* and *thinking systems* to ensure your elephant is tranquilised. It's about you personally and will equip you *to think as smart as you are.*

Finally, *in Part Four*, we will look specifically at the Business Laws of Nature so you can effectively control the other elephants running amok in your workgroup. We look at how you can influence the working environment to tranquilise the herd. It's not about trying to change people – we all know that doesn't work! Instead, this section explains how incorporating simple, replicable, important behaviours in any workgroup imposes a framework to begin harnessing those elephants, without trying to change anyone. This framework allows you to align the workgroup to the Business Laws of Nature and prosper.

When you become a skilful elephant manager, you can direct your own and other people's pachyderms toward what the business truly needs and wants. Learn how to do that and the problems you currently face will be irrelevant because you will have a solution that works consistently across all aspects of your business and personal life.

PART ONE
THE ELEPHANT METAPHOR

What we need to know to make a lasting and consistent difference to the performance of our business always seems to be lodged in many different places. There is no shortage of books touting various solutions to a variety of challenges – from productivity issues to problems of leadership or operation – written mostly by specialists who look from a narrow perspective only at their particular area.

On the upside, they usually do a thorough job. On the downside they effect little lasting change. Why? Because biology is the culprit and it's seldom if ever recognised, let alone addressed. We are not as productive as we could be because we have not learned to manage our thinking. Instead we have a reaction-based elephant running amok in our lives and wonder why it's not working out so well!

The real problem is so pervasive, we fail to see it – like the fish oblivious to the water it swims in. It's not like we can compare our thinking to something else's ... the brain we have is the only one we've ever had.

Discussion of our biological shortcomings, easily found in the biology section of the library, seems to have not yet made it into the management catalogue. Scientific advances that point to our evolutionary quirks are reported in specialist journals but rarely make the transition into leadership textbooks. Consequently, the true causes behind the universal challenges we are dealing with are seldom, if ever, put in a business context. As a result, the connection between the causes and the effects goes undiscovered.

> New specialised fields of research are shining much needed light into previously misunderstood areas of human development.

This is changing, however, and this book is my contribution to that vital work. In the past few years, there has been an explosion in neuroscience. New specialised fields of research are shining much needed light onto previously misunderstood areas of human development. For example, for decades it was believed the brain was hardwired and that its neural circuits could not be altered. This is completely false. In truth, your brain is a marvel of flexibility and adaptability. This neuroplasticity means you really can change your mind! Not just your mind but, according to Norman Doidge[13], author of *The Brain That Changed Itself*, you can and do change your brain, too.

These new insights into how we function as human beings must, by definition, affect every area where human beings function – including business and leadership. Understanding the challenges we face simply because of the way we think can make a huge difference to our productivity. In management texts, this has not been made clear enough.

This book is as much about the clarification of the problem as it is about the explanation of the solution. Because once you really grasp the implications of the genetic and biological bases of the problems you face, you can then see their ramifications and how they cause challenges, not just in business but also in every aspect of your life. You will see yourself in a new light with a better appreciation for what is really (the conscious) you and what the rest of your genetic inheritance is. And you will learn how to differentiate between the two and manage each of them appropriately to make a massive difference to your performance and your happiness.

1

The Performance Gap

Let's begin by addressing the fundamental challenge of how to improve performance.

When we are faced with business challenges, we automatically assume the solution exists outside of us, in one of two directions:

The Knowledge Gap = the difference between what you know and what you don't know

The Performance Gap = the difference between what you know and what you apply

The logical conclusion is that we are either *missing some new information or knowledge* (and that once we are aware of it, the problem will miraculously be fixed) or, *for some reason or another, we are not applying the knowledge we already have.*

At the very start of my business coaching career, I too, was fooled into believing that if we could just close the knowledge gap, then the performance gap would automatically close. I was driven to offer many good business solutions based on a lot of practical experience. Yet the performance gap remained. And even when performance improved for me, it never presented the anticipated paradigm effect for my clients.

It took me a while to realise that there was often no need to add more business information because there was nothing wrong with the many solutions already on offer. New information was merely a decoy, a placebo to make us feel better about our persistent inability to convert ideas into action and reach the potential we know we are capable of.

The frustrating part of the new knowledge strategy was that sometimes this approach worked and sometimes it didn't. No one could explain why. The mercurial nature of that solution's success made for an elusive challenge where an individual hoped to replicate it. After all, knowing something works but not knowing why it works, hardly makes it a reliable solution.

> Many of the solutions happened to fix certain symptoms but never really got to the cause of the symptoms in the first place – they were business antibiotics and nothing more.

Many of the solutions happened to fix certain *symptoms* but never really got to the *cause* of the symptoms. They were business antibiotics and nothing more. The underlying problem, or cause, emerged in the form of a variety of common business challenges and what was missing was clear, definitive understanding.

We live in a world where there is no shortage of problems, including business productivity problems. We have literally hundreds of thousands of consultants specialising in every facet of business, from productivity to logistics to human resources. They have made it their life's work to name, categorise, and describe the various types of business problems so they can then set out to provide solutions.

The business improvement industry – personal development, training and consulting included – is not unlike the computer virus protection industry or the pharmaceutical industry. All three could be charged with enjoying somewhat self-perpetuating niches. Cynics amongst us would argue that these industries have no real interest in finding genuine solutions because if they did they'd put themselves out of business, so they simply treat the symptom and bank the revenue. This is a situation likely to change only if there's a paradigm shift that alters their reasons for existence.

> **Problems are lucrative! Is anyone really searching for a solution or are they simply profiting from the perpetuation of the symptoms?**

Somewhere in a gloomy little bedsit, some bright spark comes up with a new virus to wreak havoc on an unsuspecting, computer dependent world. The virus protection industry responds swiftly. The new virus is given a name, if it doesn't already have one, and programming resources are swiftly engaged to neutralise its impact. Sometimes within hours they have a solution and the software 'upgrade' is rushed out to a suitably distressed market, willing to pay as necessary for such services.

Virus protection upgrades provide only 'temporary fixes'. Then the next geek comes along. It's a global problem and one that costs companies billions of dollars a year. It is also a lucrative business. And there are currently no viable ways to totally prevent software vandalism. Instead of a problem that could potentially be eradicated, we are forced to accept software terrorism as a *fait accompli*.

It's the same with the pharmaceutical industry. Massive sums of money are dedicated to 'raising awareness' of new conditions and diseases for which the industry can provide the 'solution'. Are huge drug companies interested in eradicating the cause of illness? Or are they more interested in treating the symptoms, maintaining the cause, and bolstering profit margins? Again, there are no viable ways to totally prevent illnesses and we are forced to accept a 'curative' industry... until a fully 'preventive' one can replace it.

Is anyone really searching for a solution? Or are they simply profiting from the perpetuation of the symptoms? Problems are lucrative! It stands to reason that more effort is made to alleviate problems than to solving them once and for all.

The 'business improvement' industry is in the same position when it comes to addressing the performance gap. Billions of dollars are generated in the process of naming, describing, and providing so-called 'solutions' to business productivity problems, yet businesses fail in alarming numbers year in year out.

At least anti-virus software or painkillers provide some temporary relief to their respective problems, whereas the much-anticipated benefits of various business solutions rarely do even that.

What these three industries have in common is that they address symptoms not causes. Therefore, while the symptoms may be appeased, the underlying problems are never really addressed, certainly never eradicated.

Sure, it would be unrealistic to expect computer software that is not susceptible to viral infection. Likewise, it is unrealistic to expect that disease will no longer threaten our health. In contrast, however, I believe the methods I offer have the potential to markedly reduce early business failures.

Symptoms vs Cures

Instead of just addressing symptoms, we're going to find real cures. How? Simple – by avoiding the misdiagnosis of the fundamental problems.

Let's say, for instance, you are 15 kilograms overweight, eat fast food three times a day, and believe that hunting for the TV remote constitutes regular exercise. Then you run up a flight of stairs and wonder why you have chest pain. Well, you'd be considered an idiot. You might be hoping your doctor will phone to confirm a genetic weakness and prescribe, god forbid, a new drug to assist with your breathing. But such measures won't address the problem. The problem is not that you have chest pains when you run up a flight of stairs. The problem is that you are fat and your body is struggling to cope with the stress your excess weight is putting on your system.

Earlier in my coaching career, with the business challenges perceived by my clients, I too accepted that the causes were the real ones.

I focused on trying to fix those and, like so many others, I was chasing misdiagnosed business problems.

My own search for definitive solutions took me from Robbins to Wilson Learning, from Macquarie University to Deacon University, from consultants to trainers – too many to mention. I attended countless courses, seminars, and presentations. And it was during one of these events that I started to see the proverbial wood for the trees.

While we waited in hushed anticipation for the arrival on stage of a world-renowned speaker, I reflected on the extravagant claims of the promotional material and the high expectations of those who'd parted with hundreds of dollars to be there. As participants, we were looking for, and expecting answers to, a long list of business challenges that had been skilfully identified and quoted in the marketing literature.

As I looked around the room on that red-letter day, I saw eager faces, people from all walks of life, many people I knew – smart, hard-working people. And I wondered if it was a question of motivation, ability, sincerity, or even personal honesty for us to be there. Many, I knew, had been to several such gatherings before, yet I was certain that nothing new would emerge from the experience; at least, nothing spectacular and/or lasting.

What if that long list of business challenges, eloquently identified in seminar brochures and millions of business books, was nothing more than a list of symptoms of an as yet unidentified cause?

We all know that eradicating the symptom is unlikely to cure the disease. So could it be possible that the forthcoming 'new information' was, in fact, not part of the solution, as we were led to believe, but part of the problem? New information that would suppress the symptoms long enough for us to be fooled into thinking we had healed our businesses and were on the way to financial success and recovery... only to find ourselves with a different symptom of the same disease, months down the track.

This moment of realisation ended my quest for the Holy Grail and, after a time, revealed to me the correct nature of the challenges we faced – they are, in fact, as deep as our biology. Exactly what I am proposing is that the challenges we face in business are not due to lack of motivation, skill, knowledge or ability. They are a function of our biology. It is the lack of any attempts to even begin to tackle *that* challenge that haunts us and holds us back.

The challenges we face in business are not due to lack of motivation, skill, knowledge or ability; they are a function of our biology.

Say, for example, you are having team management issues. You assume the difficulties in your team are because there is something wrong with your team. So you book them into a 'weekend warrior' workshop where they build rafts and join forces to solve challenges. For the while, the team seems to work well together and you assume the weekend was worth it. What you don't consider is that the reason they worked well together is that they all got drunk on the Saturday night and talked freely about work, putting their issues on the table and ended up with a better understanding of each other. It had less to do with the weekend's scheduled activities, than the biology of the thinking that went on.

The weekend allowed people to get things off their chest and appreciate each other's perspectives. It allowed them to communicate better. At least for a while. It also provided a framework where external distractions were minimised because there was a trainer managing the information flow and directing the outcomes. So the elephant was tranquilised in that setting.

To gain long-term benefit for the business from the event, follow-ups are essential such that the temporary harmony with the participants' elephants is made permanent. The weekend may have tamed the elephants for a couple of days, but it would do little for the business, unless that tranquilising environment was made permanent. (The subject of Parts Three and Four.)

The irony of the Performance Gap is that if we used all *that we already knew*, we would be far less concerned about what we didn't know. And rightly so – our performance would be so much better that *what we didn't know* would seem unimportant.

Performance Gap vs the Knowledge Gap

The crazy thing is that we try to solve the Performance Gap by working on the Knowledge Gap. The presumption is that the Performance Gap is *due* to the Knowledge Gap. In other words, if a business or an individual does not perform to their best, if they are not the living expression of their potential, they respond by seeking additional or new knowledge. And that is just a red herring.

Consider this: Despite being sceptical about the worth of business development seminars, they provide me with a forum to present my arguments about their inefficiency. My opening line is pretty much standard. I begin by asking the audience . . .

"Who already uses every good idea they have ever heard? Whose business and lifestyle is supported by bulletproof protocols – agreed, documented routines that ensure each day is an expression of the best they already know or could be?"

> We try to solve the Performance Gap by working on the Knowledge Gap. The irony of the Performance Gap is that if we used all that we already knew we would be a lot less concerned about what we didn't know. Why reach out for new ideas when you are not yet fully using the ideas you already have?

As I wait for the question to sink in and the cogs to turn, the answer is invariably the same – nobody. The next question is therefore obvious . . .

"So, what the hell are you doing *here*?"

"Why reach out for new ideas when you are yet to fully use the ideas you already have?"

This last question is specifically designed to illustrate to the individuals present that, of the ideas they already have, and of the new information they are about to acquire, few are translated beyond theory into reality.

Straight away it forces people to question why they continue to seek more.

It is this gap between knowledge and translation or application of knowledge that fascinates me. And it is this gap that the 'business coaching' profession seeks to address – with very mixed results.

I continue with my audience, "So if you are not using all the good ideas you've ever had and, if it's your business to improve things, how likely is it that your employees or colleagues are using all of *their* good ideas?"

You are in the same situation if you don't employ people but rely on others to do *their* job well, before *you* can do *your* job well.

We can't stop looking

My theory is that everybody's brain has an unused new-idea-ometer. We may not use all our good ideas but we seem to derive a sense of security and satisfaction from at least *knowing* we have some good ones.

We say to people, "Oh yes, I had that idea once" or, "When I get around to it, I'm gonna..." But because we don't use our good ideas, we forget them. Eventually we run out of new ideas. Once our meter falls below a certain point, we panic. So we race out and gather new good ideas. We may read a new book, go to a seminar, or take a training course. Once the gauge is back above critical stock level, we relax again into our comfort zone and enjoy the false sense of security of believing 'at least I have good ideas'.

Chapter Summary

- When we are faced with business challenges, we automatically assume the solution exists outside of us in one of two directions:
  - The Knowledge Gap = the difference between what you know and what you don't know,

THE ELEPHANT METAPHOR

- – The Performance Gap = the difference between what you know and what you apply.
- The crazy thing is that we try to solve the Performance Gap by working on the Knowledge Gap.
- New information is a decoy, a placebo that makes us feel better about our persistent inability to convert ideas into action and our consistent inability to express the potential we know we are capable of.
- Most 'solutions' fail or achieve only hit-and-miss results because they address the symptoms not the cause. Therefore, while the symptoms may be appeased, the underlying problem is never really addressed and is certainly never eradicated.
- The cause of the challenges we face in business is not a result of lack of motivation, skill, knowledge or ability. It's a result of our biology. The lack of any attempt to even begin to tackle *that* challenge is what haunts us and holds us back.

2
Enter the Elephant

"I think therefore I am."
DESCARTES

When Descartes uttered that line, perhaps his words were jotted down for posterity before he'd finished his sentence. Possibly his scribe was distracted by a busty wench and missed recording what Descartes *actually* said: *"I think therefore I am . . . still stuffed because that pesky elephant doesn't care what I think!"*

On a more serious note, let's try to appreciate the impact your elephant has on your daily life. We may start the day full of enthusiasm, with a long list of tasks we aim to knock over to make some real progress toward our objective. Then stuff happens. At the end of the day, we look at our list only to discover that nothing we considered important has been done. Instead, we've lost 10 hours dealing with other people's problems and other people's dreams. Granted, some of them may have been important and, in business, you have to manage what comes up. *But* at what expense?

> Fundamentally what we consider thinking isn't actually thinking at all.

The problem is, time and time again, we beat ourselves up about this situation. It's not a one-off. It's a normal business day for most people. The result is persistent frustration and consistent lack of productivity

THE ELEPHANT METAPHOR

because our elephant and external events continuously hijack what we believe to be important. We assume, wrongly, that this is a personal failing. But it's much deeper than that.

Fundamentally, what we consider thinking isn't actually thinking at all. Real thinking has been disguised by the elephant's knee-jerk conditioned responses. These allow the thinking process to be interrupted by internal assumptions drawn against a myriad of external situations.

I used the terms conscious and subconscious mind in the introduction for ease of exposition. But it's important that you understand exactly what I mean by those terms. When I talk of 'subconscious', I use the term in the strict psychological sense: operating or existing outside of consciousness. When I use the term 'conscious', I mean the opposite: operating within what appears real. For the rest of this book, I will try to minimise my use of the two terms.

The brain is a complicated piece of equipment and is still largely a mystery. Even the best neuroscientists in the world don't yet have all the answers. A most useful and practical explanation of the conscious and subconscious mind is documented in the excellent book *Evolve Your Brain – The Science Of Changing Your Mind* by Joe Dispenza[14]. In all the research I've done, the book has by far the clearest explanation of how the mind works. If you want to know more than is covered within the scope of *this* book, I highly recommend you read it. In particular, Chapter 6 of Dispenza's book, offers a thorough explanation of the many parts of the human brain, their structure and anatomy, their functions and their interrelationships.

According to Dispenza, there are two elements of consciousness. One, which he calls *subjective consciousness*, is the consciousness we recognise as the 'you'. It maintains your individual free will and allows you to express yourself as a thinking self. This element is our self-conscious identity.

The other element of consciousness, Dispenza refers to as *objective consciousness* or *subconscious*. This is the intelligent awareness that gives us life every day. Fortunately this system is separate from our consciousness because it is this intelligence that keeps our bodies working; it pumps the blood and processes millions of automatic functions without us ever being aware of them.

What this part of our mind does on a daily basis is truly staggering ... [15] Every 20 to 60 seconds, each blood cell makes a complete circuit of the body, travelling more than 9650 kilometres through the vascular channels that take up only three per cent of our body mass. There are 100,000 chemical reactions taking place in every one of your estimated 70 to 100 trillion cells every second. Ten million cells die every second and another 10 million take their place. Those that die are swept up and eliminated. Your kidneys are filtering your blood faster and more efficiently than the most sophisticated dialysis machines on the planet. Communication between your cells occurs at lightning speed. And all this started from just two little cells in the back of a Ford Cortina.

Considering that many of us forget to pick up the dry-cleaning on the way home from work, that most of us miss appointments and forget to pay bills on time, this evolutionary reality is not only fortunate but also necessary to our survival as a species.

The brain itself is just a lump of grey matter. Mind is the brain at work. The electro-chemical processes of the huge, intricate network of its neuron cells *are* what we call thinking and what constitutes our consciousness. That is, the brain encompasses our *conscious mind*, which can make choices and exercise free will on the one hand and, on the other, a *subconscious mind* that makes sure you have a functioning body to direct. These two are largely situated within two separate but interconnected 'lumps', namely:

Neo-cortex = the 'conscious' mind
Midbrain, cerebellum and brain stem = the 'subconscious' mind

What follows is a short lesson (I promise) in evolution and biology. It will be crucial to your appreciation of the systems that make up you and your elephant. These are not New Age philosophies or wacky spiritual theories without base in science. They are simple biological and evolutionary facts.

Evolution

From an evolutionary perspective, there are three brains. I'll talk more about this in later chapters but, for now, those brains are:

1. The Reptilian Brain (also known as the R-complex)
2. Midbrain (also known as the mammalian brain or limbic system)
3. Neo-cortex (often referred to as the cortex)

In the millions of years of our evolution, the brain has developed in that order[16]. Each brain acts as a separate but interconnected bio-computer system. The reptilian brain includes the brain stem and the cerebellum. It first appeared more than 500 million years ago, although how anyone can know that is beyond me. This first brain is responsible for coordination, body movement and function, and controls the fight or flight response.

The midbrain or *limbic system* appeared some 300 to 150 million years ago. This wraps around the brainstem and has come on in leaps and bounds in the past 3 million years. The midbrain is home to our involuntary *autonomic nervous system* and is also sometimes referred to as the emotion centre of the brain. It regulates chemical production and therefore has an impact on the body's internal state.

Finally, the part that truly makes us human – the neo-cortex – appeared about three million years ago and moulded itself around the other two. This is the seat of our conscious awareness. Its size and

> Although the workings of all the lobes of the neo-cortex are part of the conscious mind, for the purposes of explaining the contrast with your elephant the frontal lobe is all that really matters. The 'you' that you understand to be you is only possible because of the frontal lobe.

complexity gives us unique capabilities including free will, language, and complex learning. It also makes it possible for us to choose, reason, and plan for the future. The neo-cortex is the seat and enabler of characteristics that humans – and only humans – experience, including feelings like *fear-uncertainty-doubt*, the combination arising out of our uniquely conscious sense of the future[17].

Biology

From a biological perspective, the neo-cortex or crown of the brain is the conscious thought centre. There are four lobes in the neo-cortex – the frontal lobe, parietal lobe, occipital lobe and temporal lobe. The big daddy of those, in terms of what you understand as being 'you', the person that is reading these words, is facilitated through the frontal lobe.

Although the workings of all the lobes of the neo-cortex are part of the conscious mind, for the purposes of explaining the *contrast* with your elephant, the *frontal lobe* is all that really matters. The 'you' that you understand to be you is only possible because of the frontal lobe.

Many primates have a frontal lobe but none is as large or complex as the human brain's. This disparity has raised questions about a missing link but as yet no one knows why or how the human frontal lobe became so large relative to our nearest cousin. Recent studies, however, have revealed that there are vastly more interconnections between many more nerve cells in the human. These factors explain our greater mental powers.[18]

Primates have larger brains than other mammals because of the larger size of their neo-cortex. The neo-cortex accounts for typically 10 to 40 per cent of total brain volume in other mammals, but begins at 50 per cent for the most 'primitive' of primates, rising to about 80 per cent in modern humans. Research conducted by British anthropologist and evolutionary biologist

In this context, therefore, the elephant is everything except your frontal lobe. It is everything that slips under your conscious radar.

THE ELEPHANT METAPHOR

Robin Dunbar and his co-workers demonstrated that neo-cortex volume correlates to social complexity, especially in relation to the frontal lobe. It is this advanced frontal lobe that essentially separates us from our primate cousins and embodies all that we associate with 'being human'. The frontal lobe allows us to have self-awareness – to be aware of our actions, thoughts, behaviour, feelings, and our environment.[19]

Other lobes are involved in creating the pictures, ideas and abstract concepts we have. They are also involved in the filtering of data through the senses to give us what we view as reality. But it is the frontal lobe that decides what to do with that information. So, while your other lobes may alert you if you are too hot, they will not formulate possible action steps to alter that situation, other than causing you to move. As the seat of your awareness, the meaning you attach to those pictures and ideas, and the ability to hold them wilfully in mind, is purely down to the frontal lobe. It is responsible for all the so-called higher functions such as reasoning, planning, intellectualising, learning and remembering, creating, analysing, and verbally communicating – to name a few. And it has an interest in commerce.

In this context, therefore, the elephant is everything *except* your frontal lobe. It is everything that slips under your conscious radar. The frontal lobe is your elephant rider and, although you (frontal lobe) may think you're in charge, there is some *serious* horsepower beneath you. And, unless you understand the ramifications of that, you'll continue to get poor results, particularly in business.

I say 'particularly in business' for a reason. And it's a very important point. Our brain has evolved through human development as a means of survival. If you look at the evolutionary timeline, we have been pretty well focused on survival for the vast majority of our evolution. Business is a very late entry in the human logbook. Business, trade and barter emerged from the early advanced civilisations such as Babylon, Egypt and China. Yet if you look at human development in the context of the millions of years we've been around, we're still in business kindergarten.

In modern times, starting with Adam Smith, the economic theories of Capitalism explain much of what applies in business today. *What we need to add now is the realisation that we are not biologically designed for business; we are biologically designed for survival.*

Your elephant will almost certainly cause you challenges in your personal life. That's what makes us human. Life without emotions and passion, without spur of the moment stupidity, would be dull. But emotion and spur of the moment stupidity don't usually help in business. We are encouraged to leave our emotions at home, yet it's not possible to go anywhere without our emotions or any of the other unconscious reactions.

Our elephant comes with us everywhere, whether welcome or not. This is a mixed blessing, for we can say the elephant has kept us, as a species, alive for all these years. But bringing it into a workplace? The results are predictable and often devastatingly counterproductive.

For the sake of relevance and focus, we need to imagine that everything *except* your frontal lobe is your elephant. And it is this source of unconscious knowledge, reactions, emotions, and beliefs that is the real problem when it comes to you being a living expression of your potential.

If you seriously want to close the performance gap for yourself and the people in your workgroup, then you have to understand the elephant and learn how to direct its power . . . its truly incredible power. Do you realise, for example, that not only does your elephant know things 'you' have long forgotten but it also knows things 'you' never even knew? Stop for a moment and think about that. Your mind is so powerful that it knows things your conscious memory has forgotten and it also knows things your conscious waking self never knew! We may only be aware of some 2000 bits of information, but we apparently store much, much more.

> **If you seriously want to close the performance gap for yourself and the people in your workgroup, then you have to understand the elephant and learn how to direct its power.**

THE ELEPHANT METAPHOR

As Dispenza says, "This subconscious intelligence [your elephant] knows so much more than what our personality self [elephant rider] knows; even though we think we know it all. This is a universal, fundamental aspect of every human being, independent of age, gender, education, religion, social status or culture. Few ever stop to acknowledge its power, will and intelligence."[20]

Chapter Summary

- Fundamentally, what we consider thinking isn't actually thinking at all. Real thinking has been disguised by the elephant's knee-jerk conditioned responses. These allow the thinking process to be interrupted by internal assumptions drawn against a myriad of external situations.
- The brain is a complicated piece of equipment and is still largely a mystery. Even the best neuroscientists in the world don't yet have all the answers.
- Author Joe Dispenza describes the difference between the conscious and subconscious mind in his book *Evolve Your Brain – The Science Of Changing Your Mind*. One aspect, which he calls *subjective consciousness*, is the consciousness we recognise as the 'you'. It maintains our individual free will and allows us to express ourselves as a thinking self. It is our self-conscious identity. The other element of consciousness, which he refers to as *objective consciousness* or *subconscious*, is the intelligent awareness that gives us life every day.
- Objective consciousness or subconsciousness is an evolutionary blessing to us because it ensures that the billions of daily tasks required for our body to stay alive are done without our conscious intervention or the need for a 'to do' list.
- These two minds are embroiled in two complex systems: Neo-cortex = the 'conscious' mind. Midbrain, cerebellum and brain stem = the 'subconscious' mind.

- These brain structures have evolved at different rates over millions of years. The neo-cortex is the most recent, and is the conscious thought centre. The neo-cortex is made up of four lobes.
- Although all the lobes of the neo-cortex are part of the conscious mind, for the purpose of explaining your elephant, the *frontal lobe* is all that really matters. The 'you' that you understand to be you is only possible because of the frontal lobe. In this context, the elephant is everything *except* your frontal lobe. It is everything that slips under your conscious radar.
- The frontal lobe is your elephant rider. And, although you (frontal lobe) may think you're in charge, there is some *serious* horsepower beneath you. Unless you understand the ramifications of that, you'll continue to get poor results, particularly in business.
- If you seriously want to close the performance gap for yourself and the people in your workgroup, then you must understand the elephant and learn how to direct its power.

3

A Very Expensive Elephant

By now you may be wondering about the damage this pesky elephant is causing. So let's take a moment to quantify that damage to find out how much it is costing you and your business. After all, why would you consider spending several hours of your life reading this book unless you could be assured it was worth your while?

If, as I'm suggesting, a large portion of your business challenges is not down to laziness, poor performance, being unable to hire the right staff, or anything else you can think of, but instead is thanks to an unruly elephant – then the question we need answered is how much does that elephant cost?

What price are we paying if we don't apply all we know and we consistently ignore good ideas and valid advice because it contravenes the expectations or beliefs of either our own or someone else's elephant? How much money is lost down the gap between what you *know* and what you *apply*?

Incentive to Pay Attention – the commercial consequences of the 'Performance Gap'

The Performance Gap – the difference between potential performance and actual performance – is *the* problem most business leaders are seeking to solve.

The figures and calculations below are derived from the outcomes of coaching businesses and coaching coaches over a decade-and-a-half in the field. The data collected covers every business type and industry involving more than 20,000 people in business and 4000 workgroups.

The Staff Value Equation

Let's say 100 per cent represents the capability of a staff member who is *applying* everything they know on the job, and whose good ideas are all actioned. That 100 per cent represents someone who has no unutilised potential and who can honestly look back on their performance and say, "I could not have done that better".

Based on that definition ... What score would you give yourself on a scale from 0 per cent to 100 per cent?

To clarify, consider that yesterday your every move was recorded and you had the opportunity to watch your performance. How many times would you cringe and think to yourself, "Mm yeah, I could have improved on that. I could have done that better"? With this in mind, again ask yourself what score you would you give yourself, on a scale from 0 per cent to 100 per cent.

At the time of writing this book, I would have posed this question to more than 4000 business owners or workgroup leaders. The answer was typically somewhere between 55 per cent and 70 per cent. For the sake of this demonstration, let's be conservative and take 60 per cent.

If you have 10 staff members paid, on average, $50,000, you have an annual wage bill of $500,000. If you're getting 60 per cent of their potential, then that equates to $300,000. You are paying half a million dollars to get $300,000 worth of their potential.

In this case, the 'Staff Value Deficiency' is $200,000.

> Will you ever eliminate the Staff Value Deficiency? No, because people are people, not machines.

Wage Bill	$500,000
Percentage of Potential applied @ 60%	$300,000
Staff Value Deficiency	$200,000

Figure 1 The Mathematics of Staff Value Deficiency

This Staff Value Deficiency of $200,000 is the difference between what you are *paying for* and what you are actually *getting from* your staff. I am yet to come across any like-sized business that is comfortable wasting $200,000 a year.

But what happens to your *wage* bill if you close this potential gap?

Nothing. If you behave in a way that lifts the team's performance to 80 per cent or 90 per cent of their potential performance, your payroll costs do not increase. OK, if you sustain this then turn up for work in a Ferrari, having traded in the Commodore, the team might tap you on the shoulder and talk pay increases. So, in time, there may be some wage pressure, but not initially. Not until it's working and you are reaping the benefits anyway.

Will you ever get 100 per cent? No, because people are people, not machines. But you should be able to get 80 per cent or 90 per cent. And that can mean a huge difference to your profitability or productivity without spending an extra cent.

Scary Facts

I'm sure you are expecting more evidence than this simplistic anecdotal demonstration. As mentioned, we've 'unpacked' and 'rebuilt' more than 4000 workgroups – dissecting each as we facilitated their self-assessment of performance in every process. Our analyses support the estimates about how big this gap is and how far typical workgroups fall short of their potential.

This deconstructing and rebuilding happens in a closed workshop, off-site, over the course of two days and is facilitated by a trained Business Coaching System practitioner. It is an interactive process where the coach encourages participants to share their experiences, noting the information on a whiteboard. Many techniques are employed to protect anonymity in assessment, so that genuine results are extracted. In those two days, we break down every function of the business in order to understand where improvements can be made.

The following four-step examination leads to many amazing and alarming statistics.

Step One

First we ask, "In which areas do your workgroup's major deliverables fall?" The workgroup will then identify their top 10 areas. We call these Core Functions.

Sample Core Functions list for a *motor vehicle repair shop*

1. Planning	
2. Finance	
3. Sales and Marketing	1 to 6 are 60% universal to all business
4. Administration	
5. Technology	
6. Human Resources	
7. Quoting and estimating	
8. Stock control	40% unique to specific business – in this case auto-repair
9. Vehicle repair	
10. Customer service and quality	

Step Two

We then ask the workgroup to break these Core Functions down into their key processes. Invariably they will determine that there are around 270 to 330 tasks that, in total, make up those Core Functions – tasks that when completed to an *agreed* standard deliver the full outcome for the workgroup.

Some of these lists may have 21 items. Some may have 28, some 35. But, on average, with 10 lists there will be about 300 different things that need to be done for a business or workgroup to deliver what it promises.

Curiously enough, where the workgroups are between 13 to 16 people – the size of the average workgroup – these numbers *rarely change* whether you're a football club, a bakery, or a real estate business.

THE ELEPHANT METAPHOR

Sample task list for Finance in the *accident repair shop* (remember there is a separate list for each of the 10 above)

1. Accounts payable	12. Salary reviews
2. Accounts receivable	13. Supplier selection
3. Aged payables	14. Supplier review
4. Aged receivables	15. Produce monthly reports
5. Debt collection	16. Draft narrative
6. Reconciliation	17. Finance meeting agenda
7. Cash flow management	18. Finance meeting minutes
8. Regular report schedule	19. Bank liaison
9. Statutory accounts	20. Internet banking
10. Liaise with external accountants	21. Filing
11. Internal audit	

Step Three

We analyse each of those 300 activities one by one and challenge the workgroup on its performance. How well do they feel each task or activity is done?

One of the acceptable answers is:

"This task is done as well as could be expected by this team, taking into account the skills of our team and the resources at our disposal."

That is, *at most*, they are allowed to say to the coach, "With the people we currently have, and the tools at our disposal, we do this as well as we can".

Remember the context... Imagine the coach standing in front of the workgroup – they have listed the 300-odd procedures that make up their business. Then the coach asks the above question in relation to *each and every one* of these 300-plus discrete activities. What percentage of them do you think would be counted in the category of tasks *done as well as could be expected?*

A VERY EXPENSIVE ELEPHANT

The answer is always in the vicinity of 15 per cent – an outcome that surprises almost everyone.

A typical response from our database

Sample task list for Finance in the Accident Repair Shop	Could Improve	Done as well as could be expected
1 Accounts payable	X	
2 Accounts receivable	X	
3 Aged payables	X	
4 Aged receivables	X	
5 Debt collection		X
6 Reconciliation	X	
7 Cash flow management		X
8 Regular report schedule	X	
9 Statutory accounts	X	
10 Liaise with external accountants	X	
11 Internal audit	X	
12 Salary reviews	X	
13 Supplier selection		X
14 Supplier review		X
15 Produce monthly reports	X	
16 Draft narrative		X
17 Finance meeting agenda		X
18 Finance meeting minutes	X	
19 Bank liaison	X	
20 Internet banking	X	
21 Filing	X	

The response above means that 85 per cent of the tasks performed by this workgroup (typical of most workgroups), related in this case to Finance, have been identified as having 'potential to improve'. It's important to note that 'potential to improve' in this context means doing so with the existing team and existing resources.

THE ELEPHANT METAPHOR

Step Four

Last step of the process is to have the workgroup tell us how each of these processes *should* be done. Effectively, they are setting their own benchmarks.

Now, how long do you think it would take the workgroup, having agreed that performance could be improved, to set each individual benchmark for improvement?

Answer: In a heartbeat!

Why? Because they knew the answer, even before the coach arrived. Think about that for a moment...

They already know that, in the course of their day, 255 of the tasks they do (which represents 85 per cent of the functions of the business) can be improved. They also know how to improve them.

Our experience confirms that the team is correct... about 80 per cent of the time. In other words, of those 255 activities they *think* they can fix, they actually *can* fix 204 with existing resources and personnel. The remaining 51 can then be solved after more intensive analysis.

More often than not, we know what we should be doing but, for some reason, we don't seem to do it. I think I know why. And it's not about motivation.

A classic example that most people could relate to is health and fitness. It's not rocket science. Everyone knows they should eat more fresh fruit and vegetables, less fat and sugar, and exercise at least three times a week. Yet how many people actually do it? Is it just laziness? Or is there more to it than that?

Clearly it isn't laziness and clearly there is more to it. This book is about describing the reasons for this gulf between theory and practice, knowledge and action, desire and outcomes, so that you can start to bridge the knowing/doing gap in all areas of your personal and business life.

So, after a summary, we'll turn to the *real* problem.

> In theory there is no difference between theory and practice. In practice there is.
> – Yogi Berra

A VERY EXPENSIVE ELEPHANT

Chapter Summary

- When asked about performing to capacity, most people state that they are working to 60 per cent in terms of doing the best job with what they have at their disposal. If you have 10 staff members and you pay them, on average, $50,000 – that's a $500,000 wage bill every year. If you're getting 60 per cent of their potential, that equates to $300,000. So you are paying half a million dollars to get $300,000 worth of their potential. In this case, the 'Staff Value Deficiency' is $200,000.
- You'll never get 100 per cent because people are people not machines.
- But you should be able to get 80 per cent or 90 per cent and that can mean a huge difference to your profitability or productivity without spending an extra cent.
- Increasing efficiency and workplace productivity does not incur increased wage costs – at least not initially.

PART TWO
THE ELEPHANT DECONSTRUCTED

Do you remember those blister packs of playdough you used to get as a kid, where there'd be separate strips of red, yellow, green, blue – and maybe white or purple? Once you started to play with that stuff, the playdough strips merged together in an inevitable mess of colour. Swirls of red twisting through the yellow and pockets of white or green. It always ended up brown. Even if you could find little hotspots of colour, you could never restore it to its initial separate parts.

In Part Two, we show how your elephant is engineered with characteristics I call *thinking limitations*. Although each of those limitations is separate – much like the strips of coloured playdough – once in motion, they become virtually inseparable in their combined effect on your thinking.

This section explores those individual thinking limitations and surveys the havoc they cause. You need to remember that, more often than not, your 'thinking' is being affected by a combination of many of the separate thinking limitations. They tend to blend together, just like the playdough, and it's this indistinguishable muddle that impedes *smart thinking*.

By appreciating their individual challenges toward clear thinking, you will also appreciate their collective power. More importantly, you will then appreciate why the solutions put forward in this book work.

4
Default Settings or Your Elephant Is Lazy

Have you ever driven home to find yourself there with no memory of the journey? Have you ever been asked a question and trotted out the answer you've given a thousand times before? Have you ever said, "That doesn't work around here", "You'll never get that past management", and "Customers won't go for that"?

Imagine you've just bought a personal computer. It's probably taken you a fortnight to decide which one but, thankfully, it's now sitting on your desk ready to go. You turn it on and see that it's already loaded with pre-set 'default' settings. These might cover things such as the language you are using, the time and date based on your location, spelling dictionary, margin width, common fonts, etc. If you are not computer literate, you would naturally assume these are hard and fast rules of the machine. Of course, they are not. The default settings are in place only to allow you to operate your new PC as quickly and simply as possible. The computer manufacturers know that people are impatient and want to get started as soon as possible.

Your elephant is just the same.

Think of the case of driving home oblivious to the journey. You've no doubt driven that way so often that the whole journey was on automatic pilot. That's scary when you consider how many of us are driving around in city traffic without engaging our brains. You get in your car and, by accessing the default setting 'drive home', your elephant takes over. Only when your normal route is obstructed does your brain engage in the challenge and require you to make a decision about what to do next.

Automatic responses and default settings are a serious hindrance to clear, objective thought. They act as shortcuts, which your elephant loves because thinking can be avoided and because your elephant is impatient. They offer him a perfect solution.

> **These automatic default settings are a serious hindrance to clear, objective thought.**

These defaults are developed over time and are part of our learning process. The cerebellum plays a crucial role in the development of default settings, as it coordinates movements and facilitates automatic hardwired memories and behaviour. The hippocampus, which turns short-term memories into long, is also involved. It associates experiences with emotional memories for processing vital information during learning and for encoding long-term memories.[21]

Basically, human beings learn by association. We make sense of the world by filtering the information we receive through our five senses and classifying that data for future use. In his book *Evolve Your Brain*, Dispenza[22] uses the example of a child throwing a rock at a beehive. His action results in the new experience of seeing bees swarm toward him, the angry buzzing of the bees, the numerous stings he receives, the consequent pain they cause and the first aid he receives. The brain will encode this new experience into wisdom, so that, in the future, the little boy won't make the same mistake again. This is Basic Survival 101. If we failed to learn from our experiences, say with a sabre-tooth tiger, we would not survive.

In the case of our little mischief-maker with the bees, his brain immediately scans the environment to log associated facts. Although he's not conscious of this process, his hippocampus is taking note of all the people, places, things, time, location, and events that categorise the experience.

When this little boy is older and smells the calamine lotion his mum put on his stings immediately after the incident, he will be flooded with memories of that incident. The more the emotional intensity of the event, the more hardwired are the responses.

This is supposed to ensure that, when little Johnny is bored and looks for a suitable target to hurl a stone at, he will think twice about choosing a beehive. If the experience was painful enough, he may even think twice about picking up the stone in the first place.

These associative memories are essential for learning, allowing us to use the familiar in the process of understanding the unfamiliar. For example, little Johnny learned to ride a pushbike and, 20 years later, he decides to buy a bright red Aprilia racing motorbike. In his quest to quickly master his new possession, he will automatically use his pushbike experience in learning how to balance and steer the motorbike.

> Basically, human beings learn by association. We make sense of the world by filtering the information we receive through our five senses and classifying that data for future use. Associative memories allow us to use what is familiar in the process of understanding what is not familiar.

Sometimes the associations we make aren't that accurate or helpful. Say, for example, you had to present to your class when you were nine years old. The day of the presentation, you had a tummy bug and didn't feel well. Your mum made you go to school anyway because she thought you were just trying to get out of it. You get to class and, when it's your turn to make your presentation, you throw up on Charlotte with the pink pigtails sitting in front of you. Chaos ensues. The kids in the class are screaming. Charlotte is crying. The room smells of sick. And your teacher is livid. Already feeling seriously unwell, you rush out of the room feeling humiliated as well. If this was your first ever presentation in front of a group, it's likely you will form associative connections between 'giving a presentation' and the smell and feelings of extreme discomfort and humiliation.

You may not remember the incident consciously 20 years on, but your elephant never forgets. When you are required to make a presentation, you feel sick to your stomach, you dry retch and feel very uncomfortable. Needless to say, presentations are not your strong point.

The truth about your incident at age nine, is that you were just unwell. Your being sick was not connected to giving a presentation at all. But your brain, in its eagerness to teach you and protect you from a similar experience in the future, has inappropriately coded the experience. That programming is now affecting your career. Remember some of these associations are formed when your brain isn't fully developed, so they are often flawed. You also have to consider the extreme physical reaction. Giving a presentation isn't, to the best of my knowledge, physically threatening. This is an overreaction due to biological software that hasn't been effectively updated for thousands of years.

It's not just presentations that are affected. These default settings or automatic behaviour patterns can be triggered by an association to even a single feature. So in the future, which would explain discomfort around, say, a woman in pigtails (weird though a woman in pigtails may seem regardless)?

Think how many of these associative connections you've made over your lifetime. Over time, some of them become hardwired into what scientists call conditioned responses. Hence our propensity to disengage from true thinking. So many of our thinking obstacles are caused by these knee-jerk reactions that we pass off as thinking.

Everyone has heard of Pavlov's dog – the experiment famous for demonstrating how quickly and efficiently an automatic response could be conditioned in an Alsatian. Regularly during the experiment, just before they were given food, the dogs heard a bell. After a while, they would salivate at the sound of the bell, even when no food followed.

The bell became the 'shortcut' to salivation. Conditioned responses like this, happen just as readily in human beings.

Consider, for a moment, your response when someone asks, "how are you?" Probably it's along these lines: "Good thanks. How are you?" or similar. It's a global default setting. What a banal thing to say, yet we don't even think about it. The question is asked, the default clicks 'play' and we respond like we have a thousand times before.

If a response comes back: "Are you sure? You don't look too great". It's only then, when an external force has questioned your conditioned response, that you consciously engage in the question and answer. It's only then, that you really engage in thinking.

Default settings are automatic. They 'kick in' once there's enough evidence to fit a pre-determined conclusion or point of view. This shortcut appeals because it means we can stop thinking and either get back to what we were doing or move on (aka *survival*).

> It is the knee-jerk reactions that we pass off as thinking that cause so many of our thinking obstacles.

In the case of the presentation phobia, it's not a fear of presentation that is causing you distress, as such, it's a consequence of the way the elephant operates. As soon as you are asked to give a presentation, it instantaneously flicks through your internal Rolodex for every past experience that involves 'giving a presentation' so it can classify the request and determine if the response should entail fight or flight. If past experience wasn't great, it will trigger a flight response and you start to feel queasy. As a survival tool, it's really quite smart. But as a business tool, it's a potential disaster.

By nature, we pull in these default settings from our past and make quick judgments – often based on nothing more than a single trigger point – instead of assessing each situation on its own merit. Rather than engaging with the challenge and assessing all the information, we scan the information to find familiar characteristics so we can dismiss it and move on. This is what's happening when you hear things like, "But we have always done it that way", or "That won't work around here".

Your elephant is not interested in taking the longer view. His assumptions are made in a nanosecond. Reassessing the information from a new perspective to make sure the judgments he's made on the information are still accurate or not is of no concern to your elephant.

These lazy or default settings also help us to cope with all the decisions and information that constantly bombard us.

> The lazy or default settings are automatic; they 'kick in' once we have enough evidence to fit a pre-determined conclusion or point of view. We rush to them because it means we can stop thinking and either start doing something or move on (aka survival). They also enable us to cope with all the decisions and information that constantly bombard us.

Let's examine this in 'real' life. Consider what people had to think about three generations ago. Compare that to what we have to think about now. The difference is enormous. Back then, they didn't have to wonder, for example, about what to wear because their destination determined what they'd need to wear – i.e. church, factory floor, bakery, etc. And they didn't have to wonder how to get there because there was typically only one way to get there. These days you probably make more decisions between waking up and getting to work than your great-great-grandparents made in an entire day. Yet the biological equipment we use – the brain – hasn't changed at all in those three generations. The information flow, however, has grown exponentially, taxing both our minds – the elephant's and 'yours'.

If, as modern scientific understanding[23] would suggest, we are being bombarded by billions of bits of information via our five senses, then to be instantaneously aware of all of it would render us insane. Your nervous system, therefore, reduces the amount of information you process or become conscious of. In fact, so dramatic is this reduction that we ignore more than ninety-nine per cent of all potential information.

Default settings free you from having to consciously process the vast majority of the data you receive. They are predetermined conclusions, stored and derived from past experiences – the brain's equivalent of reflex actions. When the doctor taps your knee with his little rubber hammer, your leg kicks out. Default settings are your mental equivalent.

Evolutionary psychology, also known as *modern Darwinism*, is a discipline that has gathered both momentum and respect. It merges research, genetic discoveries, neuropsychology, and paleobiology, among other sciences. From the perspective of evolutionary psychology, the associative learning model we are dealing with is referred to as *classification before calculus*[24].

Effectively, these theories point to the same conclusions: in an effort to make sense of changing and uncertain events and circumstances, the human brain classifies all experiences instantaneously for future use so that each new experience doesn't need to be reviewed from scratch and can, instead, be matched against past learning. Because of the sheer volume of information in our lives now, this skill has become well honed and we've developed prodigious capabilities for sorting and classifying information. Even in the pre-literate tribes in existence today, researchers have found that tribe members have encyclopaedic knowledge of their environment and that they have totally systemised and categorised their world[25].

The ability to classify everything in a nanosecond proved useful not only in terms of whether to eat the red berries or the blue ones, but also who in the tribe to align to. Instantaneous assessment of people occurs today as we make judgments about new staff or how effective the new manager will be, based on the colour of his tie or, more seriously, on his gait, his height, his hair or his vocal signature.

We instinctively form opinions about people we meet in five seconds or less.

Classification makes life simpler and certainly saves time but it's an automatic response that you need to know you're making. Therefore you have to learn how to question that knee-jerk reaction, not only in your own decision making, but also in the decision making of your team.

This has been extremely important in our evolution because reacting quickly goes hand in hand with staying alive. For example, in the Stone Age, unknown person in cave = danger. A quick response here would certainly have been useful. However, new boss who happens to remind me of my uncle Albert = I don't like him, is not.

This ability to classify without thinking is the key biological basis for the default settings we are talking about. *Classification* makes life simpler. It certainly saves time. But it's an automatic response you need to know you're exhibiting. You have to learn how to question that knee-jerk reaction, not only in your own decision making, but also in the decision making of your team. Otherwise you're missing opportunities. Guaranteed.

If you take the time to read the manual for your new computer or attend a computer training course, you may be astonished to discover how capable your machine is. Once you know how to use it properly, its efficiency and usefulness go through the roof. The same is true of your thinking (or lack thereof). At least if you're aware that you may be making knee-jerk reactions without proper assessment, you are in a position to do something about it. In that moment, become a more skilful rider and rein in your elephant.

Be warned, however – this isn't always easy to do on your own. Because our default settings are second nature to us we often cannot see them. Like the fish that doesn't see the water it swims in, we don't notice all the things we so readily take for granted. It's only when questioned by someone external to us, that we are able to see our knee-jerk reactions for what they are.

How to detect a default setting

When I give a presentation on this material, the question of default settings and how to identify them sparks great interest.

A good way is to listen for absolutes, generalisations, and open-ended phrases. You may hear yourself or someone else say, "That would *never* work here" or, "You *always* do that" or, "We've tried *everything*". When someone uses such absolutes, it's highly likely that a default setting is being engaged.

Unlock the default by using specific questions to get to the truth of the situation. For example, in response to, "We've tried everything" you might ask, "What specifically have you tried before?" You would continue seeking clarification, "How often did you try that? Did you attempt doing it any other way? So did that work?"

Inevitably, you'll get the truth, which is probably more like, "The guy before me tried that once in 1974".

Your elephant is lazy – What does it mean in business?

Scenario One

You are hiring someone and you make an immediate assessment of their ability based on an unconscious default setting. You hire this person because they remind you of someone you like. The appointment turns out to be a disaster.	
Perceived problem 1. The person has been dishonest about their experience 2. You made an error of judgment 3. The role was not specified adequately	*Perceived solution* 1. Insist on checking references 2. Employ a recruitment specialist to make senior appointments
Real problem You made your decision almost immediately and all the information you paid attention to after that point simply confirmed your immediate "gut" response. Fact is, even if you had checked the references you would have heard only what confirmed your quickly formed opinion.	*Real Solution* Recognise that you and everyone around you are making these knee-jerk reactions all the time and put a system in place that will demand verification and real evidence. Learn to question all your assumptions and expect validation before final analysis is made. Insist on evidence. This is where the saying "Don't tell me, show me" finds its application.

THE ELEPHANT DECONSTRUCTED

Your elephant is lazy – What does it mean in business?

Scenario Two

> You launch a new initiative and the workgroup makes some encouraging noises only to bury it a few weeks later. You are frustrated and can't seem to get your team to embrace change.

Perceived problem	*Perceived solution*
1. Your team is inflexible 2. You need to get rid of the complainers 3. They are just being difficult	1. Sack the trouble makers 2. Force compliance 3. Let the change slide
Real problem	*Real solution*
In business, we live in the past. You know this if you are a workgroup leader. Hebb's Model means we pattern all new information against the old. The leader is trying to drag the workgroup forward yet the workgroup is grounded in the past, the known and the safe. It's not personality; it's biology.	As leader, you must use the past to paint the future. When you are explaining a new initiative or venture, refer to past efforts and point out the similarities and the differences. You might say, "It's a bit like the customer loyalty plan we implemented last year, only we won't be expecting you to do X, Y and Z and we are reducing the amount of paperwork you need to complete so the customer and you benefit." Use the past to give your team context. If the past experiences have not been positive, then make sure you point out how this situation is different from the past situation or they will draw their own conclusions and block the initiative. You will hear the penny drop if you use this type of language.

The two scenarios in the inset boxes illustrate challenges and solutions when the impact of the elephant's lazy fallback to default settings is recognised and neutralised.

Chapter Summary

- Imagine you've just bought a PC or laptop. You turn it on and realise that it's already loaded with pre-set 'default' settings covering the language preference, time and date based on your location, spelling dictionary, margin widths, common fonts, etc. If you are not computer literate, you'd naturally assume these are hard and fast rules of the machine. But, of course, they are not. These default settings are in place so you can have your new PC operational without delay. Your elephant, likewise, is geared to your default settings.
- These automatic default settings are often a serious hindrance to clear, objective thought.
- Human beings learn by association. We filter the information we receive through our five senses, classify that data and form associations for future use. These associations are essential for learning and allow us to use what is familiar in the process of understanding what is not familiar.
- The associations, however, are not always accurate. Nevertheless, they can still become what scientists call conditioned responses. Such responses are nothing more than knee-jerk reactions that we pass off as thinking but are, in fact, obstacles to our thinking.
- Default settings are automatic. They kick in once there's enough evidence to fit a pre-determined conclusion or point of view. This shortcut appeals because it means we can stop thinking and either get back to what we were doing or move on (aka *survival*).
- These lazy default settings also help us to cope with all the decisions and information that we are constantly being bombarded with.
- These days you probably make more decisions between waking up and getting to work than your great-great-grandparents made in an entire day. Yet the biological equipment we use – the brain – hasn't changed at all in those three generations. The information flow, however, has grown exponentially.

- Your nervous system, therefore, reduces the amount of information you process or become conscious of. In fact, so dramatic is this reduction, we ignore more than 99 per cent of all potential information.
- Evolutionary psychology, also known as modern Darwinism, is a discipline that has gathered both momentum and respect. It merges research, genetic discoveries, neuropsychology, and paleobiology, among other sciences. From the perspective of evolutionary psychology, the associative learning model is referred to as *classification before calculus*.
- *Classification* makes life simpler. It certainly saves time. But it's an automatic response you need to know you're making. You have to learn how to question that knee-jerk reaction not only in your own decision making, but also in the decision making of your team. Otherwise you're missing opportunities. Guaranteed.
- At least if you're aware that you may be making knee-jerk reactions without proper assessment, you are in a position to do something about it. In that moment, become a more skilful rider and rein in your elephant.
- A good way to identify default settings is to listen for absolutes, generalisations and open-ended phrases. You may hear yourself or someone else say, "That would *never* work here" or, "You *always* do that" or, "We've tried *everything*". When someone uses such absolutes, it's highly likely that a default setting is being engaged.

5

The Greatest Default of All or Your Elephant Is Pessimistic

While we are on default settings, let's consider the most powerful default of all.

You drive home and, on the way, an ambulance speeds past you (*what are you thinking?*). You turn into your street and, as you approach the bend before home, you glimpse the unthinkable: the stationary, flashing lights of the ambulance (*what are you thinking?*). You round the bend and see the ambulance parked in front of your home (*what are you thinking now?*).

Now, let me add some additional observations and *listen* to your thinking...

- The ambulance is parked in your driveway.
- The back door is open.
- The gurney is out.
- Your front door is open.

Notice please, how your thinking went systematically from, "I wonder what poor sucker needs that ambulance?" to, "Oh my God, what has happened?"

There may indeed be certain people who are naturally more optimistic than others; however, in the absence of information, we are all programmed to default to the worst probable conclusion.

You see, default settings that inhibit your thinking are both *genetic* and *behavioural*. I believe we've just demonstrated that the most basic of the *genetic* default settings is 'automated' pessimism. Certain people may indeed be naturally more optimistic than others; however, *in the absence of information*, we are all programmed to default to the worst probable conclusion.

Think about it. When a company announces its intention to shed 10 per cent of its staff, all 100 per cent start worrying. Any meeting now called by a workgroup leader will invariably make people nervous. When your child is late home, you can imagine the identikit picture of the kidnapper. If a friend doesn't return your call, you confirm they are not on leave and have indeed received your messages. You soon start wondering what you may have said to offend them.

The reason for this 'automated' pessimism is survival. We can be better prepared if we envisage the worst-case scenario and, therefore, be ready to take effective action to avoid or minimise it. Say your family holiday involved a route you've never driven before. In planning your journey, you realise you don't know where any petrol stations are located along the way. Would you be optimistic about reaching your destination on half a tank of fuel? Or would you assume the worst-case scenario and make sure you never passed a petrol station if you had less than half a tank of petrol? In Australia, most people would opt for the latter, simply because the country is so vast.

The point to note is that we are programmed to expect the worst when we do not have the facts to indicate otherwise. From a business perspective, it's crucial to understand this. If you own a business and you're considering a merger or if significant changes are in the pipeline, and you choose to tell your staff nothing about it, any assumptions they draw will be negative.

This 'automated' pessimism makes communication more important than ever. If you don't communicate effectively with your staff, they will always default to thinking of the worst-case scenario in the absence of information. People fill in the gaps left by ineffective communication and, as a result, will assume all manner of unhelpful, stressful and destructive outcomes. So even if you can't tell them everything, tell them what you can, or at least assure them, if possible, of the positive nature of any changes. If they are not positive, tell them anyway because at least they can hear the truth from you, rather than imagine the worst for themselves.

Lack of knowledge means worst likely case. Worst likely case means many things, including fear. Fear means engagement of the survival mechanism, courtesy of the midbrain. The fight/flight reflex is, in effect, our deepest, oldest, and most instinctive response. This survival response is initiated by the sympathetic nervous system, which prepares the body for physical action by increasing heart rate, pulling the blood flow from the organs to the extremities, releasing adrenalin and opening up the lungs ready for fighting and/or running. This active survival response numbs the frontal lobe[26].

The ramification of this is that you stop 'thinking' and instead react. In other words, when you're scared, it might also look like you're stupid. When threatened, the body reins supreme. It will initiate a series of actions to ensure that it survives, regardless of how stupid it might look in the process. An ill-informed workgroup is a scared workgroup and will probably behave like a stupid workgroup.

As Bruce Lipton states in his book *The Biology Of Belief: Unleashing The Power Of Consciousness, Matter & Miracles*, "The simple truth is, when you're frightened, you're dumber. Teachers see it all the time amongst students who 'don't test well'. Exam stress paralyses these students who, with trembling hands, mark wrong answers because in their panic, they can't access cerebrally stored information they have carefully acquired all semester."[27]

By the way, to be a pessimist or optimist isn't a personality issue. An optimist is a pessimist who thinks faster. In our ambulance example at the start of the chapter, the pessimist *ends* with, "Oh my

> To be a pessimist or optimist isn't a personality issue. An optimist is a pessimist who thinks faster.

god, what's happened?" The optimist goes further in their thinking. They go past that and consider, "I'll check my mobile – no missed calls. The kids are at school. My partner was fine at 3pm, when we spoke. Of course! My daughter mentioned she was dating a paramedic. Now, that explains everything except the gurney. Maybe there is something else to think about?"

Don't be fooled – given the same limited information, we all start at the same point: pessimism.

One of the findings of evolutionary psychology[28] that is pertinent to this aspect of pessimism is 'gossip.' In days gone by, the ability to keep your finger on the pulse of the tribe and anticipate any changes that would necessitate shifts in loyalties was a valuable skill. The social hierarchy of the group was constantly changing, not least because people would go off to hunt and fail to come back. The gossips in the group survived because they were able to quickly align to new leadership and manipulate others.

The same can be said to apply today to the modern business workgroup. If we are hardwired to be pessimistic *and* we are also hardwired to rely on gossip then, in an organisational setting, if proper channels of communication are not maintained, you will only harvest the innate pessimism.

You can't stop people gossiping. So expect that they will fill in the blanks even before the authoritative person (that's you) emerges to tell them the truth. Why not manage by walking around, keeping your ear to the ground and plugging into gossip networks? Knowing who the gossips are in your organisation can be extremely helpful. These are people who consistently know things before everyone else. They seem to talk to the right people at just

> **One of the findings of evolutionary psychology that is particularly pertinent to this aspect of pessimism is 'gossip'. You can't stop people gossiping, so expect they will fill in all the blanks before the authoritative person emerges and tells the truth.**

the right time. This is politicking at its best. There's no point trying to stamp it out because it's the gossips, not the corporate memos, whose fingers are on the pulse of your employees.

Chapter Summary

- Default settings that inhibit your thinking are both genetic and behavioural. The most basic of the *genetic* default settings is 'automated' pessimism. Certain people may indeed be naturally more optimistic than others. However, *in the absence of information*, we are all programmed to default to the worst *probable* conclusion.
- From a business perspective, it's crucial to understand that this 'automated' pessimism makes communication more important than ever. If you don't communicate effectively with your staff, they will always default to thinking of the worst-case scenario in the absence of information.
- Lack of knowledge means worst likely case. Worst likely case means many things, including fear. Fear means engagement of the survival mechanism, courtesy of the midbrain.
- The survival response is initiated by the sympathetic nervous system which prepares the body for physical action by increasing heart rate, pulling the blood flow from the organs to the extremities, releasing adrenalin and opening up the lungs ready for fighting and running. This active survival response numbs the frontal lobe. The ramification of this is that you stop 'thinking' and just react. In other words, when you're scared, it can also look like you're stupid.
- An ill-informed workgroup is a scared workgroup and may therefore behave like a stupid workgroup.
- To be a pessimist or optimist isn't a personality issue. An optimist is a pessimist who thinks faster.

- According to scientists in the burgeoning field of evolutionary psychology, our thinking hasn't changed much despite tens of thousands of years of evolution.
- One of the findings of evolutionary psychology, particularly pertinent to this aspect of pessimism, is 'gossip'.
- You can't stop people gossiping, so fill in all the blanks with the truth.

6
Emotion and Reality Are Mutually Exclusive or Your Elephant Is Moody!

Watch a movie and you'll get an idea of how moody your elephant is. Have you ever watched a romantic movie of love and loss and cried like a baby? Have you ever suffered a couple of nights of insomnia after watching a horror flick? That it's just make-believe makes no difference to your elephant. It's in a flood of tears or terrified.

All your logical faculties, as well as your commonsense, know it's just actors doing their bit and that everyone is fine. But these reactions are based, in part, on the associations and defaults you have. If a film resonates with you in some way, the emotional reaction will be more swift.

Say Karen and I watch *Braveheart* together. She is likely to have a significantly greater emotional reaction to that film because she is Scottish and brings with her generations of Scottish heritage that I don't have. So that emotional, associative fast-track has her in tears before I've even got the nachos out.

So, like the playdough we referred to earlier, Karen's unconscious awareness (elephant) is combining with shortcuts of associative thinking, or default settings, as mentioned in the previous chapter. These combinations activate the emotional response leading to a completely illogical outcome. Even more illogical when you consider the lead part is played by the decidedly non-Scottish Mel Gibson.

Emotion is not only subjective, it's automatic. It had to be for us to make it this far. How people react emotionally is uniquely individual, often triggered by an associative connection or default setting. In many very real ways, emotion is what makes us human, yet we assume that, as soon as we enter the workplace, we somehow leave that vulnerability at the door. We don't. And, consequently, emotion influences our perception of events and can seriously interfere with our thinking.

Evolutionary psychology offers a new paradigm on how the mind evolved and suggests that the characteristic of emotion-before-reason was an essential part of survival.[29] Obviously, when facing danger, if we stopped to think too long, we would die.

In an uncertain world full of large carnivores with big shiny teeth, those who survived had their instinct button switched to 'on' all the time. As we evolved, our emotion-driven reflexes remained switched on and became hardwired into the human conditioning. And that undoubtedly kept us alive. Emotion is like an early warning system and its role hasn't really changed much in thousands of years.

Emotion can never be suppressed, according to evolutionary psychology. That would explain why even the most level-headed employee can go into meltdown after a review. People will always hear bad news loudest, regardless of what positive things are also said. When emotion – the expression of default settings – enters the picture, everything else is overshadowed or even forgotten.

> Evolutionary psychology says that emotion can never be suppressed, and that explains why even the most level-headed employee can go into meltdown after a review.

Psychologists since Sigmund Freud have spoken of perception being dependent on the individual. Carl Gustav Jung believed that perception was projection. What we consider to be reality, he concluded, is nothing more than our own traits and characteristics reflected back to us in life. The event itself means nothing until the individual applies meaning to the event – meaning that usually arises from earlier experiences the brain has classed as 'similar'.

There's a famous story making the rounds of the motivational circuit about twin boys whose father was in prison for armed robbery. One twin went on to become a successful lawyer. The other ended up in prison, like his father. When quizzed about what drove them in such diverse directions, they both pointed to their father's incarceration: "My father went to prison... what other choice did I have?" The lawyer, seeing his father's situation as a lesson, took a very different path. The wayward twin saw it as his fate and took the same path as his father. Same genes, same situation, same mother, same father, same upbringing – radically different perception and outcome.

John Ratey discusses this conundrum in his book *A User's Guide To The Brain*[30]. "All of our brains have the same general features that make us human, but each neural connection is unique, reflecting a person's specific genetic endowment and life experience. Circuit connections remain stronger or weaker throughout a lifetime according to use." Each twin in the story chose (whether consciously or not) to think different thoughts and interpret the environment in different ways, which created different brains and different outcomes. Neurologist and Nobel laureate Gerald Edelman[31] calls this process *neural Darwinism*.

Our brains are much more pliable and flexible than we've been led to believe. We do not become 'hardwired' unless we choose to become hardwired. Regarding the age-old debate of nature versus nurture, Ratey goes on to say, "In reality there is no debate. Most of who we are is a result of the interaction of our genes and our experiences".

This is hugely important to understand. Popular belief states that we are the product of our genes; that if we have a genetic disposition for a disease, for

> "In reality there is no debate [about nature versus nurture]. Most of who we are is a result of the interaction of our genes and our experiences."
> – John Ratey

example, it's virtually inevitable that we will get that disease. There are even cases of young, healthy women removing their breasts because of a family history of breast cancer. But science is discovering that this assumption is *not* true. Genes alone do not seal our fate. The environment exerts a major influence on how those genes are expressed and it is their combined roles that yield any specific outcome for an individual[32].

A huge part of this is how we perceive the world and the environment around us and what we make of those perceptions. When you analyse perception, you realise that emotion plays a decisive role in interpreting reality. How we feel at any given moment dramatically affects our perceptions of what happens around us. Our perception of reality is a subjective, emotion-fuelled interpretation.

Emotion is what makes life juicy but it can cause havoc in a business setting.

Imagine: you just got to work and you are checking your emails. Previously, before leaving home that morning, you had opened your snail-mail and discovered that your partner had made a large purchase on your joint credit card but hadn't told you. You're still angry about it. And here you are now, at the office, checking your email to see a message referring to a query on delivery time. Normally, you'd read the email and respond rationally. But right now, you're livid and you perceive the email from that perspective. You assume the sender is also angry and respond in an unhelpful manner.

Your emotions have polluted the situation, even though your anger has nothing to do with the email. The sender wasn't harassing you and had only asked a valid question. Email communication is a disaster waiting to happen because it rarely includes adequate information or any certain clues to the attitude of the sender. It's hardly surprising that emails trigger misunderstandings.

Imagine: you are sitting in traffic. You're late for an appointment and getting more and more upset. Suddenly, from out of nowhere, somebody runs into the back of your car. Now you are really mad. You jump out of your car, slam the door and storm toward the offending vehicle, armed and ready with some choice expletives. But the driver of that vehicle is ... your sister.

All of a sudden, a knuckle sandwich turns into, "*Oh no ... are you okay?*"

The event is the same. But the interpretation, the meaning and the emotions you attach to it are completely changed.

How often, in business, do we charge into meetings simmering with resentment and internal knuckle sandwiches that can so easily distort our judgments about the real situation and affect our decision making?

The part of the brain most concerned with emotion is the limbic system – specifically, the twin structure called the *amygdala* – one part in each hemisphere, perched above the brainstem. Joseph LeDoux, a neuroscientist at the Centre of Neural Science at New York University, was the first to connect the dots between emotion and the key role of the amygdala. Until LeDoux's research, it was thought that information received via the senses was first analysed by the neo-cortex and, based on that assessment, emotion was then added. However LeDoux[33] showed this to be inaccurate.

In actual fact, the amygdala often takes control before the neo-cortex, or thinking part of the brain, even knows what's happening

This is demonstrated in Daniel Goleman's best-selling book *Emotional Intelligence*. In his book, Goleman[34] refers to a friend who was on vacation in England, eating brunch by a canal. Taking a stroll along the water's edge afterwards, he came across a little girl, frozen with fear, looking at the water. Before he even knew what he was doing, he had jumped into the water fully clothed and saved a toddler who had fallen into the canal.

LeDoux's research explained why this sort of situation occurs. When information from the five senses reaches the thalamus in the brain, it sends two simultaneous signals – one goes to the neo-cortex for processing and decision

The amygdala often takes control before the neo-cortex, or thinking part of the brain, even knows what's happening.

making, the other crosses a single synapse to the amygdala. This means the amygdala often hijacks the information and reacts to a situation before the thinking brain has a chance to respond. So the man at the side of the canal jumped in at the behest of his amygdala before his thinking brain even registered there was a toddler in the water … or that his own physical wellbeing might be at risk.

The amygdala, it would seem, is a psychological gatekeeper looking to keep trouble at bay. It scans the signals it receives from the external world, assesses any potential danger and initiates the fight or flight response when necessary. If danger is perceived, response is automatic and you experience an emotional reaction that will fuel the body in the event of danger. Even a single trigger can set off the reaction. The emotional response is often linked to past conditioning or the default settings we covered in the previous chapter.

The exchange between limbic and neo-cortex activity is at the heart of many of our thinking challenges and goes a long way toward explaining those passionate outbursts we later regret. Emotion is the fuel we use to achieve our dreams and emotional expression is one of our greatest strengths. However, if it goes unchallenged in the decision making process, it becomes our greatest weakness. LeDoux said, "Some emotional reactions and emotional memories can be formed without any conscious, cognitive participation at all."

This non-cognitive aspect is responsible for another of your big grey challenges. Research clearly shows that emotion doesn't need facts and details prior to engagement. It will fire up at the mere whiff of a familiar 'danger' signal, possibly getting all involved into a world of trouble. Without even trying, we instinctively race to conclusions within milliseconds. We unconsciously interpret any situation or event, decide whether we like it or not, present that to our awareness as 'fact' and happily form an opinion about it – all in a matter of seconds. Your emotions literally have a mind of their own. And that mind is not necessarily in sync with the mind you think of as 'you'.

Logically it's best to get all the data before you act. We all know that. And we are reminded not to jump to conclusions but it's biologically difficult not to. The associative model means the brain is pushing you to a conclusion.

But, as with so many things, the first step toward improvement is acknowledging the problem. The truth, as we all know, is that once emotion enters, waiting for those facts to arrive is then impossible. It's too late – you're already emotional and now you are part of the problem. You won't even recognise the difference between emotion and reality. Your emotions are an innate part of your thinking process.

Emotion can so easily warp understanding. This can be valuable in helping to kick-start action. But it is also the easiest way to lead to manipulation.

> Our emotions quite literally have a mind of their own and that mind is not necessarily in sync with the mind we recognise as 'I'. What really needs to happen, in non-life threatening situations like commerce, is that all the thinking should be done before emotion is engaged.

In non-life threatening situations, such as commerce, what *really* needs to happen is that all the thinking should be done before emotion is engaged. In our view, the ability to do this consistently is a trait of great leaders.

Emotion is a powerful force that is often experienced in the strangest of places. I can vividly remember being at a football game – my team playing the enemy. In this particular game, my team kicked a field goal from about 30 metres out with seconds left on the clock. We won the game and I cried like a baby.

Let's think about that for a second. A guy kicks a piece of leather filled with air. It sails right between two sticks. The kicker happens to be wearing a white jersey with a big red 'V'. The year before, he was wearing a blue-and-gold jersey and three years from now, he'll be wearing a different jersey again. But on that day, he was wearing our jersey. We won and I had tears in my eyes.

This is not logical. If something significant happened to someone close to me, I'd cry. You might conclude, therefore, that I feel as much emotional attachment to my football team as I do to my family. I can honestly say that this is not true. But it does show how easy it is to trigger emotions – especially when the object involves sport, religion and brands. In the book *Buy-ology*, Martin Lindstrom explains how we buy anything that can be wrapped and presented in some form of emotional packaging[35].

Manipulating Emotions (Religious Rallies and Motivational Speakers)

The growth of the Personal Development industry has shown how easy it is to manipulate and control emotion. Many of today's seminars are more akin to a Billy Graham revivalist meeting than a business conference.

Now I am not criticising this format. Obviously it works for some of the people who attend. A few people do change their lives – but only because they are among the rare breed of individuals who can translate an idea into action (more on that later). For the vast majority, the format doesn't offer any long-term solution. The initial enthusiasm and proclamations of impending transformation are, more often, followed inevitably by a swift crash back to reality/normality because the emotional intensity of the revival-like format cannot be sustained.

What's happening in this arena is that information is being given to participants when they are in a heightened emotional state – either through music or exercises. It's not brainwashing – although I think we all need our brains washed occasionally; it's simply the use of emotion to create a memorable or compelling 'learning' environment.

The information given and the emotion felt are often completely separate, even mutually exclusive. In the head of the participant, however, the information has been attached to 'feeling good' – therefore, recall of the material is easier, yet the likelihood of implementation, in many cases, decreases.

It's similar to dieting. The seaweed and grapefruit diet may help you loose 5kg over two weeks but you will never maintain it – just as seminar junkies never maintain their high. Long-term weight loss requires small but consistent lifestyle changes, not seaweed and grapefruit. In the long term, you are so much more likely to implement and maintain changes that are logical and rational and exercised regularly in small doses, than those built on hype and razzmatazz given in one big dose.

Using emotion to engender change is a hit-and-miss approach because it's not based on structured, well thought-out reason that is relevant to the individual. Emotions can help with the recall of the ideas or ideals but they don't contribute to the *translation* of ideas into action. As a result, most people leave on a high and stay there for a week or so. In the meantime, they drive their family and friends nuts with enthusiasm before realising, to their dismay, that they don't have the ability to apply or implement what their own emotions would wish. They still have the emotion. They just can't apply it in everyday life as presented at the seminar. There's also now a different emotion. Anticipation has turned to remorse – or worse: booking in to the next event.

The evolutionary rationale for emotion is that it is *designed* to stop you *thinking* about threats or opportunities but instead *doing* something defensive or aggressive about them. In love, that might be useful or appropriate, but in commerce, it is not.

The Business Impact

When you get emotional (e.g., experience fear), you stop thinking and start *doing*: fighting or fleeing. Our ancestors 'used' fear as a key survival tool. It made them

> The evolutionary rationale for emotion is that it is designed to stop you thinking. In love, that might be necessary, but in commerce, it's not!

run and it made them hide. Then when they were safe, having made a spear, they emerged to fight.

To deal with someone who is anxious or concerned (i.e., emotional), you need to turn the emotion tap off before you can turn on the tap of logical information. Invariably this was done by a Charlton Heston slap to the face of the distraught leading lady in the old westerns, but it's not recommended for use at a workgroup discussion.

The problem, for most of us, is that often the emotion tap is stuck open. Evolutionary psychologists would say that's how it is for all of us. I'm certainly not saying this is necessarily a bad thing. And I know that emotion is what makes life enjoyable. However, if you are trying to get the best out of your business, department, yourself, or your team, you would do well to recognise the influence of emotion so you know who is working the controls – your emotion or the facts. And it's not just because it makes discussion difficult. Emotion is extraordinarily powerful when you are trying to manipulate a situation. It, therefore, has inherent dangers in the workplace. The exercise below illustrates this point.

Exercise – Watching Your Emotions

Try this experiment. Read the facts below and, while you do, try to gauge your emotions as each new piece of information is added.

The story is true. *(Adapted from a story in Uncle John's Absolutely Absorbing Bathroom Reader by the Bathroom Reader's Institute. 12th Edition)*

The Story of Augustine Le Prince
- Thomas Edison was a famous inventor.
- Augustine Le Prince was not.
- Augustine Le Prince was a French inventor who, in 1885, developed a prototype motion picture camera.
- In 1888, he received the first patent for a movie camera, both in France and the United States.

- He demonstrated the camera to officials at the Paris Opera House in 1890.
- Despite being well received, he returned to his workshop in Leeds, England, to perfect his machine.
- Six months later, he disappeared on his way to meet up with his wife, Lizzie, and their children in New York to launch his now perfected camera.
- Every morgue and asylum was checked and he was never found.
- In the search for him, a family friend (not realising the significance of his invention) may have destroyed vital proof of Le Prince's great achievement when he cleaned out his workshop.
- Le Prince never patented the last design of his movie camera.
- He did, however, reveal his discovery to a few close friends including his patent lawyer, Clarence Seward.
- In applying for the earlier patent, Seward removed a crucial clause that would have given Le Prince broad protection for his invention.
- Months after Le Prince's disappearance, Thomas Edison claimed to have invented the motion picture camera.
- Seward was also Edison's patent lawyer.
- Edison's invention infringed Le Prince's patent and, despite being heralded as a breakthrough, it was actually much more rudimentary than Le Prince's original machine.
- When Lizzie Le Prince tried to sue Edison, she learned that, under US law, a person is not declared dead until seven years after their disappearance and, as long as the holder of the patent is deemed to be living, only they can sue for infringement.
- Edison had a reputation among fellow inventors for being ruthless. Le Prince was, at one stage, going to collaborate with Edison but was strongly warned against it.
- Lizzie discovered that Seward's partner, Guthrie, was in Europe at the time of her husband's disappearance.

How do you feel about Augustine Le Prince? And how do you feel about Thomas Edison?

However, consider also...

- Inventors are often involved in patent battles.
- Edison had a reputation for being ruthless but he was not known to be violent and there was no evidence to suggest a connection.
- Seward was a prominent patent lawyer of the day.
- Le Prince was an alcoholic and plagued by debt.
- We only have Lizzie Le Prince's word that her husband had perfected the camera.
- The clause that was dropped from the original application was very complicated. In fact, the patent office itself didn't understand it until Le Prince went there and explained it to them.

So what can we conclude? *Nothing!*

But, as you read through the information given, it probably aroused different feelings toward each party. This is how easily emotion is manipulated. It takes real courage to wait until all the information is in *before* making a decision.

So should we attempt to remove emotion from business? Of course not. For a start, you will now have gathered that it's impossible to do so. Emotion is often the secret ingredient of brilliance and innovation. But you need to appreciate the challenges it creates and navigate around those while learning to harness it.

In business, rational thinking and logic are the steering wheel and should be used to determine directions for the organisation. Emotion is the accelerator that should be applied once that direction is established. This way you can move the business in a logically chosen direction as quickly as possible. Learning how to harness workgroup emotion and use its power to achieve goals is smart business. Allowing it to run amok is not.

Your elephant is moody – What does it mean in business?

Scenario
You have a performance appraisal to conduct on a member of staff. On the whole, you are happy with the performance but there are a number of things you would like to see improved. You deliver the feedback and your employee becomes extremely emotional and storms out of the room.

Perceived problem	Perceived solution
• The person is unstable – you were only giving feedback • Perhaps you were too harsh	• Call the person back to calm him down (which never works) • Make a note in the file that he is emotional, erratic • Ignore it

Real problem
Human beings are emotional and even when most of the news is good they will hear the bad news loudest. The employee as a rational, hard-working individual did not hear your feedback because their elephant is already on the rampage. The elephant felt threatened by the negative comments and went into fight or flight mode. In addition, it is possible that the elephant was reminded of a previous appraisal that did not go well and expected the worst probable outcome.

Real Solution
You need to mutually agree in advance what the Key Performance Indicators (KPIs) are for the role. How it will be measured and what the rewards and consequences are, should they be met or not met. When all parties know what is expected of them then a framework is superimposed around the elephant's natural instincts and emotion is greatly lessened or removed from the situation.

A "surprise" appraisal means the boss hasn't prepared properly. In a commercial framework the person being appraised should know beforehand:
i. What outcomes are expected from their work,
ii. What indicators will demonstrate they have achieved those outcomes,
iii. What evidence will be used to answer their indicators, and
iv. What rewards success will bring them?

Chapter Summary

- Just how moody your elephant is can be demonstrated by watching a movie. Have you ever watched a romantic movie of love and loss and cried like a baby?
- How people react emotionally is a uniquely individual experience – often triggered by an associative connection or default setting. In many very real ways, emotion is what makes us human, yet we assume that, as soon as we enter the workplace, we somehow leave that potential vulnerability at the door.
- Emotion is like an early warning system and it hasn't changed much in ages.
- Evolutionary psychology says that emotion can never be suppressed, which would explain why even the most level-headed employee can go into meltdown after a review – people will always hear bad news loudest, regardless of positive things being said before or after. Once emotion enters the picture, everything else is forgotten.
- Psychologists since Freud have spoken of perception being dependent on the individual. Jung believed that perception was projection. What we consider to be reality, he concluded, is nothing more than our own traits and characteristics reflected back to us in life.
- How we feel at any given moment has a huge impact on how we perceive what is happening around us. What we perceive as reality is subjective – it is an emotion-fuelled interpretation. And it is that perception driving emotion that creates what we consider to be reality.
- The part of the brain that has most to do with emotion is the limbic system. Specifically, the twin structures called the amygdala – one in each hemisphere of the brain, perched above the brainstem.
- Joseph LeDoux, a neuroscientist at New York University's Centre of Neural Science, discovered that the amygdala often takes control before the neo-cortex, or thinking part of the brain, even knows what's happening.
- The amygdala, it would seem, is like a psychological gatekeeper looking to keep trouble at bay. It scans the signals being received from the

EMOTION AND REALITY ARE MUTUALLY EXCLUSIVE

external world to assess any potential danger and will initiate a fight or flight response when necessary.
- This means that the amygdala often hijacks the thinking brain and reacts to a situation before the thinking brain has a chance to respond.
- Emotion is the fuel we use to achieve our dreams, and emotional expression is one of our greatest strengths. However, if it is allowed to become an unchallenged contributor to the decision making process, it becomes our greatest weakness.
- Your emotions literally have a mind of their own and that mind is not necessarily in sync with the mind you recognise as 'you'.
- What *really* needs to happen in non-life threatening situations, such as commerce, is that all the thinking should be done before emotion is engaged.
- The growth of the Personal Development industry has shown how easy it is to manipulate and control emotion. Many of today's seminars are more akin to a Billy Graham revivalist meeting than a business conference.
- Using emotion to engender change is a hit-and-miss approach because it is not based on structured, well thought-out reason that is relevant to the individual. Emotions can help with information recall but they don't contribute to the *translation* of ideas into action.
- The full impact of the emotions is that they are actually *designed* to stop you thinking. In love, that may be appropriate, but in commerce, it's not.
- If you are trying to get the best out of your business, department, yourself, or your team, you would do well to recognise the influence of emotion so you can know who is working the controls – your emotion or the facts.
- Emotion is often the secret ingredient of brilliance and innovation. But you have to appreciate the challenges it creates and navigate around those while learning to harness it.

7

Language Has No Unambiguous Dictionary or Your Elephant Isn't Verbal

"One great use of words is to hide our thoughts."
VOLTAIRE

Have you ever asked someone to do something and they return later with great enthusiasm and fanfare to declare the job complete ... yet what is done bears no resemblance to what you thought you asked for? Have you ever looked at a set of instructions – say for a video recorder, or the mildly complex children's toy you gave your niece for Christmas – and found "just follow these simple instructions" became a test of patience and endurance? The same with flat pack furniture. Or have you ever said to someone, "Sorry, that may be what I said but it was not what I meant"?

We've established that your elephant is impatient, pessimistic and moody. The next issue messing with your mental play dough is that your elephant is also non-verbal. This shouldn't be a drama as we all participate in non-verbal communication regularly. For a simple example of conscious non-verbal communication, consider when you're about to drive to meet someone on the other side of town and you decide, 'in your conscious mind', the route you'll take. You don't describe the route to yourself in words. You do that only if you get involved in a dialogue with someone else.

The subconscious mind, however, does not communicate in words. The reptilian brain and limbic system are not having a conversation with the frontal lobe in any way that we traditionally understand the word 'conversation'.

This conversation is all chemical. The amygdala is the radar that detects the environment and produces chemicals – chemicals to direct your responses, either in the form of action or not. There is no middle ground. No debate. No discussion. It scans the environment for a perceived threat, cross references clues with past experiences and, if there is a match, even a vague match, then action will be taken, whether that takes shape as an emotional outburst, as a feeling of discomfort, or in fleeing the situation. These chemicals are the brain's language.

In essence, emotions are the language of the subconscious mind and they also send signals to the conscious mind (B. H. Lipton)[36]. Of course, non-verbal communication – using 'the language of thought' – also takes place within the conscious mind, albeit less frequently than in verbal terms. (Evolutionary psychologist Steven Pinker is a preeminent authority on the subject of the language of thought and his many books on the subject are both recommended and illuminating.)[37]

Communication involving the elephant is non-verbal, below awareness, yet we try to interpret the meaning of those signals using language. Language is supposed to allow us to exchange views and ideas, and share information and knowledge. The concept is sound but the execution is flawed.

The communication tools we use cause problems because:

- Language has no universal dictionary;
- 'A picture paints a thousand words' yet, invariably, we use words not pictures to communicate;
- Hidden communication through body language can make interpretation confusing.

We need to be able to communicate with each other in order for us to function. In business, we need to articulate our vision and our expectations to our team so that we can arrive at the predetermined destination as quickly and easily as possible. We need a common language with which we can communicate those things. Yet the constraints of our everyday communication tools make that extremely difficult – so difficult in fact that, if you and your team do indeed envision the same destination, it'll be a bloody miracle.

> Communication within the brain is non-verbal, below awareness, and yet we then try and interpret the meaning of those signals using language.

Imagine you, the business owner or department manager, are the server computer within a local area network and all your staff or employees represent the workstations in that computer network. Separately, the workstations are valuable but together, they are even more powerful. So you need a way to connect them up to work as a team. The protocol – agreed, documented routines – that allows that to happen is language, the version of which we can think of as software. For instance, the software we are using to write this book is English. However, there is an important distinction between language-as-software and real software. If I enter the same information on two computers loaded with Microsoft Excel, I can confidently expect the same output. But that is not the case with language software. In fact, I can give the same information to two people 'loaded with the same language software' and I can confidently expect a different output. Why? Because their elephants are different.

Karen has a great story that illustrates this point perfectly. She has a friend who moved from Sydney to live in Edinburgh for a couple of years. The friend was phoning around for an apartment to live in and spoke to a nice Scottish young man, asking him innocently, "So how big is your unit?" There was a long pause, followed by a rather indignant, "That's none of your business". You see, in Australia, apartments are called units. In Scotland, they are not. He was confused by the question and, in the absence of information, his pessimistic elephant assumed she was asking a very personal question. Both were using the English language, yet two *very* different interpretations were drawn.

The only thing you know for sure when two people agree on something is that they have two different interpretations of what's just been agreed upon. It's only the degree of difference that requires examination. That there is a difference is beyond debate.

As a business owner, manager or team member, I'm confident you've had the experience of asking a team member to do a certain task, then been surprised when the result they produced was nothing like what you imagined you asked for. And the reason for this is one of the three constraints of language listed earlier and elaborated below.

Factor 1: Language has no universally consistent, unambiguous dictionary

> The only thing you know for sure when two people agree on something is that they have two different interpretations of what has just been agreed upon.

There is no universal, unambiguous common meaning to all words. Everybody has a slightly different interpretation of the same word. In fact, everybody's definition or vision for every word is based on their history, their knowledge, their education, their experience and their personality. The shortcuts to understanding words have evolved through their own unique experience and, since no two histories are the same, no two dictionaries are the same either.

To give you an idea of the size of this problem, consider that the English language contains 615,000 words, according to Bill Bryson's book *Mother Tongue*.[38] Add technical and scientific terms, and the number increases to more than a million words. That's a lot of words, most of which could mean different things to different people.

This is why, at the start of this book, we were so touchy about the meaning of 'subconscious mind'. Without clearing up semantic differences, if you went with your initial understanding of that phrase, my use of the term may have confused you or triggered different conclusions to what I was intending. This happens all the time in business.

Here's a true example to illustrate the point. I have three CEO clients who each use three different words to describe successful outcomes they're seeking in their respective businesses – "awesome impact on the bottom line", "phenomenal impact on the bottom line" and "scary". One says *scary*, one says *awesome* and one says *phenomenal*. If I used the *scary* word with the *awesome* guy, his thought process may take him to a completely different place when he hears the word *scary*. He may end up thinking, "Is John suggesting I should be scared of this rapid growth?" This particular person's use and application of that word is completely different to the other person's.

Let's say I have a 'label' that I use when my business is going really well. Let's say that label is the word "awesome", which then acts as a connector to a specific place in my thinking. What if a different word is then used to label that mental picture? If *you* use a word like, say, "scary" to describe *my reality*, then consider the *thinking* I have to go through to get to the meaning of *your* expression.

My thinking goes something like ... "Surely he doesn't mean 'scary' as in *The Texas Chainsaw Massacre*? And we are talking about my business. So maybe he's using 'scary' in a different context ... It's probably a word that can be used to describe a good outcome. In fact, it's probably some teenage expression that means 'great', like kids these days use the expression 'that's sick' to mean 'that's really good' ..." and so on and so on.

Note that such trains of thought happen. We don't decide to have them, they happen all by themselves ... because we are not in charge of our thinking. They are triggered by others, not us.

It doesn't matter how quickly it happens, it dilutes the quality of the thinking that follows. Now apply a multiplier to this for each person in the equation ... you start to appreciate the problems of language.

Words connect to pictures. The 'dictionary' your target audience is using is more important than yours. The fundamental irony is that if

I want to communicate with you, then I need your dictionary to be sure the communication is accurate but I have no way of accessing it.

The importance of the other person's dictionary and perspective is critical in business. In marketing, we are constantly told to step into the shoes of our customers. So why doesn't the same principle apply across all business? Far from trying to ease understanding and mutual appreciation of the subject, in many cases 'business communication' is an oxymoron. We seem to have developed a flat one-dimensional, convoluted way of speaking to one another, the apparent purpose of which is to devolve responsibility and increase complexity so as to deliberately diminish understanding. The legal profession is notorious for hijacking language but it permeates just about every corporate memo and business letter ever written.

Take the following example:

It has come to our attention that the pre-agreed employment hours as stipulated by your contract are not being met. Indeed it would appear from information gathered that this agreement is being consistently and flagrantly dishonoured. Please desist from this behaviour immediately; otherwise the company will have to follow the official procedure to rectify the situation.

As opposed to:

You have been late four out of five mornings for the past three weeks. Fix it or you will be sacked.

They both mean the same thing but the first is dressed up in jargon and innuendo rather than stating the plain candid truth.

Business communication is also partial to the passive voice, which is weak, evasive and safe. It allows the writer to complete his or her message without taking responsibility for it, without making a personal commitment to what is said and, therefore, enables them to hide behind the corporate entity. God forbid that business communication should elicit action. Stand tall, damn it. Throw back your shoulders, take a deep breath and make your communication sing. If you have something to say, say it with conviction and clarity or don't say it at all. (I warned you I'd be prescriptive, didn't I?)

Language and complexity – example of difficulties with writing instructions

Imagine someone asks you to write instructions for how to drive a car. You would probably write something like this:

"Get in the car, put on the seat belt, depress the clutch, turn the key, take the handbrake off, put the car in gear and take your foot off the clutch".

If a complete novice followed those instructions, they would probably stall the car ... if they even got that far. Why? Because the depth of information you gave about the nuances of driving a car has moved from something you *used to* think about to something you no longer have to think about. Your familiarity with driving has resulted in it becoming 'automatic'.

What a complete novice would require is something more like this:

"Open the car door and get into the driver's seat, which is the one with the steering wheel. Pull the seat belt out and clip it into the holder between the two front seats. Make sure the car is in neutral. To test this, move the stick shift from side to side. It should be in the bar of the 'H'. When you are sure the car is in neutral, push your foot down on the clutch. The clutch is the leftmost pedal. The easy way to remember the order of the pedals is ABC, from right to left – Accelerator, Break and Clutch. Turn the ignition key. With your foot pressed down on the clutch, shift the gear stick into first gear. First gear can be located and engaged by pushing the gear stick as far left as possible, then pushing it up. Look in the rear-view mirror and the driver side mirror to check for traffic. When you are sure you are clear of approaching vehicles, turn the steering wheel in the direction of the lane you wish to enter and slowly let your foot off the clutch as you simultaneously press slowly down on the accelerator (the rightmost pedal) while releasing the handbrake by your side."

Because driving a car becomes second nature after a while, you forget all the little, but crucial steps that you go through every time you get in the car.

This is generally what happens when someone gives instructions. They start to explain how to, but huge chunks of knowledge or simple little details are unintentionally forgotten or ignored. So the DIY advice only works for the 10 per cent of users who happen to think in the same way as the author. The potential for interpretation hurdles increases when the previously explained language variables enter the equation.

Words do indeed fail us. Even in the example above, room for misinterpretation is massive. As you read through the expanded version, how many images appeared that were potentially misleading? And questions, too ... What's a clutch? What is neutral? What exactly do I mean by the bar of the H? These instructions might make sense to someone who happens to think like me. But for everyone else, it could be double Dutch.

Factor 2: A picture paints a thousand words

Another inherent language challenge is describing pictures with words. When we try to communicate using words, what we really hold in our mind are pictures. Unfortunately, we rarely articulate the full pictures we 'see'. For example, if I use the label 'awesome' to conjure my image of when my business is going really well, then I assume that everyone else appreciates that same picture. Therefore, I don't articulate in detail exactly what I mean.

But I need to because *a picture paints a thousand words*. Using a few words is never enough, let alone one word like 'awesome'. People are not in a position to connect the same picture to the same word. And, as we don't all have the luxury of communicating in pictures, relying on words instead, our expression and explanation of what we mean is a mere fraction of what is needed for unambiguous understanding between the parties communicating. Figuratively speaking, if a picture paints a thousand words, we probably deploy between 70 to 100 words per picture. Upwards of 900 words we leave for the other party to make up.

Despite the overwhelming descriptive shortfall, we leave meetings and briefing sessions assuming the other people involved have a complete grasp of what was said. Meanwhile, attendees are happily filling the gaps in our communication with *their* experience, shortcuts, skills and knowledge, and not with *our* experience, shortcuts, skills and knowledge.

We don't have a universally accepted and collectively acknowledged platform for communication. Hence we experience confusion often. The result is a situation in which people interact every day, regularly missing the entire point of their communication.

This principle of '*a picture paints a thousand words*' is effectively demonstrated with a group of people. I'm sure you've seen it done before. A seminar presenter will get a volunteer up on stage and show him or her a picture that only the two of them can see. The presenter then asks the volunteer to describe the picture to the audience. The objective is to describe the picture in such a way that the audience can actually perceive it and recreate it.

> **Figuratively speaking, if a picture paints a thousand words and we probably deploy between 70 to 100 words per picture, it means there are upwards of 900 words we leave the other party to make up!**

What happens is that the picture envisioned by audience members and inspired by the volunteer's description bears little resemblance to the actual picture. The disparate images result not only between the audience and the volunteer, but also within the audience. Having interpreted the volunteer's instructions differently, everyone has created different representations. That's because a picture needs thousands of words to fully describe it. And as discussed already, even those thousands of words will probably mean different things to different people.

Even if the presenter said, "Draw a cat", the variations between audience members in how that cat looked and what it was doing would be vast. Why? Because each person, irrespective of artistic talent, is drawing from a different associative learning model, or default setting, of what a cat looks like. One may draw a tabby cat sitting on a windowsill because it reminds him of his Auntie Anne's cat, Fluffy. Another person may hate cats and the emotional reaction occurs so fast she finds herself drawing an alley cat, back arched and hackles raised. The instruction, "Draw a cat", however, was the same for all participants.

If you think of the brain as the computer and your native language as the software, until we load the data, the software on its own will be useless. Without the numbers, an accounting package is useless. Unless you start to enter text, a word processing package is useless. In this analogy, your brain relies on your life experience as data – the equivalent of numbers in an accounting package or the words in a word processor. To deliver an outcome of value, you need to provide direct, consistent and very specific language that everyone will be able to interpret in identical fashion. And this is impossible.

There is another aspect: the *context* created by the person asking the question. How we respond (frontal lobe and midbrain alike) to a question is significantly impacted by who is asking. More about context shortly.

Factor 3: Hidden communication through body language can be confusing

All communication is not done through verbal language. The non-verbal nature of the elephant goes some way to explaining why body language plays such a crucial role in communication. Body language is your elephant making himself understood. Have you noticed that from Moscow to New York, from Madrid to Chicago, everyone knows what "angry" looks like – with or without words?

In conversation we are minimalists, so we communicate using body language and many other nuances, such as tone and accent on particular words. We also interpret those same things as a means to further decipher the communication. In his book *Kinesics And Context*, anthropologist Ray L. Birdwhistell[39] explains that the effect or impact of our communication is less dependent on words than we may think. In fact, his research reveals that 55 per cent of the effectiveness of any communication is due to the physiology of an individual, whereas 38 per cent of the communication is a result of the vocal tonality, and only 7 per cent of the effectiveness of the communication is a result of the spoken words.

To demonstrate the power of vocal tonality, read the following sentences out loud, putting emphasis on the highlighted words.

> When there is a discrepancy between what is said and what is indicated via non-verbal information, people will pay more attention to the latter.

Why did he ask me that question?
Why **did** he ask me that question?
Why did **he** ask me that question?
Why did he **ask** me that question?
Why did he ask **me** that question?
Why did he ask me **that** question?

These identically worded sentences each instil radically different meanings, depending on the accent. And that's just the variation caused by tonality.

More than 60 per cent of communication is based on visual messages that are especially important in the first few moments of contact. Interestingly, when there is discrepancy between what is said and what is indicated via non-verbal information, people will heed the latter. Or should I say, your elephant will. Remember, he's non-verbal anyway, so he's not bothered with the 7 per cent word content.

Body language is your elephant's favourite language – it will protect you by ignoring the words and paying attention to everything else.

LANGUAGE HAS NO UNAMBIGUOUS DICTIONARY

You can gauge (or guess) a mood, a response or a level of enthusiasm from body language without the person uttering a single word. For example, how many times have you witnessed someone who was asked to stay back late at work respond with a "Yes" but their body language screamed "No"? We are in situations daily where the words being spoken are not congruent with the messages being transmitted through body language. As much as we would like to, we simply cannot dismiss it. Body language is a vital part of communication.

When someone takes on the role of instructing, their body language is usually very animated. You'll see a lot of hand movements, for example. These gestures are perfectly designed to make it clear to the 'explainee' exactly what it is being explained. There is, of course, no interpretation protocol for those hand movements (or for the concentrated look of determination).

When you look at the person receiving instructions, what do you see? Typically, you'll see a lot of head nodding. If the person receiving instruction is male, you'll see two or three times more nodding than if that person is female. I suspect this is because women are less ashamed to ask if they don't understand something. Testosterone, on the other hand, often prevents men from admitting they don't understand. Sometimes they feel compelled to act as if they understand the instructions *even before they are given*. (Please ... no letters!)

So what you end up with is a lot of nodding that slowly builds to a crescendo of, "A-ha, yeah, I get it, no-problem, leave it with me", followed closely by the recipient of the instructions thinking, "What the hell was that all about?"

The sheer volume of daily discussion is so high we are always on the lookout for shortcuts in our explanations. Remember, our elephant is naturally impatient. So it's constantly scanning the environment for clues that will allow it to classify the discussion, close it down and move on. Body language plays a pivotal role in that process, albeit unconsciously. And, while you may be unaware consciously of body language unless it's very obvious, your elephant is interpreting every nuance in an effort to find a match from its long list of default settings.

It's difficult to say which is the greater of two evils: that we use body language to qualify the communication, believing it adds to a congruent message; or that we think our interpretation of someone else's body language is correct.

A synthesis of the three challenges

These three factors conspire against us. Let's look at how – using a real situation that arose while Karen and I were working on a presentation. It illustrates perfectly all three of the previous pitfalls.

We were going to need an audio production and this was the start of the discussion . . .

> John: *I want you to produce an audio cassette.*
> Karen: *Uh huh.*
> John: *Can you do that?*
> Karen: *Sure.*

I knew Karen had some experience working in the audio production industry, hence my question. Enter Major Challenge One: our interpretation of "produce an audio cassette". It was wildly different . . . as we found out. Add to this Major Challenge Two: every time she made a positive statement or response, I used fewer words in explanation – I painted less of the picture. The final nail in the coffin of our understanding was her body language, which was very relaxed and laid back. I interpreted this to mean that she knew what I was talking about.

Within the space of perhaps two minutes, Karen had accepted the project. At that stage all she knew was the names of the interviewees.

Shortly after, we decided to analyse our interaction . . . just to see how guilty we had been of breaking our own rules. We also wanted to ascertain if the project would be heading in the right direction.

John: *Think of the job you just agreed to do. You've obviously built a clear picture in your head of what we're talking about. What are the chances that picture is anything like my picture?*

Karen: *Umm... probably nothing like it.*

John: *OK, let's start again.*

John: *I want you to produce an audio cassette.*

Karen: *What do you mean produce? What's the role you'd like me to play?*

John: *Well, I've got the people I need to be interviewed. But I'm concerned that we'll get hung up on the discussion and not be objective. I need somebody to represent the listener, because the audio technicians can't and the interviewees certainly will not be objective about the topic.*

Karen: *So what you're saying is you want somebody to direct and edit the recording.*

John: *Well, yeah.*

This is just a snapshot of the conversation. But I hope you can see how things can, so easily, go wrong through one simple word and two very different impressions of its meaning, with a body language misinterpretation thrown in.

Every time Karen gave an affirmative response in the first instance, I would start to delete words about what I specifically wanted and I interpreted her positive and relaxed body language as confirmation of her understanding.

For all I knew, Karen could have been thinking about what she was going to have for dinner that night. But I was lulled into a false sense of security by my interpretation of her responses and her matching body language. And Karen was lulled into a false sense of security by assuming I might actually know the technical difference between directing and producing. Would it have been any wonder then if she came back with something I may not have even recognised? It didn't happen because we applied some thinking to correct it. But it could have easily gone very wrong.

The lesson: Talk in the right direction

Simply by getting into the habit of talking in the direction in which you think, many of these would-be disasters will be averted.

The widest point of the communication gap is due to our tendency to verbally communicate in a different direction to how we think. Our instructions, demands and expectations are usually given as conclusions. That they were inspired by a series of preceding observations or experiences is overlooked. The fact is, if you communicate the thinking *behind* your conclusions, expectations and/or demands, you may not even have to *make* instructions.

Instead of asking Karen to do the last thing I thought of, it would have been better by far to share with her the thinking that preceded my request. What I should have said is something like this:

> "We are recording an audio cassette for business. The people being interviewed know their stuff but I'm concerned the interview will degenerate into jargon and miss the mark for the audience. I figure you know this audience well and you could probably pick us up if we disappear into a maze of pet topics and irrelevancies. Maybe you could even guide the questions a little..."

> Interestingly enough, effective business leaders do naturally share their thinking and, as a result, they are much more effective in getting the solutions they need.

This was the *thinking* that led to my *thought*, which was to ask Karen to produce the audio cassette. Had I given her this thinking instead of the concluding thought, she probably would have responded to my request that she *produce* it with, "Sure John, I'll *direct* it!"

Both parties need to take responsibility for giving and receiving accurate and specific details. The fact is, Karen's view of the world is different from mine. But if we understand that and work towards precision, then we are moving toward perfect thinking and communicating.

Effective business leaders do naturally share their thinking. They are, therefore, much more successful at getting the solutions they seek. As they move toward their objectives, the pictures they paint in the minds of their audiences leave less room for misunderstanding.

Implications for business

Language has the potential to be a precision instrument to be wielded with power and clarity. Alas, in the face of the restrictions discussed earlier and the many anomalies, it often degenerates into a blunt, lazy and altogether clumsy communication tool capable of causing confusion and widespread frustration.

We've convinced ourselves that our thinking is more adaptive than it truly is, perhaps assuming that quality communication is instinctive. Running might be instinctive. But becoming a Gold Medal athlete requires commitment and dedication. Basic communication is instinctive. But high-quality communication requires training.

To give you an idea how all these factors come together to cause big grey problems that can impede your success, I want you to imagine the following scenario:

You are at work. Your manager asks to see you in his office. After you enter, he closes the door behind you both. You've just sat down in front of his desk when he asks you, "Were you here last night at 6pm?"

What just happened in your mind? In the absence of information regarding why he's asking you that, you immediately assume the worst. You start scanning your memory for something you might have done wrong. You're immediately reminded of a similar experience in the past, which sets off an emotional reaction and you start to panic. You can't find the words to say anything. If any words came to mind, you'd stammer. Your elephant is in full control of your behaviour in that moment and there is nothing 'you' can do about it. Unless you know how to 'internally pat' your defensive pachyderm and tell him to chill out, you will have all sorts of trouble with the question. But calming your elephant takes practice and, above all, awareness that he's even causing such havoc.

Language inconsistencies can cause problems. They are exacerbated when emotion steps in, which can easily happen because of tonality, body language, or because of who the person doing the talking is. Emotions can also step in because of your own emotional state when spoken to, as well as the emotional state of the person addressing you. And finally, you are being influenced by the context of the situation. In the scenario above with your boss, had it been someone from a different department or a friend of yours who asked you that question, you wouldn't think twice about the question or the answer.

When you don't know why you are being asked about something, your default response will be to assume the worst. In the absence of information, human beings will *always* assume the worst likely scenario.

So if our language is, at best, imprecise; if our emotions influence our thinking with no real bearing on reality; and if our mind has created default traps that lead us to decisions before all the information is gathered . . . then no amount of 'new ways' is going to tame that elephant and help you bridge the performance gap. This is the crux of the problem and needs to be addressed first. I believe that, until now, no one has taken these challenges and their combined effect seriously.

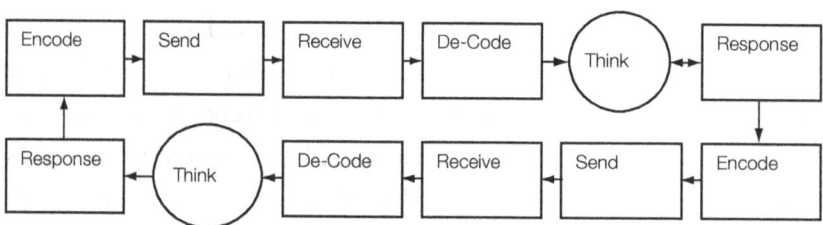

Figure 2 Communication: the loop of Encoded/De-Coded language and the thinking/processing needed before responding

Chapter Summary

- We've established that your elephant is impatient, pessimistic and moody. Your elephant is also non-verbal – your subconscious mind does not communicate in words.
- In business, we need to articulate our vision and expectations to our team so we can arrive at the predetermined destination as quickly and easily as possible. We need a common language to convey these things. However, the constraints of normal communication make it extremely difficult . . . so difficult in fact that, if indeed you and your team do arrive at the same destination, it will have been a bloody miracle.
- The only thing you can be sure of when two people agree on something is that they will both have different interpretations of what has just been agreed upon.
- Words connect to pictures. The 'dictionary' your target audience is using is more important than yours. The fundamental irony is that, if I want to communicate with you, then I need your dictionary to be sure the communication is accurate, yet I have no way of accessing it.
- If a picture paints a thousand words, we probably deploy between 70 to 100 words per picture, which means we leave upwards of 900 words for the other party to make up.
- Another aspect is the context created by the person asking the question. How we respond (frontal lobe and midbrain alike) to a question is significantly impacted by who is asking it.
- That the elephant is non-verbal goes some way toward explaining why body language plays such a crucial role in communication. Body language is your elephant making himself understood. Have you noticed that from Moscow to New York, from Madrid to Chicago, everyone knows what 'angry' looks like – with or without words?
- More than 60 per cent of communication is based on visual messages. This is especially important in the first few moments of contact. When

there is discrepancy between what is said and what is indicated via non-verbal information, people will heed the latter.
- If you communicate the thinking *behind* your conclusions, expectations and or demands, you may not have to *make* instructions.
- Effective business leaders do naturally share their thoughts. As a result, they are much more effective at getting the solutions they seek. As they move toward their objectives, the pictures they paint in the minds of their audiences leave less room for misunderstanding.
- Language has the potential to be a precision instrument to be wielded with power and clarity. Alas, in the face of the restrictions discussed above and the many anomalies, it often degenerates into a blunt, lazy and altogether clumsy communication tool capable of causing confusion and widespread frustration.
- Language inconsistencies can cause havoc. They are exacerbated when emotion steps in, which can easily happen because of tonality, body language, or because of who the person doing the talking is.
- So if our language is, at best, imprecise; if our emotions influence our thinking with no real bearing on reality; and if our mind has created default traps that lead us to decisions before all the information is gathered . . . then no amount of 'new ways' is going to tame that elephant and help you bridge the performance gap.

8

Your Elephant is Unqualified for Business

Here we are in the 21st century, thinking we are smart, intelligent business people. We study hard in school to get good grades. We go off to university to acquire qualifications for our chosen profession, along the way developing a few other qualities that may not be quite so useful. Eventually (certainly as far as our parents are concerned), we graduate and start our life of commerce convinced we've indeed learned the skills necessary for business success in our advanced, post-industrial world.

How wrong could we be . . . at least about how far, in our mentality, we have really advanced?

Evolutionary psychology essentially says that, despite inhabiting a vastly different world, we still operate with the ingrained mentality of Stone Age hunter-gatherers.

We think we have progressed and that the differences between our cave-dwelling forebears and the modern businessperson are eons apart. But are they really? With so much information existing outside our awareness and with so much so clearly left in the hands of a large, powerful, unconscious aspect of ourselves, are we really so advanced?

Expressed as a percentage of time we – as a species – have been in business for 0.125% of our existence – not a lot of experience.

Homo sapiens evolved on the plains of Africa some 200,000 years ago. The strong, fit and fast survived and passed on their genetic advantages via the process of natural selection. Business organisations, on the other hand, emerged some 250 years ago when *homo sapiens* moved into factories and offices.

Expressed as a percentage of time, we – as a species – have been in business for 0.125 per cent of our existence. And that's not a lot of experience. Business has been a one-minute-to-midnight addition to our evolution and one that we consciously fabricated.

Evolutionary psychology finds that we are hardwired to work best in groups of eight to 12 people – a number that mimics the traditional family or hunting groups from life on the African plains 2000 centuries ago. We are social creatures, living and operating best in tribes of 150. Any more and we start to split off into factions.

We instinctively screen information – first on emotion – not on facts or rational discussion. Your elephant, which is running your life in a far more profound way than you may imagine, is constantly scanning the environment for threats that appear similar, even vaguely, to past incidents. It's not just our own experiences that define or govern us. Emerging sciences have proved that characteristics are passed from generation to generation in our genetic make-up.[41]

We function on gossip, adhere naturally to hierarchy and instinctively display status through competition and one-upmanship. And we are protective of territory. In an uncertain world, all these features kept us safe. But put each of them in a business context and they manifest as a myriad of common organisational problems.

> Business is not what we were designed to do. The biology of our brain is still fundamentally operating under pre-historic conditions.

Business is not what we were designed to do. The biology of our brain is still fundamentally operating under pre-historic conditions. And we think that when we go to the office, we can easily disengage our biology, our innate makeup, and leave it at the door. We think we can be logical, rational and sensible. Not a bloody chance.

In an article in the *Harvard Business Review* called "How Hardwired Is Human Behaviour", author Nigel Nicholson, a professor of organisational behaviour at the London Business School, suggests what I have long believed to be true: managers may be working against our inner circuitry. Or, as he so eloquently puts it, "You can take the person out of the Stone Age, but you can't take the Stone Age out of the person".[42]

If we are fundamentally *not* designed for business and each of us is a complex product of genetic inheritance, culture and personal experiences, then it makes sense to accept that learning to navigate such complexity would lead to better results.

Your elephant's impatience, moodiness and pessimism is a genetic inheritance – an inheritance, remember, that is responsible for our survival for 200,000 years. It's not going to suddenly change in 250 years. We may have no woolly mammoths to contend with now, but large parts of our brain don't yet appreciate that.

Evolutionary Psychology is shedding scientific light on the hardwired patterns of behaviour, common among human beings across the board. It is not suggesting we are all the same, but it is highlighting aspects of our human-ness that we have not, until now, considered. In certain situations – commerce being one of them – we face all sorts of challenges caused by our hardwired patterns.

The investigations of Evolutionary Psychologists are even starting to look into how organisations can be designed to work in harmony with that biological inheritance, instead of trying to change it.[43]

Accepting that you can't change this inheritance is essential. It's who we are at a very basic, ancient level. And unless we start to appreciate that and acknowledge its implications, then we will continue to

> "You can take the person out of the Stone Age, but you can't take the Stone Age out of the person."
> – Nigel Nicholson

waste valuable resources trying to figure out solutions to problems that are nothing more than symptoms.

Luckily for you, I've already spent 20 years investigating how these issues play out and identifying the Business Laws of Nature that allow businesses to adapt. And remember, it's not just your elephant you need to tame; you need to learn ways to manage all the elephants in your workgroup. And that's what I'll be addressing in Parts Three and Four.

Chapter Summary

- Here we are in the 21st century, thinking we are smart, intelligent business people. However, Evolutionary Psychology essentially says that, despite inhabiting a vastly different world now, we continue to operate with the ingrained mentality of Stone Age hunter-gatherers.
- Human beings have been evolving over thousands of years. *Homo sapiens* evolved on the plains of Africa some 200,000 years ago. Business, on the other hand, emerged some 250 years ago when *homo sapiens* moved into factories and offices. Expressed as a percentage of time, that means, as a species, we've been in business for 0.125 per cent of our existence – not a lot of experience.
- We function on gossip, adhere naturally to hierarchy, instinctively display status through competition and one-upmanship and, finally, we are protective of territory. These features kept us safe in an uncertain world, but in a business context, they manifest as a myriad of common organisational problems.
- In an article in the *Harvard Business Review*, called "How Hardwired Is Human Behaviour", author Nigel Nicholson, a professor of organisational behaviour at the London Business School, suggests what I've long believed to be true: managers may be working against our inner circuitry. Or, as he so eloquently puts it, "You can take the person out of the Stone Age, but you can't take the Stone Age out of the person".
- Your elephant's impatience, moodiness and pessimism is a genetic inheritance – an inheritance, remember, that is responsible for our

YOUR ELEPHANT IS UNQUALIFIED FOR BUSINESS

survival for 200,000 years. It's not going to suddenly change in 250 years.
- Evolutionary Psychology is starting to look at how organisations can be designed to work in harmony with that biological inheritance instead of trying to change it.
- The good news in all this is that I've already spent 20 years identifying how these issues play out and how to manage your organisation around the inevitable challenges they create and *still* succeed.
- Remember, it's not just your elephant you need to tame; you need to learn ways to manage all the elephants in your workgroup. And that is what Parts Three and Four of this book are all about.

9

It's Not All About the Elephant

Before we get to the solutions offered in Parts Three and Four, there are a few more issues that you need to be aware of. I refer to these as 'the miracle of being in business'. I want to put all the cards on the table in terms of exactly what you're up against in business. But be assured, there is good news at the end. This step is essential for you to gain a complete picture, hopefully causing a change in your perspective. Such a shift is necessary if you are to take action on what you read and make a really positive impact on your business.

Going into business is like having a child. No one can prepare you for the almost overnight metamorphosis from 'party animal' to 'parent'. The concerns you have prior to the birth pale into insignificance as you face the reality and enormity of the change. It can be the most wonderful experience in life but, at times, it's terrifying. Going into business, especially for the first time, is much the same.

The BCS team and I have worked with more than 4000 businesses and have seen this unknown and unconscious metamorphosis occur time and again. I've experienced it first hand myself and regard it as one of many business conundrums. When I first became involved in the field of business coaching (that term wasn't even around then), coaching was a hobby of mine. Over time, through trial and error, I invented a special coaching tool for solving problems. I tested it on a few willing guinea pigs and it manifestly helped them and their businesses improve.

So I decided to turn my hobby into my profession. I started a consultancy. My methodology worked and business was thriving, as were my clients' businesses. It was fantastic. I was doing what I absolutely loved and everyone was winning. Each new client was a new adventure – an opportunity to fine-tune the methodology and study further how we process information and how we think. It was a series of live, interactive explorations of the 'being in business' experience and seeing how we tick as individuals and members of workgroups. I was in seventh heaven. What I didn't realise at the time was that I was designing a way to help myself and others gain control of their elephants.

I soon realised I didn't really enjoy some of the work – such as developing the marketing collateral to promote and explain the business, or developing the technology platform to record and process data and extract information, or producing output reports from the workshops.

Naturally, the thought occurred to me that if somebody else did those jobs, instead of me, then life would be perfect. So I decided to build a company to answer that challenge, developing a team of committed fellow coaches and providing an environment where we all did only things we loved doing. Meanwhile, the things we don't enjoy would be done by dedicated people who do enjoy that type of work. So I hired coaches and trained them to teach my methodology and I hired office staff to handle the administration. Perfect, right? No, not perfect. I ended up spending my time managing people which, of course, meant I rarely got to do the stuff that made me want to start the business in the first place!

Like thousands of people before me and thousands of people after me, I thought

> **I, like thousands of people before me and thousands of people after me, thought I was going into business to do what I love (coaching) – but I was wrong: I went into the elephant management business.**

I was going into business to do what I love – coaching. But I was dreaming. I woke up to find myself in the elephant management business and I was not at all prepared for it.

If you are a business owner then I can almost guarantee your experience has been similar. You were probably very good as a technician of your business. You then decided to create a business from that. And suddenly you found yourself expected to be an expert in everything but the thing you were trained in. This happens all the time with staff, too. You have a brilliant salesman and then you decide to promote him to sales manager, in charge of a team of 20 other sales people. You are left scratching your head as it turns into an unmitigated disaster. The individual goes from star performer to donkey overnight. And not only that, s/he is miserable.

Consider this – there are six ubiquitous or near-universal business core functions:

1. Planning
2. Finance
3. Operations
4. Sales & Marketing
5. Human Resources
6. Technology

Add to these the specific functions arising from whatever the business does. Each of the near-universal core functions is a discipline in its own right with tertiary qualifications available to their practitioners. Some people dedicate their *lives* to being good at *just one*. Those of us who go into business are, for practical purposes, expected to have degrees in all six.

The performance gap is a significant contributor to the astronomically high business failure rate. Yet when you look at it from this perspective, the miracle

> Some people dedicate their lives to being good at just one discipline! Yet when we go into business we are expected to have six degrees!

is not that so many businesses fail, but that any succeed at all. And succeeding is more often than not down to sheer bloody-minded determination, owner commitment and plain hard work.

In addition to the biological elephant-based challenges and the fact that you're expected to be a genius to succeed in business, there are three simple, yet profound observations about human nature that also hinder good performance.

The three 'Observations' are:

1. Invention is a primary motivator
2. Turning ideas to action is a talent not everyone has
3. Adults cannot be taught

Let's look at each one.

Invention is a primary motivator

In his classic book *Utopia*, Thomas More hit the nail on the head when he said, "And verily it is naturally given to all men to esteem their own inventions best."[44] In other words, people are highly motivated by *their own* ideas.

In our quest to close the performance gap, we seek new information but, as I suggested earlier, lack of information is not the problem. The problem is translation. And one of the crucial indicators of whether or not an idea is going to be translated into action is the very source of the idea. If you have an idea for your business that will involve one of your team members doing a certain task a certain way, no matter how

People are highly motivated by their own ideas. Experience has also shown that if someone is capable of having an idea or drawing a conclusion, then with some facilitation they are typically also capable of creating the how of implementation.

enthusiastically you explain your idea to that person, statistically, the odds of it being implemented well are relatively low. Why? Because the person having to do the work is not personally attached to the idea.

On the other hand, if the person charged with the task sees the idea as his or hers, the chances of it being well implemented improves dramatically – turning that idea into reality is now personal and that's inspiring. Besides, we understand our own inventions best and trust them the most.

Experience has also shown that if a person is capable of conceiving an idea or drawing a conclusion, then with some facilitation they are typically also capable of creating the 'how' of implementation. It is rare indeed to find a case where an agreed strategy, produced via a *structured thinking* approach, cannot be readily implemented by the group who devised it.

By our estimates, when the person with the idea is the one who will implement it, most of the motivation needed to get the job done comes automatically. (As a coach, I know from experience that when the idea is generated by the workgroup, facilitating development of an implementation plan will need only half as much work as when the idea comes from me.)

You may remember, back in the Preface, I encouraged you to deface this book ... this is the reason. If you read this book and think the ideas are interesting but don't really apply them to your own situation, then they remain 'my ideas' and you won't do a damned thing with them. If, on the other hand, you scribble freely in the margins and adapt the ideas to your own particular situation, then they suddenly become *your* ideas and the likelihood of their successful implementation increases immediately.

Turning an idea into action is not innate – it's a talent not everyone has

The second important observation is that the ability to turn an idea into action is a talent. Not everyone has it. It is not a learnt skill.

You can't just teach it and it would be incorrect to assume it can be easily fostered in people. In most cases, the individual may have the knowledge to do the task differently but will lack the innate skills to instinctively see the series of logical action steps that makes implementation easy.

Interestingly, evidence is emerging from brain science showing that certain people are more biologically inclined toward action than others. The *basal ganglia* in the midbrain are responsible for integrating thoughts and feelings with physical actions, and science has demonstrated that 'doers' actually have a slightly higher level of basal ganglia activity than most people. So if you just happen to be one of these people – great news. If not, then don't worry; you are part of the majority for whom acting on ideas is not that easy or natural.

> The second important observation was that the ability to turn an idea into action is a talent and therefore not everyone has it.

Witness the personal development industry – getting thousands upon thousands of people to pay thousands upon thousands of dollars to hear how to 'change their life'. Even if the information given is excellent (and often it is not), there is an assumption that you just have to do it and make it happen. But it's the ability to 'just do it' that is a talent or biological characteristic. Some people may indeed change their lives and achieve massive results. The majority will not. Moreover, the majority are left feeling even worse about themselves than they did before they arrived. Before, at least, they could draw comfort from not knowing what it was they were meant to 'just do'. Now there's the added pressure of knowing what it is they should just do, but still can't. 'Just do it' might be a great slogan for Nike but it causes endless guilt and distress to many others.

> People wrongly assume that this inability to act on ideas is one of the causes of the Performance Gap and rush out to top up their knowledge and ideas bank.

People wrongly assume this inability to act on ideas is one of the causes when it's one of the symptoms of the Performance Gap. They respond by rushing out to top up their knowledge and make deposits in their ideas bank. Just look at your bookshelf, if you don't believe me. How many books have you actually read from cover to cover? How many were you excited about but never built on the knowledge derived from the information? Then look at your corporate training budget. Does it tally with an increased bottom line and better efficiency? Or are things much as they've always been?

> **Reverse engineering outcomes into simple action steps is a complex thinking challenge and some people just 'have it', whilst some don't!**

There are people in the workplace who, when they tell you they'll do something, you know it's as good as done. Others will tell you they'll do something and you treat their words as a reminder that you'll have to do it yourself.

To write this off as lack of commitment or application is simply wrong. Granted there are occasions when this may be so but, for the most part, people want to do a good job. They want to be good at what they do and feel satisfaction from their work. The truth is that the conversion process – reverse engineering an outcome to formulate simple action steps – is a complex thinking challenge which some people rise to and some do not.

Ask one of your chronic implementers what makes them able to turn ideas into action and they will most likely say something like, 'I just do it' or, 'It's easy' or, 'I don't understand why everyone can't do it' – a dead giveaway that implementing is a *talent*. The expression of the art is always complex, yet seems simple to the truly talented in that area. To the artist, the doing or creating seems quite natural. If you accept this, then you can liberate the people and the systems they are in from false expectations. Instead, you can support them by implementing procedures that facilitate the development of step-by-step processes needed to go from idea to action.

This facilitation is the key factor in the success of the mushrooming coaching industry. Never before have the phenomenally untalented achieved so much. A mediocre business coach can still yield amazing results for the client. Why? Coaching – even mediocre coaching – can work, because it circumvents a number of critical thinking challenges that all human beings have, and breaks the process from idea into action into manageable, accountable steps. A coach also adds that critical element of objectivity (through a process we will soon explain) called *binary thinking*. In short, a second mind greatly assists in keeping the elephant in check by questioning the assumptions and the emotional responses we so naturally rush to. Plus, that second mind brings external accountability for your dreams that can almost force you into action (more on that in the next section).

Obviously, exceptional business coaching offers so much more than that. But surprising results are possible from even an unsophisticated intervention. Even the coaching I'm talking about here is much more than just facilitating and counselling. When you add special techniques, such as *binary thinking*, to a unique formula for best ways of developing commercial plans (for strategy, operations, performance management, etc), then you have something new, something of a breakthrough.

On a four-year government-sponsored Australian Research Council grant, a leading Australian organisational research centre worked with the coaching services industry to develop an in-depth analysis and categorisation of the field. The researchers concluded that, to enable fitting the BCS coaching approach into the Business Coaching space, a special category needed to be specifically defined. This category became known as *organisational coaching*, and is differentiated from business, life, executive, and even populist 'coaching' offers.

The report from the completed study may be accessed through the websites of both UTS and BCS[45]

> **The New Discipline of Business Coaching – The UTS Research Project**
>
> University of Technology, Sydney partnered with Business Coaching Systems in a four-year research project aimed at quantifying and qualifying the validity of business coaching. The aim of the research was to set standards of excellence and best practice for this important but at the time as yet formally unregulated field of practice.
>
> At its launch, the project's rationale, methods, goals and contributors were signalled in the following manner.
>
> Business coaching combines business planning with facilitation techniques to assist in defining and achieving goals. Its recent emergence means its effects on managerial behaviour and organisational performance have not been rigorously researched.
>
> The research project between University of Technology, Sydney and industry partner, Business Coaching Systems will change that. By combining qualitative and quantitative approaches to investigate the craft of business coaching, the study will highlight what is important in business coaching – why it is important and how it works.
>
> This will lead to the development of best practice and governance methodologies, interaction norms, processes and outputs, thus bringing much-needed benchmarks to the field. Not only will this protect the clients who turn to business coaches for genuine assistance, but it will also protect the business coaches – clearly differentiating the good from the bad and the just plain ugly!
>
> By being involved in this crucial research project and working closely with respected academics in the field, such as Professor Stewart Clegg, Business Coaching Systems is part of bringing essential validation and authenticity to the industry and remains at the cutting edge of business coaching methodology.

Adults can't (or won't) be taught!

The third observation is that adults can't be taught. The reason kids ask "why?" so much is because not knowing is acceptable. And they know they don't know. But something happens between the ages of 13 and 20. Some strange biological imbalance starts to make us feel as though we ought to know *everything*. Witnessing this biological imbalance many times, both (I hate to confess) in myself and in those in business around me, led me to this third important observation.

My evidence for this proposition comes from my experience in the Financial Services industry. As Education Chairman for the industry association, I commissioned a study on the effectiveness of the courses we provided. At the time, the industry as a whole suffered from enormous 'churn', with very few field sales staff lasting longer than four years in the business. In fact, the major insurance companies owned up to the fact that 90 per cent of those who joined the industry were gone within four years.

Apart from the obvious waste of time for the salespeople and the companies they represented, this inefficiency was costing the insurance industry millions of dollars in recruitment and training.

I wanted to know if our Association programs were *positively* impacting on this statistic. The answer was 'yes'. We found that 78 per cent of people who graduated from the Association's introductory program were still active members 10 years after completing it. This conclusion was based on the records of our then 1130 members, noting when they had completed our training programs. The 78 per cent figure did not even account for those who'd completed the course and were still active, but had elected not to remain members (membership being voluntary).

This left me wondering what was different. The answer was simple – the course didn't actually *teach* anything; it allowed participants to *learn*.

The approach the course took was, "This is your assignment for next week – try this". Participants were given the assignment for actions on yellow sheets of paper. When they came back a week later with their answers on the yellow sheets, they were then given white sheets that explained the theory behind the expected actions. Basically, the training forced them to learn through experience, not theory.

I attributed the outstanding results of the survey to this approach. For me, it led to the conclusion that adults would only learn through doing and having that doing interpreted. Adults learn backwards, if you like – which is the basis for the expression 'learn from your mistakes' and seems to be the only learning we grown-ups do.

I am not the only one who has come to this conclusion. In the 1980s, researchers from the Centre for Creative Leadership in North Carolina found that managers learn by doing. What may seem commonplace and obvious today was, at the time, radical and changed leadership education and development forever.[46]

Modern understanding of brain biology also supports this idea, based on the number of nerve-cell connections that are formed as we learn new information. If those connections are actively utilised, they become 'hardwired' like well-trodden paths. Then the presence of familiar trigger points will fire off pre-existing default settings and lead to conditioned responses that will circumvent the neo-cortex altogether. So we react as we've habitually reacted so many times before and, therefore, not as much 'space' is left for learning in an adult brain. Biologically, the brain can continue to change even in old age. New knowledge and new information will create new connections. But your open attitude to learning and willingness to change your mind will play a huge part in your very ability to do so.

The best way to get an adult to develop the discipline to build a business plan, for example, is to coach them through writing one. Create an environment that will allow them to build the business plan through a series of answers to questions that are important to such a plan – not by teaching them the theory behind the planning process.

Let's say I take two business owners. One I teach the principles of a SWOT analysis, then say, "Go away and do a SWOT analysis on your business". The other I simply ask the right questions

> Adults learn backwards – which is the basis for the expression 'learn from your mistakes' because it's the only learning we grown-ups do!

> Biologically the brain can continue to change even in old age. New knowledge and new information will create new connections but your open attitude to learning and willingness to change your mind will play a huge part in your very ability to do so.

about the business's strengths, weaknesses, opportunities, threats, and record the answers.

The first business owner is unlikely to act on the knowledge. But the second now has the benefit that the knowledge – a SWOT analysis – is intended to deliver. Unless the first business owner *leverages* their newly acquired knowledge, it is useless to them. In time, if they wish to apply it, they will likely have to re-learn it. On the other hand, the second business owner has the *benefit* of the knowledge – whether they understand it or not. *And*, if they experience the benefit, they will be motivated to understand and apply it.

The miracle of being in business

Let's look at these three observations and see how they are connected.

Even if new knowledge, by itself, *did* make a difference to the Performance Gap (which I will show is changeable)[47] then, unless you thought of the idea yourself, the likelihood of you translating idea into action is statistically low, especially if you don't have the natural 'Nike' spirit. Also, if your adult mind is too cluttered with automatic reactions, then learning new information can be really tough.

For the record and before we dive into the solutions, I am not suggesting we stop seeking new information, knowledge and ideas. More knowledge is never a bad thing. However, field experience has proved time and again that for an individual or for a business, *potential improves as you journey toward it*. The more I work on converting my potential into performance, the more my potential expands.

But potential must be tempered with application. So what to do?

Well, you could spend the next 40 years in therapy trying to unravel a lifetime of conditioning. You could go to workshops to identify your limiting beliefs and set about changing them. You could wrap yourself in an orange bed sheet and chant endlessly at a candle. *Or* you could read on and learn how to apply a thinking methodology that will effectively remove the negative aspects of your elephant while harnessing his awesome power. You won't need to understand why you are the way you are ... you'll just need to learn to work with it and get on with the job.

So stop trying to close the performance gap by jamming it with knowledge. Instead, recognise the biological and genetic implications of learning and implementation, then use the concepts in this book to unlock your ability to rely on what you already have. Let that experience identify what it is you *don't know* that you really *should know*. Then go and learn those.

Chapter Summary

- On top of the challenges of your elephant, you as a business owner have other difficulties to overcome, which I call "the miracle of business".
- Like thousands of people before me and thousands of people after me, I thought I was going into business to do what I love – coaching. But I was dreaming. I woke up to find myself in the elephant management business and I was not at all prepared for it.
- There are six ubiquitous or near-universal business core functions. Some people dedicate their *lives* to being good at *just one*. Yet we go into business and are expected to have degrees in all six.
- The miracle is not that so many businesses fail but that any succeed at all. More often than not, succeeding is down to sheer bloody-minded determination, owner commitment and plain hard work.
- In addition to the biological 'elephant'-based challenges and the fact that you're expected to be a genius to succeed in business, there are three simple, yet profound observations about human nature that also hinder good performance: *Invention is a primary motivator*; *Turning ideas into action is a talent not everyone has*; and *Adults cannot be taught*.
- People are highly motivated by *their own* ideas.
- Experience has shown that, if someone is capable of conceiving an idea or drawing a conclusion, then they are typically also capable, with some facilitation, of creating the 'how' of implementation as well.

- The ability to turn an idea into action is a talent and not everyone has it.
- Reverse engineering the outcome to formulate simple action steps is a complex thinking challenge, which some people rise to and some do not.
- A mediocre 'business coach' can still yield amazing results for the client. Why? Even mediocre coaching can work because it circumvents a number of critical thinking challenges that all human beings have, and breaks the process from idea into action into manageable, accountable steps.
- Observation number three is that adults can't be taught. The reason kids ask "why?" so much is because not knowing is acceptable. They know they don't know.
- Adults learn backwards – which is the basis for the expression 'learn from your mistakes' and seems to be the only learning we grown-ups do.
- Biologically, the brain can change. New knowledge and information will create new connections. But your attitude to learning and willingness to change your mind will play a huge part in your ability to do so.
- Look at how these three observations are connected: Even if new knowledge, by itself, did make a difference to the performance gap (we will see it does not) then, unless it's your idea, the likelihood of you translating the idea into action is statistically low, especially if you don't have the natural 'Nike' spirit. Learning new information can also be tough if your over-20-year-old's mind is cluttered with automatic reactions. Unless you consciously put them aside and maintain an open mind by constantly and actively challenging your assumptions, it will not get any easier.
- For the record, I am not suggesting we stop seeking new information, knowledge and ideas. More knowledge is never a bad thing. Field experience has proved time and again that the potential of an individual or business improves *as they journey toward it*.
- But potential must be tempered with application.
- Stop trying to close the Performance Gap by jamming it with knowledge. Instead, recognise the biological and genetic implications of learning

and implementation and use the concepts in this book to unlock your ability to rely on what you already have. Let that experience identify what it is you *don't know* that you really *should know*. Then go and learn that.

PART THREE

MANAGING YOUR ELEPHANT THROUGH SMART THINKING

We all have an elephant happily living in our heads, and knowing that or not will determine how good we become at handling it. Your elephant has enormous power but, by now, you would have recognised that the power isn't always directed toward assisting your positive aspirations.

Hopefully, you'll have recognised your own situation in these pages and had a little chuckle along the way. Everyone has an elephant to manage and there's nothing to be ashamed of when you realise it's been making most of your 'decisions' lately.

Left to our own devices, we are not in control of our thinking nearly as much as we might assume. Our elephant is impatient and, as a result, is always looking for shortcuts. Our elephant is moody which means that emotion arrives before the facts. Our elephant is also pessimistic – especially when there are gaps in the information. Consequently, we confuse the results we arrive at through this web of *autonomic* responses, emotional reactions and natural pessimism for genuine thinking. To top it all off, we then articulate this flawed perspective to others, using the imprecise medium of language.

Put all that into an environment we are not designed for – such as business – and it's hardly a surprise the results are often poor. You're not getting the results you want because you're not in charge of your elephant.

This book gives you the tools to turn that around. Part Three is all about how to take charge and how to foster smart thinking. It's all about you and what you can do personally to rectify the situation. This section discusses the behaviours you need to adopt as your own – if you are to master your elephant. These new behaviours will not only help you think smarter in the workplace but also to think smarter in all areas of your life.

The solution has two components: *binary thinking* and *thinking systems*. Both are important and the extent to which you use both components will determine the speed of your transformation.

Binary thinking can be thought of as an external solution to an internal problem. Binary thinking is the reason coaching – even mediocre coaching – can make a huge difference to an individual or business.

The Thinking System, on the other hand, is an internal solution to an external problem. It is the methodology I mentioned earlier that will remove your elephant from the decision making process, allowing you to truly make progress. It is the Thinking System that separates average thinking from smart thinking.

> The solution has two components – binary thinking and the thinking systems. Both are important, and the extent to which you use both components will determine the speed of your transformation.

10

Binary Thinking

In his book *A User's Guide To The Brain*, John Ratey writes, "...when you hit your knee on a desk, you probably rub it to make it feel better. Why does rubbing a spot that has just been injured reduce the pain instead of aggravating it? Because the act of rubbing sends a second set of the tactile signals to the brain. As the brain is finite and will have to pay attention to both signals at once, the second stimulus leads to a reduction in the perceived severity of the more intense first one."[48]

If it's true that a second stimulus – rubbing the knee in this instance – can distract your elephant, then what could a second stimulus do when it comes to problem solving?

Have you ever had a stranger at a party engage you in a discussion about your own business and, despite having no knowledge of your business, lead you to the solution to a particular business challenge you are facing? Have you ever discussed a personal problem with a friend and, through that discussion, found a best next step, even though you had imagined that none was available. Have you ever observed someone undertaking a task, suspected something was amiss, drew

Binary thinking is simply the presence of a second mind which in theory allows objectivity and subjectivity to happily co-exist in the discussion for the first time.

their attention to it with a question, and their response was, "Oh gee, I'm glad you picked that up!" Have you ever approached someone with a problem of your own and, as a consequence of their questioning, seen the solution spring from your mind like a jack-in-the-box? Have you ever noticed the difference a facilitator can make to a business meeting?

In all of these cases, the phenomenon at play is binary thinking. Binary thinking is simply the presence of a second mind, which allows objectivity and subjectivity to happily co-exist in solving a challenge. This is critical because genuine problem solving requires subjective and objective reasoning and we don't have the benefit of subjectivity and the benefit of objectivity in the same mind at the same time ... ever. They are mutually exclusive. You can't be looking at something objectively and logically, as well as looking at it passionately and emotionally, in the same moment. Rationality and logic provide benefits – as do involvement, engagement, passion and conviction – but they cannot provide those benefits simultaneously. They cannot occupy the same thinking space about a problem at the same time.

We are encouraged by media, seminar presenters and countless books to believe that when it comes to our problems, the 'answers lie within'. And they do. Yet how many of us can actually extract them when we need them? Sometimes expertise can also be a hindrance.

Often we can't find a solution when faced with a challenge, regardless of how many times we go over it. We are literally stuck in our own thinking. In these circumstances, our brain is telling us, in the only way it can, that it is unable to do what we want it to do. It requires assistance to the internal thinking problem. Then, from nowhere, something *external* triggers a whole new thought process and the solution emerges.

That external trigger provided the impetus for the necessary *information* to be retrieved in order to solve the

> This process of involving a second mind – even one that isn't really connected with the problem – is extremely powerful and can lead to solutions that you alone would never have found

challenge. The information was always there, but you needed an external trigger or influence to activate a different search route in order to find it. Often we are so attached to the problem, or the conclusion we are searching for, that we miss the way to the solution.

We experience the power of this concept every day. Involving a second mind – even one that isn't really connected with the problem – is extremely effective. It can lead to solutions that you alone would never have found but that you actually surfaced from within yourself.

In order for our thinking to function to its potential, we must seek the solution from outside the problem, not from within it. That's because successful problem solving often requires the one thing we can't give *ourselves* – objectivity.

The Microsoft Encarta College Dictionary defines objectivity and subjectivity as follows:

Ob-jec-tiv-i-ty.
- The ability to perceive or describe something without being influenced by personal emotions or prejudices.
- The actual existence of something, without reference to people's impressions or ideas.
- The quality of being accurate and independent of individual perceptions.

Sub-jec-tiv-i-ty
- Interpretations based on personal opinions or feelings rather than on external facts or evidence.

Imagine a stranger questions you about some aspect of your business. Your response is to search for the answer. In that moment, you are demonstrating your *ability to perceive or describe something without being influenced by personal emotions or prejudices*. Now, imagine a colleague asks you the same question. Chances are *rather than thinking about answering the question*, your defences will rise and you will ask yourself why you are being asked the question.

An outsider can provide objectivity and context, allowing you to supply the answers or content without suspicion, resentment, or fear of polluting the thinking process. This is why a counsellor is always going to be better placed than your brother-in-law to assist in marriage problems. There are no sides being taken, no opinions being projected, simply questions being asked to highlight the challenges so that mutual solutions can be found.

If this lack of objectivity phenomenon didn't exist, then marriage guidance counsellors would not get divorced. They would simply give themselves the thing they give their clients – the umpire's impartial (objective) perspective. When you visit a psychologist or a counsellor, they provide the context and ask pertinent questions that will illuminate the answers you need to find for resolution. Those questions are not random. They are very deliberate questions. Powerful business coaching is the same.

In order for a thought to be *perfect*, two contributions must happen concurrently – *Subjective* (skill, knowledge and experience matched with the target or outcome) and *Objective* (dispassionate, uninvolved questioning). The more dispassionate and uninvolved the objectivity, the purer the thought and the more powerful the outcome.

This twin power is evident in all areas of life ... Did you know for example that the earth is intrinsically dependent on

MANAGING YOUR ELEPHANT THROUGH SMART THINKING

the moon? In his highly recommended book, *A Short History Of Just About Everything* Bill Bryson says:

> *Not many of us normally think of the Moon as a companion planet, but that is, in effect, what it is ... Without the Moon's steadying influence, the Earth would wobble like a dying top, with goodness knows what consequences for climate and weather. The Moon's steady gravitational influence keeps the Earth spinning at the right speed and angle to provide the sort of stability necessary for the long and successful development of life. This won't go on forever. The Moon is slipping from our grasp at a rate of about 4 centimetres a year. In another two billion years it will have receded so far that it won't keep us steady and we will have to come up with some other solution, but in the meantime you should think of it as much more than just a pleasant feature in the night sky.*[49]

Our whole existence is dependent on the moon, yet nothing lives on it, nothing grows on it ... it's a big rock. Despite that, without it, we would be doomed. Our mind is the same. Another person doesn't even have to do much, s/he just needs to be present and ask the odd question. S/he doesn't even need to understand the problem. Effectively, for all it matters, they can be a big empty rock. The important thing is that they are present. For maximum impact, it helps (a lot) if that second mind has some (proven) tools and systems to follow, to facilitate a successful outcome. But benefit is still derived from just having the second mind involved and assisting.

Everything on the planet is divided into two categories.

- Things you *can* control
- Things you *cannot* control

Which do you spend most of your energy on?

Most people spend *most* of their *thinking* time and energy on things they don't or can't control. Ironically, they do preside over a huge number of under-performing elements over which they have total dominance.

If you are in total control of things you *can* control, then you are in the best possible position to *influence* things you *can't* control.

To get control... introduce a second mind. The presence of a second mind will always deliver better results than engaging just one. Human nature is such that we'll make decisions emotively, then try to validate our decisions intellectually. But that's far harder to do when someone is on hand to question your choices.

> **Most people spend most of their thinking time and energy on the things they don't or can't control.**

Your subjective perspective is not helping your business. Everything you're doing, you may be doing below your potential performance level – objectivity is needed. And, as one mind can't be both subjective and objective at the same time, you need to involve someone else's mind.

The missing piece of the puzzle is no secret to athletes who have long realised the importance of an external force. In order to get the most out of ourselves, we need to be coached, coaxed and held accountable. Athletics coaches watch you run. We need someone to watch us think.

So you can fully appreciate the relevance and importance of binary thinking, it is useful to look at the five stages of an idea. In order for an idea to travel the distance between thought and validation, it meanders through a specific sequence. Done in isolation, without the benefit of an external testing system, this process is not only complex but also highly vulnerable to early mortality.

The influence an external second mind has on the development of an idea

> **Your subjective perspective is not helping your business. Everything you're doing you may be doing below your potential performance level, which needs objectivity.**

can be better understood by particularising *the steps through which an idea typically passes as it moves from inspiration to commitment.*

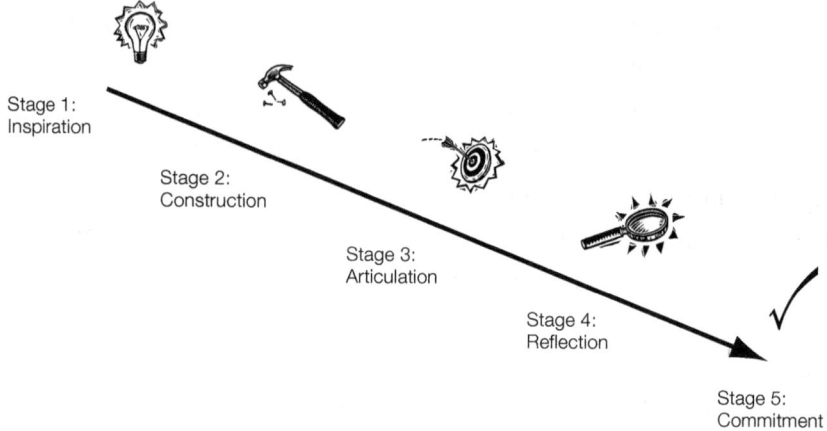

Figure 3 The Five Stages of an idea

It's extraordinary how personal a process it is. Think in those terms as you read through:

1. I'll leave the neurologists and authors, such as Arthur Koestler,[50] to explain this phenomena but we know it as an 'ah-ha' moment. You get the idea ... Let's call this stage *Inspiration*.
2. You convert the idea into an expression 'in your head'. Sometimes the idea cannot be expressed and it may die right there. Sometimes, having converted it into 'words' in your thinking, its shortcomings are exposed. Hence, in a team situation you get "Hey, I know ... why don't we? Ah, no don't worry, it won't work." Let's call this stage – where the idea takes shape in thoughts that can be expressed – *Construction*.
3. You express the idea. In other words, it survives the internal construction and is ready for public broadcast. The idea is in the public domain now and often it dies there. Someone challenges it, "But if we do that, how will we ..."? And you concede the point there and then. Often, though, it passes this test. Let's call this third stage *Articulation*.

4. Someone repeats the idea and, for the first time, a stranger is looking after your creation. Often the idea dies here because it is *different* when someone else articulates it. All of a sudden, objectivity enters and it changes the complexion of the idea. On other occasions, you hear it back and it sounds as good as it did when you told yourself. Let's call this stage *Reflection*.
5. Finally, you or someone else writes the idea down. Sometimes the idea dies here. Writing it down gives it formality and a perspective that is different and you discover its weaknesses. Alternatively, it survives. Let's call this stage *Commitment*.

In our experience, ideas that make it to stage five, particularly when they emerge intact from a workgroup, are likely to be 'good ideas'. Ideas that are thus 'chaperoned' do emerge validated because they've been enhanced along the way by input from additional sources. They are, therefore, more likely to survive to implementation, thanks to the benefit of collaboration versus sole sourced isolation.

You won't be asking yourself the questions you need to ask along the way because you are too busy thinking about the idea, not the questions. Your elephant's default settings will trap you into assumptions that are untested. And, because *you* came up with the idea, you are subjectively attached to it and the scope for emotion to cloud your judgment is huge. Without a second mind, you can get lost down rabbit warrens for years, wasting time on ideas without relevance or worth.

Think of Darwin, the man responsible for arguably the most important scientific theory of all times. He toyed in isolation with the idea of evolution for so long that he was almost pre-empted by another scientist. The second mind, in the form of fellow British naturalist Alfred Russell Wallace, wrote him a letter outlining Darwin's own, as yet unknown, theory back to him. Only then, did Darwin finally drag himself away from his beloved barnacles and focus on publishing the findings from his voyage on the "Beagle" decades before.

Binary thinking is essential for clear thinking and clever planning. But the presence of a second mind is not always enough. If, however, that second mind is equipped with a *thinking system*, then results improve exponentially.

Chapter Summary

- Binary thinking is simply the presence of a second mind, which presents an otherwise impossible opportunity for objectivity and subjectivity to co-exist in the discussion.
- Rationality and logic provide benefits, as do involvement, engagement, passion and conviction, but they cannot provide those benefits simultaneously – they cannot occupy the same thinking space at the same time.
- This process of involving a second mind – even one that doesn't really understand the problem – is extremely powerful and can lead to solutions you would never have found alone, including those you might come up with using the help of binary thinking.
- An outsider can provide objectivity and context, allowing you to supply the answers or content without suspicion, resentment or fear of polluting the process.
- Benefit is derived from having any second mind but, for maximum impact, it helps (a lot) if that second mind has some tools and systems to help facilitate a successful outcome.
- Everything on the planet is divided into two categories: things you *can* control and things you *cannot* control.
- Most people spend *most* of their *thinking* time and energy on the things they don't or can't control. Yet the irony is they do preside over a huge number of under-performing elements over which they have total dominance.
- If you're in total control of the things you *can* control, you are in the best possible position to *influence* things you *can't* control. To get control, introduce a second mind.

- Your subjective perspective is not helping your business. You may be doing everything below your potential performance level, and the only way to fix it is with objectivity.
- Binary thinking is essential for clear thinking and clever planning. The presence of a second mind is not always enough. If, however, that second mind is equipped with a *thinking system*, then results improve exponentially.

11

The Thinking System

Say a very important client, Joe Smith, is visiting your business. You want the team to clean up the office and make it look presentable for Joe's visit. The reasons behind this desire are that Joe represents 20 per cent of your turnover, exerts influence on other customers and you want to make a good impression so he stays happy and you remain profitable.

In most cases, a business owner might simply say, "Hey gang, let's clean the place up". (That is, the communication begins with the desired outcome – not the thinking behind that outcome.)

The problem with that approach is that (a) invention is a primary motivator so, because it's your idea, your request stands less chance of being actioned; (b) emotion will cloud judgment and individuals may get hot under the collar about the request, thinking it's just another demand from an awkward boss; (c) different people will interpret the instruction differently because of the inconsistency of language, so your definition of 'clean the place up' and other people's definitions of 'clean the place up' may be light years apart.

If, on the other hand, we apply our 'talking backward' technique, we would say something like this:

"Hey gang, Joe Smith is visiting us next week. He's an important customer. Twenty per cent of our business goes to his companies and a fair bit more of our business is indirectly influenced by him. We need to make a positive impression, so I want this place looking shipshape."

This is a far more productive and informed communication. The priority has been made indirectly clear and there is a disguised benefit in the form of "we all get to keep our jobs if we make Joe happy."

Let's examine what might happen if you were to apply the *business* Thinking System technique here.

The point of this example is to illustrate how right thinking produces tangible benefits. The point of this chapter is to show that there is system behind that thinking and that the Thinking System is a powerful tool in the battle with our elephants.

You:	Is everyone aware of what's happening next Tuesday?
Workgroup:	Isn't that the day Joe Smith is coming to visit?
You:	Does everyone know who Joe Smith is?
Workgroup:	*Mumbling from the group . . .*
You:	Graham, you're the man on the money. Can you just share with the rest of the group who Joe Smith is?'
Graham:	Joe Smith is our biggest client and accounts for 20 per cent of our income.
Workgroup:	Oh . . . Ah . . . Eeeh . . .
You:	Are we clear, folks, on what we are hoping to accomplish with Joe Smith's visit?
Workgroup:	Well, we want to make sure it's positive and effective.
You:	So what do we need to do to make sure his experience is positive and effective?
Workgroup:	We should put a welcome board up.

Wow! You asked a question instead of giving an instruction. And what you got is an idea that, to begin with, you didn't have and it's the workgroup's own content – unique to them.

You: That's great. Can we do that? Who could organise a welcome board? (Usually the person with the idea will volunteer.) Fantastic! What else do we need to do?'

Workgroup: We should put a pack together so he can leave with some of our new stuff. He's a big buyer of Product A, but Product B and Product C haven't yet been presented to him. A sample pack would be great for Mr. Smith to take with him when he leaves.

Benefit No. 2! – Another that you didn't have before you asked the question. But you still have your problem – cleaning the place up hasn't been mentioned. So, if you simply ask again . . .

You: That's great. What else can we do?

Workgroup: We should make sure that Mr Smith gets to spend time with all the people who are servicing his account.

My goodness . . . Benefit No. 3. Remember that you still want somebody to volunteer to clean the place up. It hasn't happened yet. So you ask again.

You: Is there anything else?

Workgroup: We need to clean the place up.

We really should make sure that reception is looking impeccable.

Bingo! Three new ideas, plus your objective fulfilled.

The point of this example is to illustrate how *right thinking* produces tangible benefits. The point of this chapter is to show that there is system behind that thinking and that the *Thinking System* is a powerful tool in the battle to tame elephants.

So what is a Thinking System?

I can remember when I got the latest album from one of my favourite bands. My first listen was all the way through while reading the cover notes. I recall thinking there were two songs on the album that stood out. The cover notes showed who wrote the songs. The first was co-written by Desmond Child. The second was also co-written by Desmond Child. My curiosity was piqued. I didn't realise it at the time, but I'd uncovered a thinking system.

We've been hoodwinked into believing that life is complex. Maybe it's quite the reverse. The expression of art is complex. Yet, to the artist, it's simple. The expression of elite sport is complex. Yet, to the athlete, it's simple. The expression of music is complex. Yet, to the composer, it's simple. Why? Because the composer knows or has worked out a *system or formula*.

Take a moment to see if you recognise any of these songs or artists:

- *If I Could Turn Back Time* (Cher)
- *Don't You Love Me Anymore* (Joe Cocker)
- *I'll Be Your Shelter* (Taylor Dayne)
- *Let's Make It Last All Night* (Jimmy Barnes)
- *Because Of You* (Celine Dion)
- *A Smile As Beautiful As Yours* (Natalie Cole)
- *Faith Of The Heart* (Rod Stewart)
- *Have You Ever?* (Brandy)
- *How Can We Be Lovers?* (Michael Bolton)
- *I Don't Want To Live Without Your Love* (Chicago)
- *I Don't Want To Miss A Thing* (Aerosmith)
- *I Get Weak* (Belinda Carlisle)
- *I Turn To You* (Christina Aguilera)
- *Blame It On The Rain* (Milli Vanilli)
- *Could I Have This Kiss Forever?* (Whitney Houston & Enrique Iglesias)
- *Give Me You* (Mary J. Blige)
- *How Do I Live?* (Trisha Yearwood)
- *I'd Lie For You (And That's The Truth)* (Meat Loaf)
- *Music Of My Heart* (Gloria Estefan & NSYNC)

- *Painted On My Heart* (The Cult)
- *Through The Storm* (Aretha Franklin & Elton John)

Depending on your musical taste, I imagine you would recognise many of them – either the song or the artist or both. You can almost sense the moment of inspiration as they walked along the beach at sunset – infused by passion, tragedy or a broken heart. The initial whisper of a melody, fragments of a song, and the occasional poetic lyric coming together in the night air. Back at the cosy beach house with the muse, the artist reaches for his or her trusty guitar and tinkers. A masterpiece is created and the droplets from heaven are recorded for the world to enjoy.

Mm ... Well, actually no. All these songs were written or co-written by a songwriter named Diane Warren. A one-woman music business. She is probably the most successful songwriter of the past 20 years, with scores of international Top 10 hits across pop, country and R&B charts. Warren, together with Desmond Child, the man I originally came across years ago as co-writer on a *Kiss* album, has written an incredible array of amazing songs for artists in all genres of popular music.

Obviously, songwriting is a system that can be based on a formula. I'm not disputing the natural talent both Diane Warren and Desmond Child have, but there is clearly a 'right way' to compose a hit. To the audience, these songs are born of pain or passion that strikes a chord in the hearts of millions (usually triggering a default setting or associative memory). To the songwriter, they are formulae.

The same can be said of successful sitcoms. We laughed at *Seinfeld* and thought it was such an original and unique idea. But was it really? Look at the *Mary Tyler Moore Show*. In both shows you find similar or corresponding character types: a relatively normal one (Seinfeld and Mary), a headstrong woman (Elaine and Rhoda), a zany one (Kramer and Ted Baxter) and a quirky one (George and Murray).

How about *Everybody Loves Raymond*? The normal one is Raymond, the headstrong woman is his wife and the zany and quirky roles fell to either Raymond's brother, his sister-in-law or his mother or father. The combinations (of the ingredients) were the same.

When we are faced with a business challenge, we (a) try to solve it on our own, and (b) almost always assume that the solution doesn't already exist and, therefore, we have to re-invent the wheel. Both views are wrong. For a start, thinking about the challenge alone is sub-optimal. Plus, we all too often miss the solution within reach.

Best thinking requires another mind, and ideally a mind equipped with a formula, a *thinking system* that can quickly uncover solutions to that particular problem. If Dianne Warren and Desmond Child could create formulae for writing hit songs, could formulae exist for diagnosing common business challenges that would work every time, regardless of business, industry or size?

After a decade of diagnosing challenges and helping workgroups and leaders close the gap between performance and potential, I discovered a haunting similarity between the challenges they all faced. Looking back, my first two years as a business coach were wonderful. Every business presented a new challenge and, around every corner, a new set of issues to help my clients navigate their way through to a solution. Clients would say, "Our place is a little different" and I would believe them. They would ask me if I had experience in *their* industry because it was "special"... and I believed them, often wondering if I was truly qualified to help them.

> If Dianne Warren and Desmond Child could create formulae for writing hit songs, can there exist formulae for diagnosing common business challenges that would work every time regardless of business, industry or size?

Then, almost overnight, the *landscape changed completely*. All of a sudden, *nothing* was different. Nothing was new. The 'our place is different' illusion was exposed for the misconception that it really was.

Since then, it has, in fact, been Year Two repeated 18 times. The important aspect has come down to the outcome desired, while the rest of the brief, although informative, has played a secondary role. When they wanted faster production, then the rest of the brief was secondary. When they wanted conciliation, then the rest of the brief was secondary. When they wanted to successfully merge two divisions, then the rest of the brief was secondary. If they said that ownership of the organisation had changed and the new team needed to develop their own strategic vision, then the rest of the brief was secondary. Why? Because the types of the challenges are universal. It is the content, or details of the challenge, and *only* the content that is unique.

If you look at anything long enough, study anything hard enough, and get close enough to anything, its simplicity emerges from the chaos. It's like those 'magic' 3D diagrams you used to get in the weekend supplement of the newspaper. Hold them up to your nose, then draw the picture away from you and suddenly, out of the chaos, you see the true picture behind the mess.

Once you have read this book, you will start to see order in the chaos. Again, while binary thinking is always better than solo thinking, it also helps if that other mind has a system – some tools and processes – to guide you through the maze of your own thinking as quickly as possible. That's what the *Thinking System* is all about.

> While binary thinking is always better than solo thinking, it also helps if that other mind has a system, some tools and processes that can guide you through the maze of your own thinking . . . and that is what the Thinking System is all about.

The business thinking systems I've developed over the past 20 years mean that when it comes to strategy development, operational excellence, performance management or any other business issue you may be experiencing, there is already a best way to elicit from a workgroup or individual the outcome they seek. You don't need to re-invent the *shape* of the wheel.

How *Binary Thinking* works in tandem with the *Thinking System*

When wrestling with any challenge and striving to produce your best thinking, there are two things you need to be clear on: *Context*, which is what you think about and *Content*, which are the thoughts themselves.

Clarity is attained by being conscious of their separateness *and* by realising that *context* requires *objectivity* while *content* requires *subjectivity*.

As we've already covered, it is impossible to be subjective and objective at the same time, which is where the need for binary thinking comes in. The second mind only deals with the *context* and questions relevant to it. This frees you up to worry about *content* only, namely providing genuine answers. As a consequence, the path toward the solution is much smoother, faster and assured.

The job of *thinking systems* is to shed light on areas that could lead to emotional reflexes and pessimism by systematically drawing out the information needed to tranquilise your elephant's most destructive tendencies. The objective facilitator minimises the natural moodiness of your elephant. In addition, their external questioning ensures that your defaults are checked and validated for facts rather than mere assumptions.

> An objective facilitator minimises the moodiness of your elephant. In addition, an external questioner ensures that your defaults are checked and validated for facts and are not mere assumptions. The job of the Thinking System is to shed light on areas that could lead to pessimism and emotional reflexes – by systematically drawing out the information needed to tranquilise your elephant. In sum: these effects counter your elephant's counterproductive tendencies.

Example of *Binary Thinking* and the *Thinking System* in action

A client of mine owned a significant business and had just acquired a subsidiary company. I asked where that subsidiary company was located. It was in another capital city. I then asked about their intentions in terms of maintaining its location. They said that Head Office would naturally retain its existing location to minimise disruption to the new subsidiary.

I continued to question them about this with the aim of identifying whether any real thinking had been applied to the ramifications of that 'decision' which, of course, was not really a decision but an assumption based on the course of least resistance. So I asked, "What are the expectations of the subsidiary company regarding its likely location?" and "What might be the advantages or disadvantages of discussing and identifying the best location?"

By applying a *thinking system* approach to the situation, a series of commitments were made that led to an opportunity for a substantial part of the new subsidiary to change location and become part of the acquirer's business.

The people in that section of the subsidiary were happy because they saw career advantages in joining the bigger organisation. And my client was happy because it offered some significant economies of scale otherwise missed had their respective elephants made the strategic decisions unchallenged.

Using default settings, they had taken their thinking only far enough to respond to their suspicion that the Head Office didn't need to move. With the application of a *thinking system* (defined and explained shortly) and the injection of some objectivity (via the coach), they were able to decide what their ideal outcome would be, then work back from that position to see if it was possible. They found that there were parts of the subsidiary that shouldn't be moved but, by examining the full extent of the decision and its ramifications, they saw the benefits of achieving a middle ground.

Looking at the story above, you may think, "but that's so obvious". And you're absolutely right. But we are outside the problem. Every one of the executives who I coached in this example would have drawn the same conclusion had they been outside rather than inside the problem. But they could not separate themselves from the issues long enough to see it, until I came along.

It's not easy trying to see past a big fat elephant sometimes. How many solutions to problems seemed obvious once articulated? Don't, for one minute, think that I am immune to this either. I am living proof of the necessity for objectivity. I can visit a business, ask questions aimed at prompting important conclusions about how they're doing something then, the next day, find myself in exactly the same trap I helped that client avoid.

Thinking systems are the answer. "What is a thinking system?" I hear you ask.

A thinking system is nothing more than *a series of questions which, when answered with integrity, will lead to the best next step.* After 20 years of practice, I can claim that this is a most powerful tool for drawing out and clarifying any context – one of two requirements for smart thinking and developing superior solutions for any challenge.

It is particularly powerful coming from the second mind and when that mind knows the appropriate questions to ask in a given setting. The thinking system, coupled with binary thinking – the other of the two requirements – means that it doesn't matter who you are or where you live, the *context* or framework required in order to solve a particular problem in the best possible way is, like a creative *formula*, always the same.

Only the *content* would vary if, for example, a different person in a different situation had that problem. The route to the solution, however, is always the same. The answers sound unique but the questions are universal. Likewise, the songs are all different but the formulae for composing them are all the same.

The *questions* making up the *thinking system* for, say, developing workgroup operational plans, are 'universally' the same but differ, of course, from those making up the *thinking system* for developing executive performance improvement plans. The *effectiveness of the questions* making up the thinking systems is a product of the experience borne by the facilitator representing the second mind.

In the case of 'professional facilitators' or business coaches, the thinking systems are often the IP (Intellectual Property) of their organisations. In a coaching organisation such as BCS, the IP embodies the cumulative experience over the years of the numerous member Coaches.

Consider another example: Imagine a friend says to you, in a way that clearly invites your assistance, that they are unhappy with their home environment. You oblige by conducting *two separate* dialogues, based on a common *thinking system*.

CONTEXT	CONTENT	
The Thinking System	**Person 1**	**Person 2**
Are you happy with your environment?	No	No
What bothers you about your environment?	Too tidy	Out of date
What would it take to fix it?	Negotiate with flatmates	Renovate the lounge room
Is this something you can do?	Negotiation is difficult for me	I don't have the money
Could you get help?	My friend is a good negotiator	I could get a loan
What stops you from doing that?	I'm a little shy	My credit rating
What could you do to fix that?	Ask my flatmates what you just asked me	Talk to my parents about helping me out

The questions asked to unveil the issues are exactly the same for both persons. You don't even need to know what the challenge is before you start. The real solution will come from their answers anyway, and those are always unique. The questions are the *thinking system* and the answers lead to the solution. But getting those questions wrong can be costly, both in time and resources. And even the right answer to the wrong question is still the wrong answer.

Thinking systems work all the time, regardless of the complexity of the situation. To illustrate: I was engaged to work with an executive group of a major telecommunications company. At our first meeting, six very senior executives were in the room, each of them at the helm of a near one billion dollar business. I was warned that it would be difficult because of the personalities and their points of view. And, naturally, I needed to understand that, for people to achieve this sort of status in a company of this size, there was going to be ego involved and they were going to be concerned and committed to presenting their opinions.

At every opportunity I've had working with this group, however, I never once experienced the tensions I was so strongly warned about – and which I was told were always apparent when I was not there. The absence of the expected behaviour, I'm reluctant to admit, had nothing to do with either my extraordinary personality or my magic skills. It was simply due to the imposed objective template into which they had to pour their subjective content. This defused the issues between them. Their elephants were thus bypassed. Emotion was mitigated by an objective second mind. Defaults became immediately obvious and countered. And natural pessimism was eliminated because all the information was put forward in front of everyone at the same time. There were no gaps for anyone to suggest $2 + 2 = 5$.

Each individual turned their energies toward an idea instead of toward each other and this led to unity, not division. Issues about which they may have argued had I not been present became, in a different context, issues for resolution down the track.

For this dynamic and eclectic group of people, we started with a simple set of questions, then a visioning exercise with the expectation that, at the very best, we would begin to nut out only the basics. Instead, over a period of a day and a half, we authored the whole thing from beginning to end – a 22-page document that ultimately became the basis for the strategic plan for the entire business. They were all surprised at the distance they travelled in that short time. Yet for me, this is commonplace – not because of any mercurial properties on my part, but simply because there is always a formula or best way. And, once you know the *thinking system* – the right questions to ask – the rest is easy.

Another case involved a major financial institution that wanted to create an offshore version of its capital markets business. A bunch of people with different skill sets had been selected to start this business. But bringing together personalities from different backgrounds with different skill sets, often with different agendas and objectives, as well as different client bases and different networks within the organisation? The concern was how to make it all happen quickly and effectively.

We began by taking the group into a room and asking them each to describe what perfect success for this new business would look like in 12 months' time. Immediately they poured their subjectivity into this objective framework – that is the context. They were not arguing with each other about what the new business would look like. They were responding to the question with a plan taking shape as their answers were stated. Occasionally, issues came up indicating emerging differences. But each time, we agreed to put them aside with a view to later applying a different context to find appropriate answers to those issues. We discovered that, ultimately, their overall vision for the business's future was 80 per cent agreed.

Everyone in the room committed to not letting the 20 per cent interfere with the picture of the future they had collectively created. At the end of the day, we had a picture of the future, we had identified the stakeholders, we had set objectives for each one and devised a plan to achieve it. Before 5pm that day, by their own admission, they had arrived at a place they thought would have taken many months to get to. Less fortunately, they ascribed the achievement to the skill of facilitation. As much as I would love to take credit for the outcome, I know without a shadow of doubt that the separation of content and context led to this result... *and* brilliant facilitation, of course!

A useful analogy to illustrate this concept more clearly is any sporting contest. You have the rules, which are the context, and you have the players and the game, which are the content. In order for the game to work, everyone must know the rules. But rules can be broken in the heat of the moment, so we have a referee, who is guardian of the context.

The referee is the objective filter for the game and must observe the game without bias. As soon as s/he has a personal stake in the outcome, their involvement is flawed and so are the game and its result. Objectivity is dissolved by emotion. If you have no particular attachment to any one side, you can observe the game from the purity of the rules and the game. When you are not emotionally involved in the outcome, you can observe the game for the level of skill shown by the players.

The same is true with any form of coaching. The coach is the guardian of the context. And what a good coach will do is provide you with the template for thinking, which is the context. You 'insert' your own individual content and are then able to draw the necessary and right conclusions for yourself and your business.

If you employed a consultant to assist you in your business, you would most likely be given recommendations based on the consultant's experiences – which may or may not be similar to the situation your business is currently facing. My belief is that it is far more valuable to guide a business to its own conclusions and solutions based on its specific situation. This requires that the outsider's expertise be in the realm of context, not content.

The route to the solution is always the same but the solutions are always different, depending on the business. With consulting, the solutions are formulaic and the system of arriving at those solutions is not. The route to the solution varies – often based on the consultant's experience, rather than that of your business – and is specifically designed to arrive at one of a handful of black box solutions.

In my prescriptive mood, I would advise you to read this last sentence again because it is very, very important that you understand it and appreciate its significance.

A word of warning about context

You only have to look at the number of people each year who are 'lost' to cults and fringe groups around the world to realise the incredible power of context. We can all sit at home on a cosy winter evening and struggle with the rationale ... What happens to seemingly normal people that they would surrender their worldly goods to people who are waiting for the aliens to arrive? Are those people mad? Do they have a medical condition? Perhaps they are just very unhappy? Or maybe they had a traumatic childhood?

Even if the answer is "yes" to most of those questions, the explanation is elsewhere ... in the hands of those who take advantage of them. The way they take advantage is by controlling the 'context'. If you control information flow and only release the information that supports a particular reality, then it becomes easy to make people believe just about anything. For the followers in question, what they have come to believe is obvious and completely rational and it is we who are living in a fantasy world. Such is the power of this concept. Ask a person the right question, introduce doubt, control the information, and sooner or later their reality *will* change.

The elephant is listening to the conversation and it doesn't know fact from fiction. If the picture is controlled, you can intentionally trigger emotion, thereby hardwiring the perception and making it a stronger thought. Stronger thoughts are more often repeated and therefore dominate. Hey presto! One more radical to the cause.

It was 20th century sociologist Robert K. Merton who first coined the phrase 'self-fulfilling prophecy'. In his book *Social Theory And Social Structure*, he states, "The self-fulfilling prophecy is, in the beginning, a false definition of the situation evoking behaviour that makes the originally false conception come 'true'. This specious validity of the self-fulfilling prophecy perpetuates a reign of error. For the prophet will cite the actual course of events as proof that he was right from the very beginning."[52]

How many *reigns of error* do we have running amok in our lives? When we expect something to happen with such conviction, we set in motion actions and behaviours that can ultimately bring about the very thing we expected. With cults, even when the 'day of reckoning' comes and goes without incident, those involved will spin a new *reign of error* to explain it, choose a new day and off they go again.

Be very careful about who you allow to mess with your context.

Chapter Summary

- We've been hoodwinked into believing that life is complex. But the reality is quite the reverse. The expression of art is complex, yet to the artist, it's simple. The expression of elite sport is complex, yet to the athlete, it's simple. The expression of music is complex, yet to the composer, it's simple. Why? Because the artist/athlete/composer knows or has worked out the system or formula.
- When faced with a business challenge, we (a) try to solve it on our own and/or (b) assume that the solution does not already exist. Both are wrong. Best thinking requires another mind *and*, ideally, for that mind to be equipped with a *thinking system* that quickly uncovers the formula for the solution to that particular problem.

- Binary thinking is always better than solo thinking. It also helps if that other mind has a system – some tools and processes – that can guide you, as quickly as possible, through the maze of your own thinking. That's what the *thinking system* is all about.
- The business thinking systems I've developed over the past 15 years mean that, when it comes to operational excellence, performance management or any other business issue you may be experiencing, there is already a best way to reach the outcome you seek. You don't need to re-invent the wheel.
- An objective facilitator minimises the natural moodiness of your elephant. In addition, an external questioner demands that your defaults are checked and validated as facts rather than assumptions. The *thinking system* sheds light on areas that could lead to unwarranted pessimism and, as such, a *thinking system* tranquilises your elephant's most destructive tendencies.
- A *thinking system* is nothing more than a series of questions which, when answered with integrity, will lead to the best next step in finding a solution.
- It doesn't matter who you are or where you live, if you have a particular problem, the *context* or framework required in order to solve it in the best possible way is always the same.
- For a different person, living in a different place, it is the *content* that would vary. But the route to the solution is always the same. The answers always sound unique but the questions are universal.
- The questions are the *thinking system* and the answers to those questions are the solution.
- The *questions* that make up the *thinking system* for, say, developing workgroup operational plans, are the same 'universally' but they differ from those making up the *thinking system* for developing executive performance improvement plans. The *effectiveness of the questions* making up the *thinking system* is a function of the experience of the facilitator representing the second mind.

- In the case of professional facilitators or business coaches, the *thinking systems* are often the IP of their organisations. With BCS, for example, the IP embodies the cumulative experience, over the years, of the numerous coaches who are members of the coaching organisation.

12

The Thinking System in Action

One of the things we do in the role of coach is to help construct action plans. In the course of the work I do, I facilitate hundreds of action plans. As a consequence, it's not uncommon for me to be told, "Gee you know how to do a lot of things." Truth is, I know how to do one thing: how to ask the 39 questions that make a perfect action plan. They perceive me as having a purpose for each question and that I must therefore know the answers. But I don't know the answers. All I know is the right question to ask. Step by step. They know the answers. Together we can create the perfect action plan.

You might be thinking, after the previous chapter, that it can't be that easy... "A *thinking system* is nothing more than a series of questions, each of which, when answered with integrity, will lead to the best next step in finding a solution."

Perhaps it's only that easy when the challenge is that easy. If you needed to draft a business plan for a joint venture between three major financial institutions, maybe that would be more difficult, right?

Actually no, it doesn't have to be. Representatives from three major financial institutions sought my advice regarding negotiations for a highly market-sensitive joint venture opportunity. They were very concerned about how long the process would take and how sensitive it all was.

It took less than 60 minutes to get the issues on the table. It took exactly one day to exhaust the discussion and set the research parameters. In two weeks, the research was done. It took one more day to reach agreement on the terms and variables. It took 70 days from the start of discussions to a signed-off agreement between three different boards of directors, in their three different languages, with their three different sets of interpretation.

The following commentary is from that experience. At the outset, the company representatives were looking nervously at each other. I directed one of them, "*Point to one of the other parties in this room and finish this sentence:* 'the only circumstances under which we would contemplate moving forward with you are . . .'"

The exercise was repeated in sequence and, within minutes, an agenda authored by the team was in place. There are a million different potential joint ventures. But once the parties enter the room, there is only one approach. By employing a *system to extract best thinking*, you get the 'elephant in the room' out in clear view without any emotion.

The team in question agreed on a joint venture once they realised:

- It would not cannibalise their existing businesses
- They could not gain the advantages of the joint venture on their own
- They each had something unique to bring to the table
- They had a mandate from their respective board of directors

> By employing a system to extract best thinking, you get the "elephant in the room" out in clear view without any emotion.

Remember: content is unique; context is universal. Only the content, or information supplied, is unique. The questions needed to get the information out and on the table are universal.

To establish what those questions might be, one of the best ways is to 'talk backwards'. Work back from the desired outcome to determine what you need to know and do in order to achieve it. Doing so will naturally create the context for the thinking, so that the content from all the relevant places can be gathered and a clear conclusion can be attained. This means sharing the *thinking* that led to your conclusions... *before* sharing the conclusions. It is this process that creates context and forms the basis of the *Thinking System*.

Remembering the example of Joe Smith's visit from Chapter 11 will help here. You wanted the team to clean up the office to make it look presentable for Smith's visit and for him to have a good impression and stay happy doing business with you.

One alternative was to say, "Hey gang, let's clean the place up". But that would be starting the communication with the thought – not with the thinking and definitely not with assurance for the desired outcome.

The other alternative was applying our 'talking backward' technique in a series of Q&As, culminating in "*Bingo! Three new ideas, plus your objective fulfilled*".

You may be saying to yourself at this point, "Yeah, right, John... that worked well. But what happens if they never give you the answer you're looking for?"

The solution is to simply convert your request into a question. *Thinking systems* are questions, so you would simply ask, "Do you think, folks, that the place needs to be cleaned up, or are we happy with it as it is?"

> Effectiveness of the Thinking System is partly in the discipline of continuing to question and partly in the purposeful selection of the very questions themselves. And it is these questions that take your elephant and the elephants of others out of the decision making process.

Even with you providing content – "Yes we should give it a bit of a clean" – it is still them borrowing a share of the idea. They're still buying in. And you have not issued a single instruction.

For the sceptics who might dismiss this approach because it 'takes too long' – please understand I'm not suggesting that, if you are at war, in the frontline of battle, you gather the troops around and say, "Listen, I've just got this little order that's come down the line suggesting we retreat from this barrage... How do you men feel about that?"

There *are* times when this type of approach isn't appropriate; when directions just need to be given and followed. But they are rare.

The most important point, especially in an increasingly competitive environment, is that taking a little extra time led to three benefits instead of one, increased the chances for success and was a catalyst for positive culture. The technique requires less skill than patience and puts the right people in charge. And, if you regularly call on the skills, expertise, and knowledge of the people in your business and implement their ideas, you will be astonished at how productive they can be.

All you need to do is ask questions that trigger thinking which, in turn, loads the necessary information into the minds of the people you are speaking to. Armed with that information, it's only a matter of time until they come to the conclusion you're hoping for. You get the solution you're after *and* the thinking system gave you a bucket load of extra bonuses as well.

The *Thinking System's* effectiveness is partly due to the discipline of continuing to question and partly due to the purposeful selection of the questions themselves. These questions take your elephant, and the elephants of others, out of the decision making process. Ideally, the questions may even train those elephants...

It can be seen from the example how questions that make up the *Thinking Systems* are designed in reverse. In other words, first identify the conclusion, or first identify the challenge, then build the *Thinking System* backward from that point.

In practice, it is the special skill of the coach or facilitator to hit on the question that *outs* the elephant *up front* – as in the joint venture example in Chapter 11. The building and accumulation of questions will lead to such completeness that the questions become complete, invariant and thus universal.

And the system's application is clearly not limited to business.

To illustrate this, I will share a short story with you. First, some background: I grew up in an environment where, if you made a commitment to do something, you were expected to stick to it. Naturally, I had similar expectations from my children.

When my daughter was 11, she became a Girl Guide. One night at the dinner table, she said that she would not be attending Girl Guides the following Thursday because her friend was having a Halloween party.

Because of my commitment thing, I have an internal cathartic explosion...but manage to control myself. So:

John (1): (*In the coolest voice I can muster*) Tell me about the Halloween party.
Lesley: Well, it's on Thursday and it's going to be at Mary's place.
John (2): OK. And who's going to be there?
Lesley: Mary, Maria, Marlene, Melissa.
John (3): What happens at Girl Guides?
Lesley: Well, we get together and we do a whole heap of exercises.
John (4): When I pick you up from Girl Guides, you're normally just playing, running around.
Lesley: Yes, that's at the end. In the meantime, we do exercises.
John (5): What's the name of the lady who takes care of you at Girl Guides?
Lesley: It's not like a baby-sitting service, Dad. Jacqueline's actually a Guide Leader. And she works.
John (6): I understand that. So she turns up and basically just sets up some exercises for you?
Lesley: No, she doesn't. When we turn up, she's already decided what we're going to do. And she has a plan for all of us because we're all going for different badges.
John (7): So she puts a fair bit of work into it?

Lesley:	Yes.
John (8):	And how many of you are in the troop?
Lesley:	Eight.
John (9):	And how many of you are going to the Halloween party?
Lesley:	(*After a moment's thought*) Six.
John (10):	Out of interest ... When this girl – Jacqueline, you say – turns up for Girl Guides next Thursday night, having prepared for each of you, to help you grow and develop, and to push you on your journey, and finds that only two people have turned up ... Just describe to me how you expect her to feel when she discovers you are all at Mary's Halloween party?

(*Long silence.*)

Lesley: I don't have to go to the Halloween party.

All I did with my questions was to bring forward the facts that led to my conclusion, in the hope that they would 'connect'. My hunch was that, if Lesley could be brought to some consciousness about those same facts, she might – if her Mum and I had done our job properly over the 11 years of her life – also reach the same conclusion. She did.

She didn't go to the Halloween party. And, when she rang her friend, she actually applied the *Thinking System* to her friend. However, it turned out her friend's parents had simply told her she couldn't go to the party.

This experience improved my relationship with my daughter. She was never going to be allowed to go to the Halloween party but, more significantly, the decision became hers.

When a brain is engaged in this way, only the frontal lobe is activated. Lesley's brain had to answer the questions and arrived at a logical conclusion. If I had said, "You're not going to the bloody Halloween party" that would have skipped past the frontal lobe straight to the midbrain – anger, frustration, resulting in, "Dad's a bastard".

So, Vamos – ONE; Marie's parents – NIL. The same outcome... but my daughter wasn't angry with me for not letting her go to the party. The *thinking system* is a form of engagement that only the frontal lobe can handle.

Here's the above interaction represented diagrammatically:

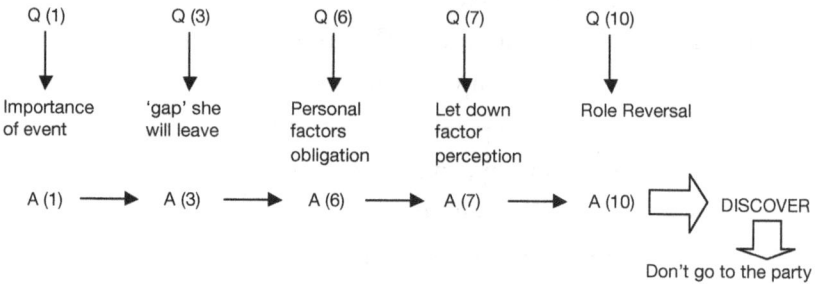

Figure 4 Thinking System in a one-on-one dialogue

Simple Thinking Systems

A simple *Thinking System* is characterised by knowing what you want to achieve, and simply converting that information into questions. These questions, when loaded into the mind of the respondent, will result in that person also 'coming up' with your answer.

I knew I didn't want Lesley to go to the party and I also knew that, if I made her aware of what I was aware of, she would more than likely come to the same conclusion. So I turned my arguments into questions that allowed her to draw the same conclusion as I had. I created an 'adult' context.

The arguments above could have, just as easily, been simple statements but that approach would not necessarily have led to the discovery I wanted her to make. This way, I was engaging her and making her think about the answers rather than just getting defensive.

Looking at the Joe Smith example and representing the questions diagrammatically, you can see it's a system being played out until your desired answer is forthcoming.

THE THINKING SYSTEM IN ACTION

The Joe Smith visit summary:

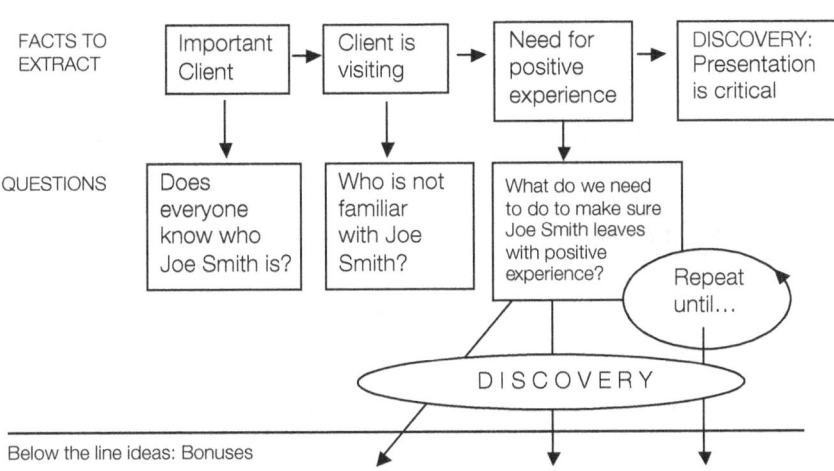

Figure 5 Thinking System in a one-on-many dialogue

Identify something that's important to you that you want your team to work on. Then list all the information that's needed in order for them to be able to draw the same conclusion. Then create questions that solicit that information in the form of answers.

I didn't want Lesley to go to the Halloween party. And, for Joe Smith's visit, I wanted our business tidied up. The former played out as a one-on-one dialogue, the latter as a one-on-many. Test it for yourself.

Complex Thinking Systems

More intricate challenges, as you will have recognised, need different systems. That is why I distinguish between two types of thinking systems – simple and complex.

Complex Thinking Systems are applied when you don't necessarily know the answer but you know the outcome you are trying to achieve. The joint venture case from Chapter 11 is a good example. It illustrates, in the case of complex situations, the importance of the way a *thinking system* can be applied. It also raises a question as to where that 'killer' opening question came from.

Answer: from the set of questions accrued over time through the skill and experience of the coach, facilitator or manager. Given experience, the questions become part of a 'universal' set accrued over time.

Exercise for constructing a Thinking System

Think of an instruction you wish to give your team – an important one that requires them to either:

a) Do something they have not yet been asked to do
b) Do something they consistently refuse to do

Now write down every reason why they need to, or should embrace the behaviour or carry out the instruction. Include selfish reasons that will help you, and others about benefits they will receive. Now for each reason, construct a question for which the answer is the reason.

Look at the logical flow. Mix the reasons up – some questions for them, some for you – and decide a balanced order in which to ask them.

Now give it a go. And remember, this apparently 'long way' of doing things is actually a natural behaviour demonstrated by successful leaders and coaches. It may surprise you how easily and quickly this will become second nature. Once you appreciate how simple and effective it is, you will never go back to your old way of working.

Chapter Summary

- By employing a system to extract best thinking, you get the 'elephant in the room' out in clear view, without any emotion.
- Remember: content is unique; context is universal. Only the content, or information supplied, is unique. The questions we need to ask to get the information out and on the table are universal. They are accrued over time through the skill and experience of the facilitator.

THE THINKING SYSTEM IN ACTION

- To establish what those questions might be, one of the best ways is to get into the habit of 'talking backwards'. Work back from the desired outcome to determine what you need to know and do in order to deliver that outcome. Doing so naturally creates the context for the thinking, so you can gather the content from all the relevant places and arrive at a clear conclusion. This means sharing the *thinking* that led to your conclusions *before* sharing the conclusions. It is this process that represents context and forms the basis of a *Thinking System*.
- If you regularly call on the skills, expertise and knowledge of the people in your business and implement their ideas, you will be astonished at how productive they can be.
- All you need to do is ask questions that trigger thinking which, in turn, loads the necessary information into the minds of the people you are speaking to.
- The *Thinking System* is partly due to the discipline of continuing to question and partly due to the purposeful selection of the questions themselves. These questions effectively take your elephant and the elephants of others out of the decision making process.
- A simple *Thinking System* is characterised by knowing what you want to achieve and simply converting that information into questions.
- Complex *Thinking Systems* are applied when you don't necessarily know the answer but you know the outcome you are trying to achieve.

13
Questions – The Essence of the Thinking System

There's a game called Outburst – the Game of Verbal Explosions, *which is a great illustration of the power of questions and the* Thinking System. *In the game, the player is asked to name 10 answers in a specific time. For example, I ask Karen to name 10 children's writers. She has two minutes to name as many children's writers as she can until she has named all those on my card. Karen named J.K. Rowling, Rudyard Kipling, Enid Blyton ... and that was it! "Pretty poor effort for a writer," I thought. If I were playing the game properly, I would have simply revelled in her discomfort. But I was trying to prove a point, so I intervened. I asked, "Who wrote Winnie the Pooh?" and "Who wrote Alice in Wonderland?" She knew the answers – A.A. Milne and Lewis Carroll. "What about the bunny?" "Oh, Beatrix Potter." However, if I hadn't asked the questions, she would have struggled to untangle what she already knew and retrieve the information from her knowledge banks to present the information in time.*

The merit and importance of questions are discussed in thousands of books but their value from our perspective is that:

a) You can't control your elephant, or anyone else's elephant, without a system that will bypass it. Questions bypass the elephant, allowing 'you' to take control.

QUESTIONS – THE ESSENCE OF THE THINKING SYSTEM

b) Questions demand conscious answers. This invokes the frontal lobe while placating the elephant. Statements, on the other hand, challenge the midbrain, involving the elephant and even encouraging it to be unruly.

When you make a statement, you disclose a position, an attitude, a prejudice. Our natural reflex is to assess statements in relation to their threat to, or at least their impact on, us.

When you ask a question, you are eliciting the respondent's attitudes and prejudices. In forming a view, the frontal lobe and midbrain work together.

> A thinking system is the questioning system that will enable you to permanently distract elephants in the workplace.

When you ask me a question, I think about me in order to answer it. When you make a statement, I think about you in order to assess it. For example, you might ask me, "Did you enjoy the film *The Matrix*?" I engage my frontal lobe to consciously think about it, asking myself whether I've seen it, then focus on remembering it and answering the question. On the other hand, you might say, "I watched *The Matrix* last night ... it was rubbish". If I think anything at all, I am assessing you by that statement. My elephant is having a field day. In a heartbeat, he's gone from, "What do you mean, you don't like *The Matrix*? It's a modern day classic" to, "This guy's a moron. Clearly I can't trust him".

A *thinking system* is the questioning system that will enable you to permanently distract elephants in the workplace. A *thinking system* is, after all, just a series of questions which, when answered with integrity, will deliver the next best step for any given challenge. That's it. Belying this simplicity, however, is great depth and breadth of application.

A *thinking system* is, essentially, a thought process that captures the right information, in the right order, to allow the correct conclusions to be reached. Capturing that 'right' information is done by formulating the 'right' questions.

The right questions are the heart and substance of *every* thinking system. They are the compass by which even the most inexperienced traveller can navigate through the maze of their own thinking to arrive at the clarity of understanding.

Questions are the compass that will navigate even the most inexperienced traveller through the maze of their own thinking to the clarity of understanding.

If you accept the paradigm 'you do not know what you do not know', you can release the power of questions to uncover what you do know *and* discover exactly what you don't know. Through these insights, you can finally analyse your own behaviour. In so doing, we can create a personal 'idiot's guide' to unlock our own unique abilities, skills and talents so their expression doesn't fall to circumstance or chance but, instead, can be 'turned on' anytime, anywhere.

The solution you want or need is nearly always in *your* head, not someone else's. When the *questions* needed to achieve this are clearly thought out and arranged in a *sequence*, they qualify as a *thinking system*. But they are still questions, their purpose is to skilfully elicit bytes of information that need to be collected and then (as if by magic) *connected*.

Questions have a magnetic quality that pulls you toward knowledge. But, just as the right question can pull you toward the right answer, the wrong question can propel you in the opposite direction, away from the truth. Again, the right answer to the wrong question is still the wrong answer.

So the challenge is two-fold: you must not only answer correctly, truthfully and with integrity but, just as importantly, you must *ask* correctly.

To illustrate: I once attended a conference where the speaker talked about his real estate business and how his agents would pursue opportunities in the marketplace by asking, "Do you know anyone who needs to talk about real estate today?"

So you can imagine, Small Town, USA ... all the real estate agents wearing big smiley-face nametags that say, "Hi, my name is Ralph. Talk to me about your real estate challenge". At the supermarket checkouts or at drugstores, the agents would say to cashiers, "Thanks, Mary. Do you know anyone who needs to talk about real estate today?"

This approach produced about a 5 per cent positive response.

In an attempt to increase that percentage, they decided to change the question. The new question was, "Who do you know that might like to talk about real estate today?"

The response increased fourfold. Theoretically, the response could have gone to 100 per cent, because everyone must know *someone* they *suspect* might need to talk about real estate. Nevertheless, quadrupling the response was a fairly impressive increase, achieved by a subtle difference in the question.

Why did the percentage of positive responses increase so dramatically?

If you've ever received sales training, you will recognise the first survey question as a *closed question* – one that can be answered with a *yes* or *no*. While such an answer might be correct, it's a case of the right answer to the wrong question. A different question is needed – the right question this time ...

What is it that prompts a different reaction from the first question to the second?

Answer: The two questions send the thinking on completely different journeys. In the first question – "Do you know anyone that needs to talk about real estate today?" – the brain's immediate response is either "Yes" or "No". If "No", then the brain immediately looks for a way to shut down the conversation and move on. Perhaps the individual being questioned had an experience with an overly exuberant Amway representative and the default clicks into "No" to avoid future recurrences. Perhaps the individual gets annoyed and emotion comes into play. Or perhaps they become suspicious and expect the worst. Whatever the reason, their brain doesn't engage in anything beyond finding the quickest way to close down the conversation.

If "Yes", then we hit the second barrier because the question mentions *'need'*. Remember, the elephant is non-verbal. So, if someone does come to mind, they are then graded against the respondent's own definition of 'need'. What does 'need' mean to that individual? For example, *my* thinking – or internal dialogue – may answer, "Well, I know that Julie is looking to move house but that is six months to a year away...so it doesn't really constitute 'need'". As a result, my thinking will discount Julie, based on my own definition of 'need'.

The real estate agent, of course, would have loved to speak to Julie so he could introduce himself. Then, when the time came for her to move house, she would think of him.

With the second question – "Who do you know that might like to talk about real estate today?" – the brain goes in a completely different direction without encountering the mental reflexes of "Yes" or "No". Instead it asks, "Who do I know?" and immediately references the internal Rolodex. In an instant, it is searching the internal database and is mentally scanning recognisable names and faces. The brain is no longer looking for ways to close down the small talk. It has actually been sent to a different place – a place where friends live. A negative response is now not logical, so the thinking has to *change*.

Both questions were aimed at eliciting the same result – to get leads. Yet one was far more successful than the other. Such is the power of the right question. It sets thinking along the right path.

If you want to improve your life, start asking better questions.

Questions drive our thinking. In effect, you are controlling the respondent's thinking through the skilful asking of questions. Whatever the thinking *is*, it is a response to your question.

> Our mind has an enormous capacity for storing and retrieving knowledge. But that capacity is useless unless we can direct it to create or carry out action. Questions allow us to do that.
> If you want to improve your life, start asking better questions.

QUESTIONS – THE ESSENCE OF THE THINKING SYSTEM

Our mind has an enormous capacity for storing and retrieving information. But unless we can direct it to create or carry out action, that capacity is useless. Questions allow us to do that.

I thought the following experiment was so clever when it came to my attention that I took the opportunity to test it at a seminar I was conducting. To the 60 or so people in the audience, I said, "Put your hand up if you remember a neighbourhood dog (the four-legged variety) when you were growing up?"

About half the audience put their hands up. I then asked, "Do you remember the name of the neighbourhood dog? If you do, write it down now".

I then asked, "When was the last time somebody asked you that question?" and challenged those who responded positively, "Put your hand up if it was more than five years ago; more than 10 years ago, etc."

A 55-year-old in the audience reflected on the fact that he hadn't entertained a thought about that dog since he was 15 years old. That little piece of information was last accessed 40 years ago. Wow!

That experiment illustrates a number of very powerful ideas. First, the incredible capacity of the human mind to find information from within its memory banks – even useless information. Second, that information abandoned for 40 years would still be there at all. (Where does all this information go? Can you imagine how much data is in there?) Third, the possibilities that are implied by both ideas: How creative, intelligent, and resourceful could you become if you could access, at will, all that you've ever discovered, learned, seen, heard, spoken, thought and experienced? If you could do that, is it possible you'd be significantly less obsessed with stuff you don't yet know?

The last powerful idea about questions is the role of the question itself.

That little piece of information about the neighbourhood dog might have stayed buried in the recesses of the mind forever if the question had never been asked. Granted, the world was not made a better place by its retrieval. But its excavation demonstrates the enormous possibilities for us.

This is not about memory. It's about the application of information retrieved from memory. Memory isn't enough. We have to be able to bring the right pieces of information together at the right time. And questions allow us to do that. *Thinking system* questions are especially purposeful because of the context they impose, as illustrated in the following paragraph.

We need to retrieve all the memories relating to X – not just one memory of X – so we can formulate a conclusion from that pool of disparate memories and the ideas they provoke. Only when we pull together all the memories of X can we see the correlations among them and the connections between cause and effect. In the case of my merger client, when all the information relating to the best location for the head office was collated, the solution was blindingly obvious. But, until that occurred, it was not obvious at all. In fact, a contrary opinion had apparently been obvious.

Gathering all the available relevant knowledge means we are in a position to negate the shortcomings brought about by our elephants. It also allows us to draw an informed conclusion about what to do for the best outcome, rather than making a reactive choice based on one aspect or one view.

> Our elephant has the habit of taking shortcuts: through default settings we mentioned earlier, instinct, emotion and inferred meaning. If not trained otherwise, this can lead to invalid conclusions and can influence our effectiveness.

Our elephant has a habit of taking shortcuts – through default settings we mentioned earlier, instinct, emotion and inferred meaning. If he is not trained to behave otherwise, this can lead to invalid conclusions and can diminish our effectiveness. By being able to see the bigger, more complete picture – especially if you have a second qualified mind to facilitate the process – you can circumvent the pitfalls of relying on those shortcuts and default settings and, instead, stick with fact and truth.

Questions are the tools for excavation. If the questions are right, then you get the right information. If the questions are wrong, you don't. Know this: once you determine the nature of the outcome you're after, there is only one best set of questions. We'll demonstrate this in more detail in Chapter 14, where we dissect the *business* thinking systems for perfect strategy, for performance contracts and for diagnosing any business challenge you may be having.

But questions are not just about gaining clarity of thought. We are rarely taught how powerful questioning is. Questions have so many powerful benefits that are often overlooked because of their sheer simplicity.

If you are lucky enough to have been exposed to sales training, you may have been introduced to the power of questions. However, even if that is the case, so much of the sales training I've seen is more about manoeuvring people into preordained conclusions, rather than a process of integrity and honesty that arms people with information to make considered judgments and draw valid conclusions.

Thinking Systems and Manipulation

You may be thinking at this point, "Hold on John . . . isn't that manipulation?" No, it isn't. Manipulation is feeding twisted information that causes the person to arrive at a polluted conclusion. Manipulation can also be achieved by limiting the information – by only asking the questions that will uncover the information to force you to make the decision I want you to make.

For example, with our earlier story in Chapter Five about the disappearance of Augustine Le Prince, I could have related only half the story and left you feeling very uneasy about Thomas Edison. That would be manipulation, deliberately limiting the information to distort the facts in order to get you to feel anger toward Thomas Edison.

Manipulation is about engaging emotion to direct a person to a particular self-serving conclusion. As you can see with the Augustine Le Prince example, it's easy enough to do. Imagine how much of what we read or see in the news every day is tainted by the emotion of the correspondent or the motives of the producer. It is the easiest thing in the world to play on someone's emotion and therefore control someone's conclusion.

On the other hand, using *thinking systems* takes courage and commitment because you are creating the framework for the truth to emerge – good, bad or ugly. It takes courage to uncover the truth and look at it clearly and objectively, without getting worried about what it might mean to you or your company's performance. But the long-term benefits far outweigh any short-term discomfort.

The *thinking system* is about asking questions that will allow a person to access all of the information necessary for them to reach the right conclusion themselves.

For example, it is easy to tell someone to do something. If you need something done, you simply identify what it is, select a person, and tell them to get on with it. Traditional business logic may even tell you that this approach is easier and quicker. It takes thought, courage and trust to replace an instruction with a question because you can't control what conclusion the person will draw from the question. You have to be open to the possibility that they may know more about this particular task than you do, in which case you will either need to be prepared with another question or have enough faith in your people to let them run with their own conclusions.

> It takes courage to uncover the truth and be able to look at it objectively and clearly, without getting worried about what it might mean about you or your company's performance. But the long-term benefits far outweigh any short-term discomfort. Questions can be designed so that the answers are less prone to manipulation.

Nevertheless, the right question puts the questioner in control of the outcome and allows him/her to control the environment with much more skill. (This sounds like sales training because selling is all about managing thinking.)

If you look at the process of negotiation, the person who asks the questions is always in control. Whoever is asking the questions drives the agenda. Agendas can give you back control of your thinking. Knowing this, if you are not the one asking the questions, you can still formulate a *thinking system* to pre-empt all the possible questions you could be asked. That way you can enter any negotiation, meeting or discussion fully armed with the answers. And that is a very powerful position to hold, whichever side of the fence you are on.

Good questions play a more important role in getting to the truth than good answers. In fact, the questions can be designed so that the answers are less prone to manipulation.

Showing our True Colours: An example of a thinking system

'True Colours' is the name we've given to a simple approach we use in facilitating a performance assessment of a workgroup. At one point in this exercise, the participants grade themselves.

The idea of True Colours often scares workgroup leaders. Their concern is that their team will overstate the quality of its performance. In other words, they will give themselves credit they do not deserve. Let me tell you, it *never* happens. Quite the opposite. During the True Colours exercise, the coach will invariably need to remind the participants that workgroup performance is measured against its own best potential outcome. Not against the best in the world, or the best imaginable, or even the best competitor. It's about how well *they* perform measured against their *own* capacity to perform.

Typically, they will tell us they perform less than 15 per cent of their processes to the best of the team's ability. Amusingly, that concerned workgroup leader will now be saying, "Oh, come on guys ... we're pretty good at that. Don't be so hard on yourselves".

This could be a very confronting and uncomfortable process if proper attention is not paid to the question and how it is asked. The trick is to separate the individuals from the process and de-personalise the entire benchmarking exercise.

When a *thinking system* is sound, then politics, 'white-anting' and manipulation do not survive. Furthermore, and better still, default settings are turned off, emotion is disconnected, a common language is distilled and the person asking the questions is divorced from the content.

If someone in the workgroup wants to manipulate the outcome – whatever their motivation – they'll need to convince the others of that false outcome. And the only way they can do that is to manage the *information flow*. Whereas a *thinking system* allows only the questioner (not the respondent) to manage the information flow.

So you can't artificially influence the data to support your case if you can't manage the information flow. But if your case is sound, then it is based on evidence and will emerge in any event.

> When a thinking system is sound, then politics, white-anting and manipulation dies. Or better still, default settings are turned off, emotion is disconnected, a common language is distilled and the person asking the questions is divorced from the content!

How to Ask Questions – the *right way* and the *wrong way*

To ensure purity of thought and eliminate manipulation, the technique we use is called Horizontal Sequential Questioning – the right way.

This means eliciting the answer to a particular issue cohesively, rather than allowing the responses to direct more questions, one after another, in search of answers to the issue. The latter we call Vertical Sequential Questioning – the wrong way.

QUESTIONS – THE ESSENCE OF THE THINKING SYSTEM

An example of Vertical Sequential Questioning would be:

Q: Hey Karen, what's holding you up with John's book?
A: John won't do his edits.
Q: How come?
A: I'm not sure. I know he's busy.
Q: Why not talk to him about it ... Hurry him along?
A: I don't want to annoy him.
Q: Will he be annoyed?
A: No, probably not. But I'm swamped anyway, with other projects.

Note: At this point, the interchange is flawed – the right answers to the wrong questions are getting nowhere. It's an endless loop. Where do you go from here?

Q: Are they more important than John's book?
A: No, not more important ... just other commitments.

This is Vertical Sequential Questioning – we keep asking one new question and getting one new answer. If we continue this way, what happens is that we end up with an unproductive stream of nonsense.

So let's do it properly:

Q: Hey Karen, is John's book progressing to schedule?
A: No.
Q: So, what's holding it up?
A: John won't do the edits.
Q: What else?
A: I've now got other priorities as well.
Q: What else?
A: I'm not sure how committed he is, or what the deadline is.
Q: What else?

A:	I've been working on and off this book for nine years and I feel a bit numbed by it at times.
Q:	What else?
A:	That's it.
Q:	OK, what have you done about it so far?
A:	He's had the re-draft for about nine months. He needs to read it, give me feedback and make some edits.
Q:	What have you done about that so far?
A:	I've emailed him a few times, chasing it up.
Q:	Did they work?
A:	No.
Q:	What options have you considered?
A:	I could call him…
Q:	And achieve what?
A:	I could gauge his commitment and set some deadlines. Plus it would give me an opportunity to explain my schedule so he knows what he can expect from me.
Q:	Would that make you feel better about it?
A:	Yes, because I do feel guilty that it's not finished. Truth is, even if he did finally get around to reading it, I wouldn't be able to get a revised version back to him for a few weeks. That's frustrating.
Q:	When will you call him?
A:	Now.

This was Horizontal Sequential Questioning. It allowed us to get all the issues out on the table early, so the discussion didn't end up in a meaningless heap.

With Horizontal Sequential Questioning, if a person tries to 'massage' the answer, they can't, because they don't know the journey they're taking. They can't see or predict that question one – a simple and apparently innocuous question – is eventually going to lead to them having to commit to action. Nor do they realise that they are simultaneously authoring their plan.

Clients always want my 'Agenda' for the off-site workshop or facilitation process. They will never get it. I'll happily tell them where they will be at the end, but the journey is none of their business. Content will be theirs. Context belongs to me.

When you observe things on a macro level, the problems on the micro level dissolve. For example, you may head into a meeting committed to making an issue out of something, then see it lined up against all the issues the workgroup faces. You are then overwhelmed by a sense of perspective and your thinking becomes clearer and more rational.

Horizontal Sequential Questioning often amplifies the 'groove' of thinking. When everyone is thinking about the same thing, the speed of thought increases and the momentum that is generated can move the workgroup ahead in leaps and bounds.

Of course, the *Thinking System* is not about trying to make people uncomfortable or 'catching them out'. It's about getting to the best thinking they can do, so that it then translates to their best action. And getting to the best thinking is all about asking the right questions. The way we achieve this is by always separating the task from the individual. Separating the task from the individual ensures collaboration rather confrontation or potential for accusation.

> By separating the task from the individual you ensure collaboration rather confrontation or potential for accusation

Questions Build Rapport

Questions also allow a person to *build rapport and develop relationships*. This is something instructions don't always do. I once had a member of staff who was responsible for administration. A large part of her day was spent mail-merging letters and sending them out. From my office,

I could see her stand up and sit down, maybe 20 times a day, to retrieve something from the printer. The printer was only a short distance away but it was on her left-hand side. And she was right-handed, which meant that retrieving the printing from her seat was beyond her reach.

Being the systems freak that I am, this setup irritated me. And I felt sure, therefore, that it must also irritate her. But rather than going to her and suggesting she moves the printer (or worse, telling her to) – which was the 'obvious, logical' thing to do – I approached it differently. I wandered over to her, as if I was just dropping by, made some small talk, then asked, "What would you change about your workstation if you could?"

I, of course, asked this question thinking she would immediately mention the printer. But she didn't. Instead, she mentioned her chair and how she would change that. She mentioned a couple of other little things that we could also fix. Then came the bombshell...

"You know what I particularly like is that the printer is on the wrong side for me. This means I have to get up from my desk and get the material from the printer. So I don't sit in my chair all day and get a sore back."

This irritation to me was a godsend to her. I learned a valuable lesson that day about questions, subjectivity and objectivity. I took my perception of the situation into that conversation and it was the exact opposite of hers.

If I had marched over to her and said, "You know, this is really stupid... Why don't you just move the printer to the other side of your desk? Then you won't have to get up all the time". I would have received any number of responses, such as, "Well, I would if those bastards in technical support would give me the cable extension I ordered six months ago" or, "Well, actually I like it that way because it helps my back. So it's not stupid to me". Either way, we would have been heading for a conversation most probably laced with hostility.

In the end, the result was that she felt 'listened to' and that I cared enough to ask about her comfort at her workstation. We got to interact in a busy day and I got to see something from a different perspective. Instead of imposing my view on someone else, my view changed.

To recap, questions allow us:

- To gain clarity of thought, which allows us to gather the necessary information and draw correct and appropriate conclusions.
- To control the outcome with more skill and to control the environment around us – the one who asks the questions is always in charge.
- To illuminate the real issues and eliminate guesswork.
- To open our thinking to allow space for creativity to develop.
- To build rapport and strengthen relationships and allow us to operate with honesty and integrity.

Exercise: Reconstructing past instructions

Think of all the instructions you've issued in the past 24 hours – by email or face-to-face. Consider how you might re-construct them so that they end with a '?' instead of a '.' Or worse still, an '!'

Chapter Summary

- You can't control your elephant or anyone else's elephant without a system that will distract it. Questions distract the elephant.
- Questions distract the elephant because they invoke the frontal lobe. Statements, on the other hand, challenge the midbrain and encourage your elephant to be unruly.
- A *thinking system* is the questioning system that will allow you to permanently distract elephants in the workplace.
- A *thinking system* is essentially a thought process that captures the right information in the right order and allows the correct conclusions to be drawn. Capturing that 'right' information is achieved by asking the 'right' questions.

- Questions are the compass by which even the most inexperienced traveller can navigate through the maze of their own thinking to arrive at the clarity of understanding.
- A *thinking system* enables us to analyse our own behaviour. In so doing, we can create a personal 'idiot's guide' to unlock our own unique abilities, skills and talents so their expression doesn't fall to circumstance or chance and, instead, becomes a repeatable system that can be 'turned on' anytime, anywhere.
- The right answer to the wrong question is still the wrong answer.
- Asking the right question sends the brain on a positive journey looking for solutions. Ask the question the wrong way and the brain will immediately look for ways to shut the conversation down.
- If you want to improve your life, start asking better questions.
- Our mind has an enormous capacity for storing and retrieving knowledge. But unless we can direct it to create or carry out action, that capacity is useless. And questions are what allow us to do that.
- Memory isn't enough – we need to be able to bring the right pieces of information together at the right time. Questions allow us to do that.
- Our elephant has a habit of taking shortcuts through the default settings we mentioned earlier – instinct, emotion and inferred meaning. If he is not trained to behave otherwise, this can lead to invalid conclusions and can diminish our effectiveness.
- It takes courage to uncover the truth and be able to look at it objectively and clearly, without getting worried about what it means for you or your company's performance. The long-term benefits far outweigh any short-term discomfort.
- Questions can be designed so the answers will be less prone to manipulation.
- When a *thinking system* is sound, then politics, 'white-anting' and manipulation do not survive. Furthermore, and better still, default settings are turned off, emotion is disconnected, a common language is distilled and the person asking the questions is divorced from the content.

QUESTIONS – THE ESSENCE OF THE THINKING SYSTEM

- To recap, questions allow us:
  - To gain clarity of thought, which allows us to gather the necessary information and draw correct and appropriate conclusions.
  - To control the outcome with more skill and to control the environment around us – the one who asks the questions is always in charge.
  - To illuminate the real issues and eliminate guesswork.
  - To open our thinking to allow space for creativity to develop.
  - To build rapport and strengthen relationships and allow us to operate with honesty and integrity.

14
Three Examples of Business Thinking Systems

We round out Part Three – the part about how to manage your elephant through smart thinking – with three examples:

1. Template – diagnosing the cause of *any* business problem
2. Strategy – constructing a perfect business strategy
3. Performance – designing a performance contract

The purpose of these three examples is to demonstrate the ways that *thinking systems* and associated methods lead to effective solutions.

1. Diagnosis of *any* business performance problem

Failure to perform tasks to the level the team regards as appropriate can be attributed to the limitations in our thinking. These limitations manifest themselves in a number of ways, such as poor morale, lack of systems, etc. As such, they are sometimes mistaken for being the problem. They are in fact only *symptoms* – a consequence of you not being in charge of your thinking. Your thinking is constrained because, below your awareness, your elephant is actually running your life. Your elephant is using past experience, associative learning and emotion to *decide* for you. And the results speak for themselves.

Examining substandard performance in thousands of businesses, we discovered that poor thinking leads to the manifestation of 10 recurring obstacles that inhibit performance. So basically, any of 10 standard business challenges can surface as a result of the lack of good-quality thinking.

I will share with you the '10 obstacles' that plague business around the world. They are simple and easy to remember. Then we will turn them into a *thinking system*, in order to convert those challenges into a set of questions to help diagnose the problem (or problems) that needs to be addressed.

There are 10 ways that poor thinking commonly manifests itself in business, creating obstacles for individuals and workgroups alike.

Lack of a System

A system is not a 'way of doing things' – that is a habit. A system is *the* way chosen from all the *known* alternatives. (Our elephants prefer habits.)

Procedures not Written Down

There is no use having a system if it is not committed in writing. Doing so provides a solution when the person who typically performs a task is unavailable. (Our elephants don't need you to tell them anything.)

No Accountability

If nobody *owns* the job, then shared blame will lead to poor execution. (Our elephants don't find it necessary to publicise that which we alone are responsible for.)

No Audit

No matter how important the task, if nobody is checking, then where's the motivation to do it better? (Our elephants don't view our performance as anyone else's business.)

Lacking Recognition of Importance

The importance of some tasks is not always recognised (until some formal thinking process is applied) and small things can often have a domino effect. Once the team can see this, they can reverse-engineer a process or two and lift their game. (Our elephants know you don't really monitor their performance.)

Lack of Skill

Occasionally, the workgroup does not possess or 'match' the skill needed to complete the task to the desired standard. (Our elephants don't realise that old skills are insufficient for new systems.)

Lack of Resources

Simply put, this refers to all the resources excluding human skills and technology. (Our elephants know you won't invest in the new/upgraded tools it needs.)

Lack of Technology

The business may not have the hardware or software to do the task. (Our elephants know you won't invest in the new/upgraded technologies it needs.)

Change in Structure

The person who used to do a particular job well left the business, or the business structure changed and the job was not reassigned. This is an extraordinarily common problem in small business. (Our elephants don't think through the consequences of their neighbours departing.)

The Benchmark is New

It may be that the team has only just latched onto the idea for improvement. (Our elephants are happy doing things the old way.)

As mentioned, these 10 obstacles are what workgroups commonly attribute to preventing them from reaching their potential. In the boxes you will find the template, based on these 10 manifestations, including a brief definition of each obstacle.

Now let's find the solution . . .

Imagine that someone has come to you with a business challenge. You are now the second (*binary thinking*) brain that is going to make all the difference. You are confident because you have a tool kit (*thinking system*) that will allow you to extract the best possible result. The tools you will use are predictable, distillable, systematic and independent of the person you are dealing with. The tool, in this case, is the template in the breakout box.

A No-brainer Thinking System – using closed questions

System (a way of doing/addressing the tasks selected from known alternatives)
   Do you have a System?
Written (the system committed to paper or electronically stored, accessible to all)
   Is it written down somewhere?
Accountability (one person in the workgroup who knows implicitly that they are responsible for the desired outcome and the process)
   Is someone accountable? Does s/he know s/he is accountable?
Audit (a way of checking that the process is followed the way it should be)
   Do you check?
Importance (a clear understanding of the impact the process has on the rest of the business)
   Do they know how important it is?
Skill (the capability or knowledge required to perform the tasks to the identified standard)
   Have they got the skills?
Resources (the tools, equipment, capital and facilities needed to do the tasks properly)
   Do you have the resources?

> **Technology** (the hardware and software needed)
>   Have they got the technology?
> **Organisation** (the structure to support the person accountable – e.g., to provide that person with specialist skills, changes in the structure)
>   Has there been an organisational change that caused the problem?
> **New** (assessment of the time needed to bring the new idea to life)
>   Is it a new idea?

Try it: Pick a problem, any problem

The person seeking a solution says, "Our supplier is letting us down. I don't know what to do about it". Let's see how the template can be applied.

You ask ...
Question 1: *Do you have a system for dealing with suppliers?*
Question 2: *Is it written down somewhere?*
Question 3: *Is someone accountable for that supplier?*
Question 4: *Do you check?*
Question 5: *Do they know how important it is?*
Question 6: *Have they got the skills?*
Question 7: *Do they have the resources?*
Question 8: *Have they got the technology?*
Question 9: *Has there been an organisational change?*
Question 10: *Is this a new problem?*

What about another problem?

The person seeking a solution says, "Part GS57 keeps running out of stock and holding up the process".

You ask...

Question 1: *Do you have a system for dealing with stock control?*
Question 2: *Is it written down somewhere?*
Question 3: *Is someone accountable for stock control?*
Question 4: *Do you check?*
Question 5: *Do they know how important it is?*
Question 6: *Have they got the skills?*
Question 7: *Do they have the resources?*
Question 8: *Have they got the technology?*
Question 9: *Has there been an organisational change?*
Question 10: *Is this a new problem?*

Or what about another? (Just to prove a point)

The person seeking a solution says, "Sally, in accounts, isn't pulling her weight".

You ask...

Question 1: *Do you have a system for dealing with performance issues?*
Question 2: *Is it written down somewhere?*
Question 3: *Is someone accountable for that?*
Question 4: *Do you check?*
Question 5: *Do they know how important it is?*
Question 6: *Have they got the skills?*
Question 7: *Do they have the resources?*
Question 8: *Have they got the technology?*
Question 9: *Has there been an organisational change?*
Question 10: *Is this a new problem?*

Now apply all your learning from this book and take your skills up a notch – this is a *real* thinking system. You have a toolkit to diagnose problems: this template.

Now it's over to you.

> ### Template or checklist for developing thinking systems
>
> **System** (a way of doing/addressing the tasks selected from known alternatives)
> **Written** (the system committed to paper or electronically stored, accessible to all)
> **Accountability** (one person in the workgroup who knows implicitly that s/he is responsible for the desired outcome and the process)
> **Audit** (a way of checking that the process is followed or the job done the way it should be)
> **Importance** (a clear understanding of the impact the process has on the rest of the business)
> **Skill** (the capability or knowledge required to perform the tasks to the identified standard)
> **Resources** (the tools, equipment, capital and facilities needed to do the tasks properly)
> **Technology** (the software and hardware)
> **Organisation** (the structure to support the person accountable – e.g. to provide that person with specialist skills)
> **New** (assessment of the time needed to bring the new idea to life)

You have the 10 factors that took 10 years and a few million dollars worth of study to distil. All you need to do is memorise the 10 highlighted words and jot down some questions that will enable you to work through the list to help your friends and colleagues find solutions to their problems.

> ### An Empowering Thinking System – using open questions
>
> **System** (a way of doing/addressing the tasks selected from known alternatives)
> Tell me about your system for tackling this. (Assumes they have one)
> **Written** (the system committed to paper or electronically stored, accessible to all)
> Where would this information typically be kept? (Assumes they document it)
> **Accountability** (one person in the workgroup who knows implicitly that they are responsible for the desired outcome and the process)
> Who would regard this as being their job? (Assumes assignment)
> **Audit** (a way of checking that the process is followed the way it should be)

> How do you know that it's not being done properly? (As 'challenge' implies)
> **Importance** (a clear understanding of the impact the process has on the business)
> Has the impact of this task on the rest of the business been explained?
> **Skill** (the capability or knowledge required to perform the tasks to identified standard)
> What is the typical skill set you need to get the job done?
> **Resources** (the tools, equipment, capital and facilities needed to do the tasks properly) What could you acquire in terms of resources to make it easier to do the job properly?
> **Technology** (the hardware and software needed)
> Tell me about the software that drives this process?

If you don't believe me, stop now and try it.

Example 2: Constructing a Perfect Business Strategy

A business strategy should be a map to establish your destination and guide you there. If it doesn't, it's not a business strategy... it's something else.

It's essential to know where you want to go before you can select the strategies that will get you there. Business Coaching Systems' *Eight Steps To Perfect Business Strategies* is an eight-step program that equips you to critically analyse the destination and direction – both where you want to end up, and what strategies and tactics will propel you toward that ultimate goal.

The Eight Steps give you new tools and new insights about how to rewrite the rules governing strategy development. A proven methodology is used to create the business future. The experienced coaches at BCS, as *objective workshop facilitators*, do not write a strategy element into the plan until it is tested for its effectiveness to move your business from where you are to where you want to be.

MANAGING YOUR ELEPHANT THROUGH SMART THINKING

The Facilitation Concept

No one can be objective about their own ideas, and trained facilitators at BCS are skilled at providing that essential component. They also map your ideas and those of your colleagues to a uniform, compatible format that permits the interplay of creative freedom and hard-nosed analysis.

The Eight Steps constitute the *Thinking System* governing an offsite workshop event. These steps are:

1. **Pressure Points** – *What factors, beyond your control, shape your business's future?*

The two-day workshop starts with collecting and clarifying the six to twelve outside pressures on your business that are compiled from questionnaires completed by your participants in the workshop preparation. Typically, they include the economy, competitor activity, technological advances, shifting market demographics and government regulation. We also conduct a historic overview to see which external factors shaped the organisation's past. This alerts us to equivalent outside pressures in the present and the future.

2. **Proximity** – *Which pressure points are closest to the bone and capable of affecting you most?*

Ranking the pressure will highlight the urgency of tackling a threat. Better, it can also reveal a window of opportunity and inspire those masterstrokes that are the hallmark of all winning strategies. Ranking the external factors means that, even if we cannot manage our way around all of them at once, we can at least manage our organisation around the most important of them.

3. **Reckoning** – *Which way are the outside pressures going?*

This vital process of evaluating the pressures themselves ensures we put the most energy into addressing those that are closest or most likely to grow with time. It's a powerful focusing device, since some pressures will emerge as already distant and diminishing with time – therefore, not worth the allocation of long-term management resources.

4. **Impact Statements** – *How would the picture look if what might happen does indeed happen?*

Businesses without a strategic plan simply wait and see. Should something impact detrimentally on the business, they then say there's nothing they can do. Circumventing this, we construct impact statements that give you a firm basis now for action. Only by taking a mental step into the future can we make tough decisions about what to do while we still have the time.

5. **Inertia** – *What would happen if we did nothing at all?*

Step 5 deliberately works the opposite way to the previous step. It's reasonable to evaluate the effect of doing nothing, given that nothing is exactly what many organisations do. This step rings some welcome warning bells. It also provides a rationale for your decisions when you justify your emerging strategy to those not participating in the workshop, such as a board or senior management.

6. **Destination** – *How would the organisation look if each major impact were correctly managed over the next three to five years?*

We now think outcomes – taking mental snapshots of total success. This gives us an advance view of the optimum outcome. It liberates us to devise, schedule and implement the steps capable of achieving the ideal outcome – which, by the way, is the only outcome worth planning for.

7. **Milestones** – *What goals must be achieved mid term to get back on track for the long term?*

This is the hands-on, sleeves rolled-up step. We leave conceptualising and get down to practicalities that will bring means and ends together. But we are still working with the ultimate end in mind.

8. **Perspirations** – *What day-to-day processes will drive our activities in the direction of the long term, via the mid term?*

Only actions that work toward achieving the milestones are included here. And the only milestones that were previously included were those that led to the final destination. This is powerful planning. It's a good feeling being on the home straight.

Within each step, facilitators draw out the information using – you guessed it – further *thinking systems*, as demonstrated previously in the examples, especially in Chapter 12.

This is just a brief window into the unique methodology of Business Coaching Systems. If you want to know more – visit www.bcscoach.com.au or call us on 02 9934 1900 (International: +61 2 9934 1900).

Example 3: Designing a Performance Contract

A Performance Contract answers a set of questions that are both practical and predictable. The questions form a *thinking system* for effective discussion between management and staff.

What people must know:
- Who am I accountable to?
- Who is/are accountable to me?
- What does the business expect from all of us?
- What does the business expect from me?
- What are my Key Result Areas?
- What are the Characteristics of Delivery?
- By what measure will I be assessed?
- What are the targets I need to achieve?
- Where do I fit in the team?
- What skills, knowledge and experience are required?
- What gaps must I address?
- When will I be reviewed?

Answers provide the *content* of the document – the contract.

PART FOUR
MANAGING OTHER PEOPLE'S ELEPHANTS THROUGH SMART WORKING DYNAMICS

We've considered the various 'gaps' that exist in business and ascertained that, at the source, our tendency to under-perform is due to our unruly elephants. Just below our conscious awareness are limitations to our thinking, mostly an expression of the elephant itself. We have deconstructed those limitations so we can clearly see them for what they are and bring awareness and understanding to the problems they create.

These limitations hinder the mode of operation in which our performance matches our knowledge and capabilities.

Many authors have written about poor attitude, lack of opportunity, lack of encouragement and other symptoms. Attempts to address those have seen the launch of studies and books in their millions and still counting. What they unwittingly perpetuate are typical workplace problems, such as lack of systems, failure to record processes or failure to foster accountability.

The solutions I have put forward in this book are *binary thinking* and *thinking systems*. Simply involving another mind in the challenges at hand will improve your results exponentially. And, if that second mind also uses powerful *Thinking System* methodologies, the results can be miraculous. They place at your disposal the tools to ensure smart thinking and put your frontal lobe in charge of your business.

But what about your workgroup? If we concede that adults cannot be taught and that invention is a primary source of motivation, then how do we control the elephants rampaging around in your workgroups, especially when their presence has been ignored?

In the international business bestseller *First Break All The Rules* by Marcus

> You can have at your disposal the tools to ensure smart thinking and to put your frontal lobe in charge of your business.

Buckingham and Curt Coffman, the authors confirmed what every manager already inherently knows – you can't change people. The book is a product of two mammoth research studies over the past 25 years undertaken by the Gallup Organization. The study gave voice to more than one million employees and 80,000 managers.[53]

What they found was that the greatest managers in the world *seem* to have little in common. They differ in sex, age and race. They employ vastly different styles and focus on different goals. Yet, despite their differences, great managers share one common trait: they do not hesitate to break virtually every rule held sacred by conventional wisdom. They *do not* believe that, with enough training, a person can achieve anything he sets his mind to. People don't change that much.

Don't waste time trying to put in what was left out. Instead, try to draw out what is left in. If you want someone to be what they are not, you have two choices: you can try to *change* them, or you can *make it easy* for them to be the way they really are. To find and nurture someone's natural talent is hard enough without trying to ignore that talent and turn them into something else instead.

Part Four isn't so much about the individual. It's about the group and how you can adapt the working environment to elicit best thinking from the individuals so the workgroup can be more effective ... despite the herd of elephants they carry with them. Part Three was about you, and about how you can *adopt* new behaviours that will help raise your thinking to new heights. Part Four is about your environment, and how it can *adapt* to facilitate the effectiveness of your workgroup.

There will be people in your team opposed to adopting new ways of operating. They won't want to use *thinking systems* or engage others in *binary thinking*. They will stick two fingers up behind your back and do whatever the hell it was they were doing before. This chapter is about adapting the workgroup so this attitude cannot prevail.

Change occurs either inside out (from the individual to the environment) or outside in (from the environment to the individual). It's a two-way process. As discussed previously, the new field of Epigenetics is upending the conventional understanding of genetic control and showing how the effects of your genetic makeup are not set in stone but are constantly evolving and changing, based on your environment and life experience. The same is true for business workgroups. If the individuals in your team don't wish to cooperate, you can still achieve your desired outcome by altering the environment and life experience of the workgroup.

Considering that adults learn best by *doing*, the way to pacify the elephants in your charge is to implement new frameworks or operating protocols – agreed, documented methods of operation – for the workgroup.

To improve business performance, we need to get people to behave in ways that address the real problems, thereby overcoming the limitations. And we need to do that in a way that works *with*, rather than *against*, the way their mind works.

Binary Thinking and *Thinking Systems* are tools we can use to compensate for limitations inherent in one-on-one interactions and bring about predictably positive outcomes. The task now is to bring about

> People don't change that much. Don't waste time trying to put in what was left out. Try to draw out what was left in. That is hard enough.
> The following six operating pVrotocols, when replicated into your organisation or workgroup, provide a way of managing the whole environment (versus an individual) to overcome the impact of a herd of elephants.

the same positive outcome for one-on-many interactions, such as in leader-to-group situations. In a nutshell, we will build on methods already presented but with slight alterations. This is far more useful than suggesting wasteful ways to try changing what can't be changed.

These alterations are replicable in your organisation and provide a way to manage the whole environment (versus managing an individual) to overcome the impact from a herd of elephants. The six operating protocols or routines presented in the following chapters reflect winning behaviours. They are, in shorthand, the Business Laws of Nature.

Aligning to the Business Laws of Nature automatically alters behaviour and combats our innate shortcomings. You and your workgroup can then enjoy the benefits of improved business performance, without individual or collective transformation.

In short, Part Four is devoted to what the workgroup leader can do in order to get the desired outcome from his team, whether the individuals in that team want to cooperate or not.

15

Setting the Scene for Taking on the Task

The Chinese Room is a thought experiment devised by the philosopher J. Searle to illustrate the difference between behaviour and understanding; to show the pitfalls in trying to assess one's capability (knowledge) by watching one's behaviour (a symptom of knowledge) alone.

Imagine a translator sitting in a room with an appropriate Chinese/English rulebook. Provided the rulebook was extensive enough, it would be feasible to supply English text as input and have Chinese text returned as output. The operator need not know any Chinese to appear to the observer to be a linguist.

Similarly, the computer known as 'Deep Blue' could be seen as having a powerful intellect, evidenced by its chess winning performances.

Lesson: You do not need to have knowledge in order to exhibit behaviour.[54]

The techniques promoted here are designed to encourage the behaviours in others. The challenge is to provide your workgroup with a framework that allows them to feel empowered, inspired, productive, valuable and needed

Remember the statistics we discussed earlier ... workgroups always feel they perform only 15 per cent of their tasks well. Note that this is the same whether the response comes from a good

SETTING THE SCENE FOR TAKING ON THE TASK

company, a bad company or a just plain ugly company. This does not negate that the performance of good and bad businesses, relative to each other, is very different. On close inspection, we realise that good companies do certain things almost 'instinctively' that bad companies just don't do.

This chapter, along with those that follow it, are devoted to what you, as workgroup leader, can do in order to get the desired outcome from the team. You'll be presented with tools you can easily use without needing to go through the years of trial and error it took to develop them. They will be readily applicable and, by *behaving* in a way that deals with the inherent challenges caused by our brain biology, they will help you convert your business into a powerhouse.

I do not pretend to be the first to recognise these behaviours and their importance. However, I am *re-stating them as outcomes* – that is, showing that if you use the suggested routines or protocols to behave, and encourage this behaviour in your team and workgroup, then you will overcome the thinking limitations and you will materially improve performance. Remember, the people who behave this way typically do so unconsciously anyway.

The theory of why they work is there for those who want it. But be assured, regardless of your understanding of the theory (as in the 'Chinese Room' example), the behaviours we explore will work.

The techniques promoted here are designed to encourage the behaviours in others. The challenge is to provide your workgroup with a framework that allows them to feel empowered, inspired, productive, valuable and needed. This not only creates a more effective and efficient workgroup but also a more harmonious and enjoyable one. And all of these things ultimately affect your bottom line.

The benefits that result from these behaviours are cumulative – each one assisting the next. Applied separately, they are powerful facilitators for change; applied cumulatively, they are exponentially so. And this cumulative benefit creates what we call a *virtuous circle*.

Vicious Circles vs Virtuous Circles

Everyone knows what a *vicious circle* is. Most of us have experienced one at some time in our lives. A vicious circle is a downward spiral, where one bad thing leads to another to another and you can't get out of the self-reinforcing negative loop.

For example, two candidates are going for the same job – one is currently employed, the other is not. They both have exactly the same skills, same knowledge and same experience. Based on that information alone, if you ask employers which candidate they would recruit, the typical answer would be 'the one who is employed'.

So the person without a job misses out on the very thing s/he needs and the person who's already got a job has an opportunity they *don't* need – although they may *want* it, they don't need two jobs. For the one who misses out, that's a vicious circle.

The lesser-known flip side to the vicious circle is the virtuous circle. Most people don't even know that virtuous circles exist because virtuous circles are either not consciously recognised or they are put down to luck or chance. The critical differences are that vicious circles are often apparent while virtuous circles are not, and also, *people will readily trace their bad luck but they don't consciously trace their good luck.*

Success and the role of Context vs. Content

Successful people don't generally know why they are successful. They put it down to various platitudes or 'just hard work'. But the truth is that, whether through luck or learning, they have worked out how to think smarter. It is probably unintentional for them and, if asked to describe how they operate, they are often unable to do so.

It's not that successful people don't *want* to tell you how they work – they *can't* tell you; *they* don't know what they do either. They can't tell you because they weren't *there*. They only participated in *content* (which is their effective behaviour) not the *context* (watching themselves behave). The day that someone points out what was so effective in their behaviour, and why, is when they get their very own 'ah-hah' moment.

You need both content and context to learn. This book is in itself an imposition of *context* on what has always been *content* for me. It has forced me to *explain* what, for me, has become historically instinctive.

So, I have now *unpacked* that instinct and we turn to the blueprint for behaviour that can be *replicated* through *simple techniques* to make your outcomes successful.

When something goes wrong, people tend to be more introspective and analyse, or at least look at, their behaviour. The question 'Why did this happen to me?' will pop up almost automatically and may not even be a conscious process. The power of questions will enforce analysis because if you ask a question your mind is compelled to answer.

On the other hand, when something goes right our tendency is just to be happy about it and celebrate. Contemplation usually doesn't occur. Yet this is exactly the key to unlocking the mystery of what is different between successful people and unsuccessful people. Successful people have an innate desire to trace their good luck as well as their bad. They know, instinctively, that if they trace the effect back to the cause, they will be able to repeat the behaviour that brought them 'good luck' and avoid the behaviour that brought them 'bad luck.'

You've heard the saying 'The harder I work the luckier I get'. In commerce, luck is overrated. It's usually a case of uncovering the patterns and behaviours that, when re-applied over and over again in the form of hard work, will yield the positive results.

Luck is what happens when opportunity meets preparation. Successful people are simply repeating positive behaviour protocols they've created for themselves or instinctively had all along.

The need is, therefore, twofold: the process of introspection, such as we do when things don't go well, is just one step in the process; we then need to ensure that we learn from the experience and do not go on repeating the same error in varying disguises.

The challenge with a virtuous circle is this: we not only have to accept that it happens but we have to consciously engage in introspection so we can find the common denominators to our success and transfer them to other areas of our life. For the most part, in the pages that follow, I have done this for you. These six Business Laws of Nature can hardwire the 'luck' into your business.

Virtuous Circles

Consider, for example, a business owner who is known for being a listener. Ask such individuals why they choose to listen to their staff. In most cases, the response would be one of surprise at the question. You see, people who do this naturally, assume that everyone does it and, therefore, the question seems strange to them – like asking, 'Why do you breathe?' After the initial surprise, a typical response might be, "Of course I listen to my staff".

But what actually happens within the business as a result of that behaviour? The two obvious things are (a) that the listeners may end up with ideas they didn't have before and (b) that the relationship between the business owner and the staff is healthier as a result.

The not-so-obvious things are the little cultural nuances that can gather their own momentum and create a positive impact in the business. Staff can see the interaction in which one of their colleagues talked to the boss and was actually *listened* to. As a result, their perception of the business is positive. They conclude that they are part of an organisation that listens. The more that evidence is gathered for this, the sooner it creates a default. The elephant has a new positive assumption.

It makes people feel valued to see that their opinion *does* count for something and it has a positive effect on the whole environment. Because the staff members sense a direct connection between what they suggest and the prosperity of the business, their elephants become less pessimistic. There is less uncertainty and elephants like that.

Others in the organisation, who are now aware that the company has listened, are consequently more likely to come forward themselves with their own ideas. Let's say the ideas that come forward (or the ideas that follow) are good, leading to savings – either less expenditure or greater revenue. There is now more money to spend on more ideas that then come more often from people who are now more motivated to share ideas within an environment that they enjoy.

Voilà ... a virtuous circle.

Most of these listening business owners would not say to you, "Well, there are a number of discreet reasons why I listen to my staff... First, it means that everybody realises I listen. This means I get more ideas from my staff and some of those ideas turn out to be good so I implement them. And then more ideas come from more people, more often. And so my business is more profitable". Instead, the typical answer is, "Well, doesn't everybody?"

The reality is that not every business owner does listen. Instead, they exhibit a very different symptom. That symptom comes from thinking, "Well, if I listen to the staff, then they'll take up all my time. Then everybody will waste my time giving me their stupid ideas. Besides, we don't have the budget to do different things. And it works just fine as it is".

Who wins the coconut for working out who or what is making the 'decision' not to listen?

In my experiences of unpacking and rebuilding (or analysing and synthesising, if you prefer) many businesses, I have observed that these virtuous circles are, in effect, the results of good behaviour.

Each of the six characteristics, or Business Laws of Nature, described in the next six chapters is exhibited by effective workgroups. As such, they have unconsciously dealt with their elephants.

Encouraging your business to demonstrate each Business Law individually is a powerful catalyst for change. When put together, the laws create a virtuous circle. Each one makes the other more possible and the outcomes spiral up to success, not down to failure. Each one is, ultimately, an expression of *smart thinking* and becomes *imposed context* – or the automatic way of thinking. Each one is a *thinking system*, expressed as behaviour or operating protocol.

Behaviour vs Knowledge – 'Fake it 'til you make it'

Let's remember, for a moment, the curious way that adults learn: they behave in a particular way which then teaches them why it works. If adults do something that results in a good outcome, they respond with, "Oh, that worked ... I might do that again". That is, if they're *surprised* the outcome was good.

They forget that, three months ago at a barbecue at their brother's home, who is also in business, someone said, "You should try this". Once they try it – possibly by accident – and find that it works, it becomes part of their automated behaviour ... as long as they recognise the connection between the action and the outcome.

Kids know they don't know and have no ego attached to that fact, so they get an idea by being given a suggested action. They then go and try it. And, if it works, they transfer that idea into knowledge. It's almost like an internal checklist, where kids try some suggested thing – it either works or it doesn't. They incorporate the resulting information as knowledge.

Adults, on the other hand, stop doing that as soon as ego shows up – which, for most of us, is some time in our teens. Suddenly, we stop trying things suggested to us and so our knowledge stagnates. For us to learn, we have to do the behaviour, witness the outcome, connect the two and come up with the idea ourselves. It's a bit like the 'fake it 'til you make it' philosophy.

The need behind this behaviour is universal; its application compulsory.

If you incorporate the Business Laws of Nature outlined in the next six chapters and don't get too hung up about why the behaviour works, then you will see results. How fast you then reverse-engineer that knowledge to create a virtuous circle is your own personal evolution. Always remember, these are behaviours that compensate for your elephant – all that information sitting just below your conscious awareness that has a profound influence on how you live your life.

I know it's hard to imagine having an elephant and not realising it ... But that's exactly what you have. The challenges this pachyderm causes are permanent biological realities that cannot be self-corrected by conscious decisions.

Let me explain the layout of the chapters and signal their value to you. Each includes six components structured as follows:

1. Title
The title introduces the Business Law of Nature and the principle behind the behaviour. In time, these laws become conscious links between your behaviour and the competent application of *thinking systems*. You will start to think and see, in your work and your interactions, Design = Ownership = Motivation (the first of the six Business Laws of Nature). Don't dismiss the chapter headings as catchy hooks, however tempting that may be. Commit them to memory instead.

2. Précis
This thought starter begins to scope the idea and explain its connection to performance. It is described in the language you might use if you wanted to explain the behaviour to, say, a team member.

3. Behaviour
This is a brief description of the 'to do' item that might indicate the presence of the right 'thinking' which, in turn, is a catalyst for the right behaviour. Successful people exhibit the behaviour and successful workgroups do, but not everybody does. Remember, the behaviour some of us have developed is a kind of

Remember: encouraging your business to demonstrate each characteristic individually is a powerful catalyst for change, but when put together they create a virtuous circle.

unconscious attempt to control the characteristics of our unruly elephant.

4. Rationale

This is a detailed look at what makes the behaviour work in our favour and, especially, how to apply it most easily. Where appropriate, specific reference is made to the thinking limitation it overcomes.

5. Workshop Exercises

These are designed to help you begin to shape your behaviour and, ultimately, your thinking. The exercises are simple and straightforward. You only add the questions which, to a degree, become self evident in the exercise itself.

6. Comprehension Check

This closing thought links the behaviours together, demonstrating how they become 'virtuous circles'

16

Business Law of Nature 1: Design = Ownership = Motivation

People are never stronger than when they have thought up their own arguments for believing what they believe. They stand on their own two feet that way.

KURT VONNEGUT JR, FROM *HOCUS POCUS*[55]

Précis

People are naturally motivated when given the opportunity to design their own plan for success and put that plan into action. When they do, it's no longer just work – they're doing something for which they can see a purpose. In other words, put the meaning back into the job and it's no longer a job; it's a personal mission.

Think about a work project that truly motivates you. It's not always that you enjoy the process. It's more often that you like the outcome because you see value in it. Workers, at all levels, respond the same way.

Behaviour

In good business, we have consistently found that decision making and inventiveness flow as easily from the bottom up as they do from the top down. The behaviour we look for is a strong meeting culture, where scheduled and disciplined meetings occur as a priority, not as an *ad hoc* necessity. This means that opportunities are hardwired into the business to allow people to 'have their say'. People will begin to see these meetings as a forum for discussion and interaction and, consequently, take a mental note of issues that might improve business performance, knowing the culture provides them with an opportunity to share their suggestions. In these businesses, there is often a strong performance management discipline as well. This means that people know the time will come when they can not only comment on their own performance but also the performance of the business as well.

> We have consistently found in good businesses that decision making and inventiveness flow as easily from bottom up as they do from top down.

Rationale

Design = Ownership = Motivation is the first Business Law of Nature. It explores the connection between personal innovation, ownership and action. People are motivated by the opportunity to design their own success. There is no greater motivator than feeling that you are the engineer of your own future. In businesses that exploit their potential best, there is, typically, contribution to design throughout the team and a culture of inclusiveness and openness.

If you can get people in the organisation to design their own solutions and take ownership, they become more motivated to implement those solutions because their elephants are also managed in that environment.

Managing thinking, securing engagement and allowing ownership mean that the elephant's desire to be moody, pessimistic and reactionary is minimised. This allows the frontal lobe to take charge long enough for the individual to deliver.

I said in Chapter Three that people are people, not machines, so you would never get 100 per cent from them. But you can improve performance by up to 25 per cent and reach 80 per cent or 90 per cent – without paying a single cent more in expenses. Normally, if you ask your staff to do more work, they will expect to be remunerated for that change in their job description. But, if you change the culture of the company to empower employees to highlight shortcomings and allow them to find their own solutions, they will become more productive and more fulfilled. Remuneration may never be an issue. Besides, if your people begin performing to a higher level of efficiency, then the business will improve. And when business is good, there's more to go around, making it possible to reward those efforts, too.

One of the characteristics of an effective workplace is an environment where people are encouraged to have control and influence over the way their job is done. This requires effective workgroup leadership behaviour. Good workgroup leadership fosters a sense of control and helps people find the answers to their questions. Allowing workgroup members to come up with their own ideas, subsequently, triggers the required motivation.

Let's talk about the sort of environment that a good leader is striving to produce, with the end in mind, because replicating it will be simple. Again, in order to replicate the behaviour, you don't need to understand the science behind it. First, you need to let people have control of the way they do their job. Let them come up with the ideas that are needed for the business to improve and provide opportunities for the team to participate in designing those answers. It doesn't mean abrogating responsibility or delegating your authority away. It means:

> **Good leadership is where the leader fosters a sense of control by the workgroup and assists people to find the answers to their own questions.**

1. Talking backwards
2. Using the *diagnosis Thinking System* detailed in Chapter 14
3. Creating opportunities to invent

Talking backwards

If you want something done for a reason, give the reason before the something. It's that easy. Wear an elastic band around your wrist, or a piece of sticky tape over your finger, or something to remind you, for a week or two, to remember this. The approach is best used when what you are about to ask:

- Should be done by someone else, not you;
- Requires a new approach;
- Will take someone out of his or her comfort zone;
- Feels in your gut like the request might offend; or
- Causes you to hesitate in any way before asking.

In these circumstances you need to *talk backwards*. This can be done through the application of a simple *Thinking System* as described in Part Three.

Using the Thinking System for problem diagnosis

Stop giving answers to questions and start asking the questions outlined in the *problem diagnosis thinking system* discussed in Chapter 14. If a staff member has a challenge and you have a solution, at the very least, take your suggestion and turn it into a question. Replace, "Why don't you . . . ?" with, "Would it make sense to . . . ?"

Can you see that you are likely to get a less than frank response if your colleague has an issue with the first expression of the suggestion, "Why don't you . . . ?" But if you express the suggestion the second way, you are more likely to invite healthy discussion and arrive at a suitable solution.

In other words, if you tell me "do this" and you are wrong *and* you are my 'boss', my thinking goes, "How do I disagree without threatening my position?" and that is not a productive train of thought. This mental response is almost completely avoided if the suggestion is couched as a question. The question is much more inclusive and will lead to conversation. Even if you disagree, you can answer more frankly with either, "Yes, but ... " or "No, because ... "

If you ask questions instead of give instructions, you allow the correct people to own the idea and find the answer. They may assume you knew all along, but so what? They will have shared ownership and that equals motivation.

Creating opportunities to invent

Convene a team meeting to discuss the business and create food for *thinking systems* to apply:

- How do you think we are going?
- What do you all think we do best?
- What's the *least* effective practice in this business?
- What's the *most* effective practice in this business?
- Around the room quickly – what's the one thing about this company you would change?
- What are our competitors doing that we are not?
- What's our point of difference?
- Who's our best customer? What makes them the best?
- Pick one other person in the room. If you were in their shoes, what would you change? And why?
- What is one initiative we committed to, but failed to deliver on? And how can we fix it?
- Have I forgotten to follow through on any promises?
- If we were to hire someone tomorrow, what additional skills would we bring in first?

Each of these questions is designed to uncover a well-known and predictable problem. As an exercise, look at each question and jot down what issues you think would or should surface.

A role of the workgroup leader is to align your workgroup to the first Business Law of Nature and foster *Design = Ownership = Motivation* at every opportunity. You need to be asking yourself, at every stage, how best to move ownership and design into the hands of those who will be doing the tasks.

> You need to be asking yourself at every stage how best to move ownership and design into the hands of those who will be doing the tasks.

Invariably, effective workgroups are found where the workgroup leader is able to communicate in the language of each individual.

I remember reading an article about Bill Parcells. Parcells is an American Football legend. His team management career is punctuated by moments when he took incredibly under-performing teams and turned them into champions. He did this on a number of occasions without the revolutionary change in playing talent you might suspect. In his article in the *Harvard Business Law Journal*, Parcells attributed his success to the fact that he manages 'collectively individually' (my words not his, but I think they sum it up). The cornerstone of his success is one-on-one communication. He manages the team by managing the individuals within the team first, then the team as a unit evolves. The understanding here is that, if everyone in the team knows what is required of him or her and what to expect, then the team will naturally thrive.

Successful communication is the result of the *questions* you ask.

The action that business owners can take here is to re-read Chapters 11 and 12 on the Thinking System and start to develop questions that can lead to these design and discovery outcomes. Remember, the secret is to ask questions that are aimed at getting the other person's mind to collect the pieces of information needed, to draw the conclusion you're after.

Conclusions vs Decisions

I'm often asked, "How will I know I'm on the right track?" My answer is always the same: you will feel it, and that feeling will emerge from *conclusion-based*, rather than *decision-based* management.

Knowing whether you've made a decision or drawn a conclusion lies in your degree of comfort — *after* you've made the call. When you draw a *conclusion* there is practically no discomfort. Why? Because the basis for drawing a conclusion is to know and feel that you have all the evidence you need – you have all the facts.

Most *decisions*, on the other hand, are part fact, part assumption, part guess and part hope.

Conclusion: I have all the facts.
Judgment: I have all the facts I can reasonably obtain.
Decision: I do not have all the facts.

Leaders are forced to make decisions when they know they have either all the information they can get or all the information that makes commercial sense to get. They have the experience to assume the rest. So, leaders are in charge of that delicate balance between how much time to spend making a decision and how much information to gather and rely on. The further down the chain of command you go, the more you find the need to be drawing conclusions.

It's a conundrum because the further up the ladder you go, the more sophisticated the thinking and the better placed you are to draw conclusions.

Now, I'm not telling you when to make a decision or when to draw a conclusion. I'm simply pointing out the difference. And if you understand the difference, you can understand *thinking systems* that bit better because *thinking systems* are the question generators for extracting the

> **Leaders are forced to make decisions when they know they've got all the information that they either can get or that makes commercial sense to get.**

facts, faster. The more questions you ask, the more facts you get. And the more facts you get, the greater the chance of being able to draw a conclusion rather than make a decision.

Design = Ownership = Motivation is about using questions to help people collect the information necessary for them to draw conclusions – often the same conclusion you may have started with. It's about asking the right questions so that you empower people to find their own answers, their own ideas and, therefore, feel motivated and inspired to achieve their own self-designed outcomes.

Whenever I have a client who does not have a best next step, I get them to ask their team. More than 50 per cent of the time the problem is solved in a heartbeat. I had a client who was wondering whether he should add a new product to his line. He was going through the pros and cons and just going round in circles. I said, "OK, let's go ask the team ... Let's just have a chat". The ensuing discussion was instantly rich and balanced, and considerations emerged that we hadn't thought of before. The decision became very straightforward for the business owner, as the introduction of this new product would have resulted in a clear conflict of offerings – a perspective he had not seen on his own. The staff didn't talk him out of it. It was just a logical next step that became obvious once all the additional ideas, opinions, and information came to the surface. I estimate that my client had agonised alone over this choice and lost sleep over it for months. Discussing it with the team solved the problem within 30 minutes. Plus the team got to feel more involved with the business and its direction, and that made them feel valued and inspired to be part of the business.

Workshop Exercise

Technique 1 – Simple Thinking Systems aid design
Design a Thinking System – select a desired outcome for your team to work towards.

BUSINESS LAW OF NATURE 1

In the boxes marked F1 through F5, think of five facts or reasons that make that outcome relevant and worthwhile. Then construct a question, to which the answer could be that fact or reason. Record the experience below, after you try it on the team.

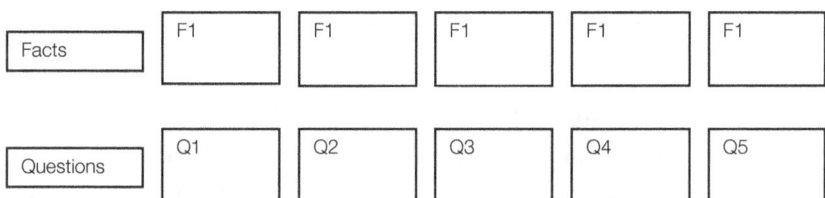

Figure 6 Developing purposeful questions

Technique 2 – Re-engineering

As mentioned earlier, the most effective way to teach an adult is to have them do something, then assess the results. Your business or workgroup must be encouraged to align with this Business Law of Nature and adopt these protocols as a matter of course.

The best way to introduce *Design = Ownership = Motivation* to the team is by adding a new aspect to your weekly meetings. Each week, assign a workgroup member the task of preparing a presentation to the group on a process they will be responsible for: why they do that process; why it's important for the business; and why it's done that particular way. That person is to share the prepared material with the workgroup at the next meeting.

As the facilitator of this process, it is important that you separate the individual from the process. So encourage the individual to say, "The company performs X task", rather than "I perform X task". This way you remove the personal attachment between the individual and the process, and invite a more impartial and open discussion in the group.

The final stage of the exercise is to open the presentation for discussion and to brainstorm different ways to do the process currently under the microscope. Remember, when you brainstorm: first, write everything down – however stupid it may seem to start with – then look at the answers as a group, consider them, discard any that are inappropriate and, finally, consolidate the best elements.

The other members of the workgroup add objectivity to the process because often they don't know that much about it. However, for this to be a valuable activity, the owner of the process must draw the conclusions as to how best to change the process. That individual will be more motivated if they get to re-engineer the process, not if everyone else is telling them how to re-engineer it.

At the end of each meeting, congratulate the participants – especially the person who owns the process under scrutiny. That person is then asked to go away to re-design the process the best way they see fit before reporting back to the group at the next meeting. At each meeting, a new person presents until everyone has re-engineered at least one of their core processes. You can continue with this exercise until all processes have been done, or move on to a different workshop.

Comprehension Check

Questions activate the frontal lobe. Empowering the workgroup with the responsibility of helping the business, brings their smartest thinking to life. Under these conditions, the elephant cannot exert a contrary influence – ownership of the design or invention means it accords with the elephant's need for keeping you safe, fed and employed. The focus for success, therefore, is your conscious self.

17
Business Law of Nature 2: Know Every Other Player's Position

Précis

Teams combine better when everyone has a clear knowledge of everyone else's job definitions. In other words, if I team up with you, I need to know if you're a front row forward, ruckman, or goalie. I will know better how I can relate to you when I understand how your job helps me do mine, and how much you rely on me to do yours. People who see meaning in their job also want to be relied upon. Being needed is great for the ego, short term . . . and great for the career, long term.

Behaviour

Successful businesses appear to have a higher level of 'collective consciousness'. The people in them seem more acutely aware of what their colleagues do, than is the case for businesses that struggle. They have sophisticated induction and orientation procedures that are written and communicated throughout. They have an organisational chart. They let staff 'talk' to each other and they have a social calendar.

Rationale

One of the things we've found while unpacking businesses and observing effective patterns is that many of the accepted truths of business are flawed. *Know Every Other Player's Position* relates to one of these paradigms. If we ask ourselves the question, "Is it good for everyone within a workgroup to know what everyone else within the workgroup does?", the answer is invariably, "Yes". The logic is overwhelming in favour of this conclusion. However, if we ask specifically *how much* people should know, the assumption is that superficial knowledge ought to be sufficient. The concern is that too much knowledge will be a burden on the individual because too much information can be confusing and would distract them from their own specific role.

Our experience tells us that, in reality, the opposite is true. We are yet to find the point at which too much information adversely affected a person's performance or productivity.

Instead, what we discovered was that providing more information has extraordinary value for the business. When I first began coaching, I found there was some resistance from people participating in the workshops – they felt they were being involved in analysing parts of the business that weren't their concern. And this meant it could occasionally get – dare I say it – boring.

By pushing on with the process, we later discovered that, whether or not people got bored, was dependent on how the coach handled the situation. If the coach encouraged people to see the value of their objective viewpoint on the process, they suddenly became 'facilitators' along with the coach. Their points of view mattered because they were truly separate or isolated from that process. We took them from zero *content* to being part of the *context*.

Going back to the elephant for a moment . . . if the elephant is non-verbal, and language is a poor medium for communication, *Knowing Every Other Player's Position* demands that more words, not fewer, are deployed to explain the individual tasks carried out by each person. As a result, everyone gets much more information, uncertainty disappears and its place is taken by understanding and tolerance. The elephant is, therefore, much less likely to get moody and rely on default or knee-jerk reactions.

Typically, in a business, if you are not the doer of a job, you are a beneficiary of that job being done, or you rely on that job being done so you can do your job effectively.

One of my observations on performance is that you can't be a part-time anything if you want to master it. That is, you can't do anything in life to lift your potential unless it's all you do. If you spend every day doing what you're doing, you'll get better at what you're doing. Eventually, you'll be the best you can be.

By taking people into parts of the business they aren't related to, I could have been accused of distracting them from their full-time jobs. Not so. What we found was that they were instead getting better at the part of the business they were involved in.

Why? Well first, I wasn't asking them to do it – I was asking them to understand it as we analysed it, so the distraction was not permanent, only temporary. Making that clear upfront immediately took the pressure off the workgroup members, and they became interested and curious rather than sceptical and suspicious. Remember, in the absence of information, people will take a pessimistic perspective. So, as soon as I gave them information that allayed their fears about having to 'do' anything extra, they relaxed. As their interest rose, they became more productive and helpful with answers or possible solutions, and so they started to see the big picture more clearly.

Let me explain...

Imagine you give some children 50 Lego pieces. They are restricted in what they can build by virtue of the fact that they have only 50 Lego pieces. They can only build a certain number of things. Correct?

But suppose you give them 950 more Lego pieces to make a total of 1000 pieces... Can they build more things? Yes they can. Of course, they can. What's really interesting is that, if you then take the same 950 Lego pieces away and leave them with the 50 they originally started with, what do you think happens?

Logic would suggest that they would be restricted to what they could build before. But they can now build different things because that experience with the additional pieces created a wider perspective about what's possible with the *original* 50 pieces.

The same thing happens in a business. If you understand where your Lego pieces fit in the big picture, then you can become much more creative in your area, as well as within the business as a whole. So it's absolutely vital that you adhere to the second Business Law of Nature and *Know Every Other Player's Position* because it will always impact – even if only marginally – on what you do and how you do it.

Note that a symptom of effective workgroups is the existence of a broad understanding by all people in all parts of the business, and that there is a transparency in the performance in all parts of the business.

Try to imagine, for a moment, that people actually do care about how their performance and their job impact on others. Then you start to see an environment emerge where people say, "Hey, I've got an idea about this thing that you guys do. I thought that if I change this, then you could do it that way, and that would be better for you. Wouldn't that help?"

Or, when somebody's unavailable to fulfil a particular task, you don't then have a complete ignoramus who says, "Well, you know, the person who normally looks after that is not here at the moment, I'm sorry..." Instead, the person can have an intelligent conversation with the customer who then feels as if they have a solid relationship with the whole business or that the business is smart. It conveys an impression to customers that it's an effective workplace they are dealing with.

The net result is that your team members understand – collectively and individually – what you want to accomplish. It makes for better team members. What we've also discovered is that this inclusive approach effectively gives workshop participants an MBA in their own company. And that's a real bonus for them, and for the stakeholders.

Colleagues often experience a real paradigm shift when we work through this process. Every time we do an Operational Plan with a workgroup – every time – at some point and, often at many points, somebody will turn to someone else and say, "Geez, I didn't realise how much you had to do". Once the coach unpacks what each individual does, the rest of the team suddenly realises what that person faces every day – the difficulties, challenges, complex processes and procedures. This allows everyone in the business to better manage their expectations of each other and find constructive, effective solutions to the challenges they face. The journey brings the workgroup together, always with renewed respect and understanding, and they become a force to be reckoned with.

Knowing Every Other Player's Position is about understanding the impact that you have on the people in the organisation, and the expectations you have of them. It's about resetting the defaults.

Workshop Exercises

Technique 3 – Virtuous Circle

The workshop for this behaviour is actually a by-product of the workshop for *Design Equals Motivation*. By choosing a process, then sharing with the group the details of that process, the rest of the group automatically becomes aware of that player's position. They may previously have known that she did a certain process, but hearing why she does it that way and what impact it has on the business, opens up understanding – not only of her role in the company but also of the business itself.

Technique 4 – The business 'Spin the Bottle'

Tell everyone in the workgroup to think of their Key Performance Indicators (KPIs) and ask them to identify their most important one.

Every week – perhaps after the usual agenda of the weekly meeting – ask a pre-elected workgroup member to challenge another member of the team with the following statement:

"I need you to do _____ *(insert name of task)*, so that I can _____ *(insert name of deliverable)*, and deliver against _____ *(insert KPI)* key performance indicator (KPI)."

For example, Louise says to Mark, "Mark, I need you to give me the sales figures for the week by no later than 12pm on Fridays, so I can complete the sales analysis report and deliver against my KPI, which is to provide the sales report to Joanne by 4:30pm every Friday".

The first 'blank' in this sentence (sales figures) will often not be a KPI for the person being asked the question. Therefore, they are not very motivated to complete that section of their job. But, when it is made clear to them how that affects this other person and her ability to meet her KPI, then they can bargain with each other.

Providing the sales figures to Louise is not one of Mark's KPIs, so he does it if he's not doing something else and it's usually the first thing to get bumped if something unexpected comes up. He might have thought Louise's boss, Joanne, was just being difficult when she hassled Louise for the sales reports every week at 4:30pm. Now that Mark understands the consequences of his actions on Louise, he is more likely to provide what Louise needs when she needs it.

What happens in this situation is that they can start to bargain and come to an understanding. For example, in this case, Louise could say, "Well, I know you are really busy on Fridays, so would it help if you didn't have to give me the stock level report until Monday morning and, instead, concentrate on the sales figures on Friday". This compromise would improve communication and rapport between the two employees and is only possible because of shared information as a result of the second Business Law of Nature – *Knowing Every Other Player's Position*. This has allowed Louise to meet her KPIs more easily, as the atmosphere is one of conscious assistance rather than unconscious resistance.

One way to incorporate this behaviour into your business is to add 'KPI re-engineering' to your weekly agenda. Each week, everyone is asked to assess one of their KPIs and break it down into what needs to happen and who is involved in the accomplishment of that KPI. Often it's not until we engage our thinking in this way that we can start to see the opportunities for improvement. KPIs are often dreaded tasks that can cause stress in the workgroup. But what we have found is that it is very rarely the KPI itself that is the disturbing element. It is the difficulties the individual must go through to achieve it.

In the above example, Louise may well have dreaded each Friday afternoon because each week it was a struggle to get Mark to produce the necessary information. It was then a rush to deliver the sales report to Joanne by 4:30pm. Mark wasn't being difficult – it was, as I mentioned before, unconscious resistance. As soon as he was made conscious of the impact of his contribution and discussion was opened between them regarding solutions and ways of assisting each other, the stress was released from the situation. Louise was able to get her figures in time and meet her KPI. Mark was happy because he was able to do this easily now that he had more time for the stock report. And Joanne was happy because she got the figures on time every Friday so that she, too, could monitor her progress in meeting the company objectives and her own KPIs.

Comprehension Check

So let's look at the cumulative effect these two Business Laws of Nature – and the behaviours involved in each – to see how they impact on each other.

Design = Ownership = Motivation means people perform better when they're given an opportunity to design their own way to success. *Know Every Other Player's Position* is about understanding what everybody else in the company does. Understanding what everybody else in the company does makes you a better designer. So, by helping people understand what everyone in the company does, then empowering them to design their own solutions, you now have somebody who's likely to design solutions that are closer to the workgroup's needs. This creates a *virtuous circle*, producing constant improvement in the business – "I design a way to do something, I find out more about what you do, I get a chance to redesign, and each time I increase my potential".

And remember: *the journey toward potential will always enhance potential.*

The elephant loses its access to "I'm the only one who can't do this", "No one works as hard as I do", "The people in Accounts are lazy", "The business is not interested in me", "The boss only wants to make a buck", etc. We are beginning to neutralise the fear, uncertainty, and doubt that drives so much of our passive resistant behaviour.

18
Business Law of Nature 3: In Time Right Becomes Wrong

Précis

This highlights that the right solution becomes the wrong solution in time. If being different in the marketplace is really a marketing advantage – and it is – then you can't create and sustain that advantage by trying to hold onto a stock strategy. If anything, the context is changing so rapidly today that any business initiative that suited a marketplace more than a few years ago is on its way to obsolescence.

You may be very attached to a strategy or tactic but commercial realities are brutal. If your competition finds a better way to do something, your old strategy, no matter how appropriate it was in its time, will cost you market share. You can be as good as you were last year, even slightly better, and still be going backwards.

Behaviour

We have found that successful businesses have a level of anticipation that sets them apart from their peers. They seem to leave old ways behind before they become redundant. Procedure manuals get updated regularly in these workgroups. Customers are surveyed to provide valuable feedback. And service is as relevant as quality. New employees are invited to be objective and speak their mind about how they perceive things. And competitors are consistently observed as a matter of course.

Rationale

If you go to the supermarket, to the perishable goods section, one of the wonderful things you find stamped on all the goods there is their 'use-by date'. This miraculous little invention makes sure that when you take the milk carton home, and pour it on your cornflakes, all the milk doesn't slide out in one big cube.

> If your competition finds a better way to do something, your old strategy will cost you market share, no matter how appropriate it was in its time.

It's one of the most useful advances of the 21st century – particularly for the unsophisticated shopper. The little known fact is that most processes in your business have their own inherent use-by-date. In their current form, they only have a certain shelf life. This can be a daunting concept to grasp because it basically sends a message to any staff member that whatever it is they're doing, however comfortable they might be doing it, it's only effective 'temporarily'.

I'm not suggesting that every process changes every other day. What I am saying is that every process is on its way to becoming redundant. And therefore, every process, depending on its purpose, reaches a point when it's appropriate to sit back, analyse and synthesise it again. In many cases, the process might be reinstated very similarly to the way it was. Change might have been minimal. The better businesses, the better workgroups, are those that constantly challenge their own processes and procedures.

Remember, your elephant loves shortcuts – so welcomes any excuse to shut down your thinking. But if you have a systematised process of checking all the procedures in your business, your elephant is neutralised by the process of inspection.

Business is a very fluid entity, constantly changing, whether we like it or not. So go with its evolution and watch the business morph into something else. Metamorphosis is the new permanent state for thriving businesses.

Living with change

My favourite line in a song by Melissa Etheridge called *Change* is: "The only thing that stays the same is change" (contrary to what the French fondly observe: "The more things change, the more they stay the same"). The new *status quo* – the normality for business – is that tomorrow everything will be a little different. Therefore, it becomes important to find the things that can be systematised so they can be self-adaptive to changing requirements, wherever possible.

This is a cultural characteristic. And the workgroup leader's responsibility and obligation is to create an environment where things are questioned. That can feel at times like 'working without a net'. The challenge is that we have never been given the tools and understanding to be able to face that challenge in a rational and logical manner. If you are given the challenge without the tools to deal with it, of course you get nervous. Remember the first time you drove? It wasn't exactly something you just jumped in and did – there was an element of adrenaline.

And being able to change a process is a skill in itself that needs fostering.

I suggest you adopt a planning discipline that regularly challenges every core process and sets a date for reconstructing that process on a rotational basis. So gradually analyse everything you do, look at each one and say, "Are we doing this

> Have a planning discipline that regularly challenges every core process and sets a date for reconstructing that process on a rotational basis.

as well as we can?" If the answer is "Yes", ask the question, "When is the next time we should look at this?" In any event, don't leave it longer than a year.

It may be that when you revisit the process, nothing needs to be done to improve it, in which case move on. But what this diarised reassessment does, is ensure that your processes are current and applicable *today*. It can also highlight where shortcuts have been made, or evolved, that are not conducive to the end result. It creates an opportunity to audit the process. (Remember: you should be doing this backwards.)

In most instances, we discover that processes are made redundant only *well after* they've become redundant. Your aim is to foster a mindset of healthy questioning, or healthy doubt about procedures, so that you account for the third Business Law of Nature. Quality workgroups are workgroups where people do challenge the entrenched aspects and procedures of the business. Don't confuse questioning with change. Questioning illuminates the need, as well as the pathway, for change.

This whole process can help take advantage of new skills and objectivity that recent additions to the team might bring. Instead of teaching new staff the 'way we've always done it', we can use the fresh eyes of the new arrivals to reassess the processes and add new perspective. You may then see something that could make the process faster or more efficient.

What you are aiming for is to program the mind to always question the process. But that's difficult because it would mean changing people. So *you* need to do it, provide the *context,* that is – provide the *norms* for reviews and redesign. It's more important than trying to make the process perfect.

I'd rather have somebody who asks about the process and challenges the process than somebody who concentrates their energy solely on making the existing way of doing the job perfect. When somebody has a healthy suspicion about, and questions, the process, they will avoid the problem of having processes questioned only *after* they've failed. In most businesses, the time when we question the way we do things is when we find evidence that there needs to be a better way – the sour milk has already been poured on the cornflakes.

When people question, the least outcome possible is knowledge. And knowledge is not an insignificant outcome for any business process. *Just because a process is questioned, it does not mean it changes, it just means its chances of being wrong are reduced.*

Unfortunately, processes in business don't carry easy-to-see warnings and, sometimes, they don't even have outward signs of dysfunction. However, if you question the process in terms of finding a better way, rather than in terms of whether or not it's still working, you will pre-empt the need for change before it is forced upon you. Don't wait until your staff and customers get a mouthful of lumpy milk before you act. Instead, be aware of when the process is likely to 'go off' and be proactive.

> Use the downtime often experienced around the Christmas period to effectively review the past year so you can sweep into the new year with the best possible processes available to you and your team at that time.

A business ought to be looking at all of its core processes on a regular basis, creating both a capacity and opportunity for the team to question those processes. I would suggest a workshop, at least once a year, to look at core processes. Use the downtime, often experienced around the Christmas period, to effectively review the past year so you can sweep into the new year with the best possible processes available to you and your team at that time. But don't sacrifice commercial reality and profitability for chasing what the dictionary defines as 'perfect'.

Workshop Exercises

Technique 5 – Innovation reporting
With the workgroup, identify the 10 most enduring processes in the business. These will be the processes that have remained the same for

the longest time. As a group, try to force yourself to come up with a different way of doing them. Be as outrageous as you like because, often, within a seemingly ridiculous idea, there is a kernel of possibility that could revolutionise the business. Make it a game. You could give points for the ideas. You could offer a prize for the best idea – voted on by the team, of course. You could have a debate – one side defends the current way, the other argues for change.

Technique 6 – Innovation culture

Put a value on innovation and set a target. Make it known throughout the organisation that innovation is rewarded in some way. It could be that the staff member responsible gets a bonus. For example, someone may highlight a way for a process to achieve the same outcome but at less expense – that person may get a percentage of the savings. Or standardise it and implement an innovation bonus scheme.

Talk up innovation. If someone does a good thing or comes up with a money-making or money-saving idea, make it your top topic of conversation for the week. Tell everyone: "Have you heard George's idea?"

Comprehension Check

In Time, Right Becomes Wrong recognises that eventually the processes and systems in the business will become out of date. Well surely, if I *Know Every Other Player's Position*, I'm more motivated to identify where the potential weaknesses in the processes are. If I'm allowed, and encouraged to be the *designer* of my own methodology or my own process, I'm more likely to be looking for those parts of my job, or those parts of my processes and procedures, that are likely to become redundant. I'm more likely to look at them because:

a) You gave me the opportunity
b) Because I now see it as my responsibility
c) I will enjoy my job more, and be rewarded for it

I'm empowered. I know that I'm allowed to – and, therefore, I'm more inclined to do it. In many cases, people don't re-engineer because they don't think it's their role or that they have the authority to re-engineer. But we've proved through our work that the workgroup does already know how to make things better 85 per cent of the time. It stands to reason that if the culture encourages individuals to make those changes, and rewards and recognises the improvement those changes make, then the business will become more effective, efficient and profitable. And the staff will be motivated and happy. Their elephants become less active when the frontal lobe is in overdrive.

According to new evidence documented in John Ratey's book *A User's Guide To The Brain*, when we learn new things, the relevant part of the brain engaged in learning that new process will gain mass[56], giving new and far reaching support to the idea of 'use it or lose it'. Our brain grows like a muscle during use. Once that new skill has been mastered, then it interacts with the other parts of the brain, turning such skills into routine. The result is evolution from conscious incompetence to unconscious competence. Getting your team to challenge and refine processes is not unproductive. It is critical. It keeps them commercial.

19

Business Law of Nature 4: Everybody Has a Right to Know the Score

Précis

Knowing you are making progress makes the job more satisfying. Every concentrated thinking exercise always establishes a clear destination ... a destination that everyone involved thinks is worthwhile. It must always include a system for letting them know what progress is being made towards the destination.

You have a right to be travelling home at the end of every day saying to yourself, "That was worth every minute" or reaching the end of the week and saying, "That was worth every day".

Behaviour

Strong businesses have strong reporting disciplines – ones in which the reporting and the performance of the *individual* is typically more comprehensive and focused than the reporting of the performance of the *business*. Appraisal disciplines are in place, supported by a succession plan. If the business is too small for any formal succession, then the workgroup leaders are sponsoring professional and personal development programs for their staff. The performance of staff is measured and reported against. There is a link between those reports and the performance of the business. The workgroup leader walks past people and says things like, "Great job on the ABC Pitch, Mary" and, "We got that shipment out thanks to you, Dave".

Rationale

Aligning to the fourth Business Law of Nature means keeping people aware of the impact that *they* have on the business. And, when it comes to the elephant, the characteristic this circumvents is its penchant for moodiness. Our elephants get moody and emotional when they're threatened or scared. In the workplace, such situations can come about from lack of information or not really knowing what is expected of us and how we are faring against those expectations. *Everybody Has A Right To Know The Score* ensures that those instinctive uncertainties and concerns that evoke emotion are handled along the way.

> This protocol is about keeping people aware of the impact that they have on the business. Everyone Has the Right to Know the Score ensures that those instinctive uncertainties and concerns that evoke emotion are well handled along the way.

There are two schools of thought regarding disclosure of information. First is the 'mushroom' approach that basically specifies that you keep your employees in the dark and feed them BS.

The second school of thought is that your team will be motivated by the opposite approach. Imagine charts and graphs all around the office that detail the company's philosophical approach, the company's targets and where the company is at in relation to those targets. Of the two, more information is always preferable to no information. But it does need to be tempered and relevant to the individual. When we have access to information and are surrounded by visual clues, they remind us about what is important and keep us on track. The boss is a 'moving' reminder, too.

Most employees of any company don't really care how the company is performing *until* they can assess how that performance relates to their own contribution. And if you want to see this reality in action, then concentrate on highlighting how each individual specifically impacts on the success of the business.

> Knowing the score is about personally attaching, or helping people understand the impact their role has on the outcomes of the organisation.

There's no doubt that effective workgroup leaders are leaders who are able to develop relationships that allow them to very quickly get into the minds of their employees and understand what motivates them.

This is why sales teams are so motivated by their performance because, typically, their sales are *their* KPIs, although their outcomes are often erroneously construed as the company's KPIs. The manufacturing crew is rarely as excitable because no one takes the time to directly connect what they do to the overall performance of the company. Only when people see the connection are they likely to be motivated by it.

> Effective workgroup leaders are those who are able to develop relationships that allow them to get into the minds of their employees and understand what motivates them.

For example, in our business, we run workshops which, in the case of a small business, can necessitate a company being 'locked up' for a couple of days off-site. We have, in the past, employed a 'Workshop Coordinator' whose job it is to book the venues. This involves selecting the venues and making sure the venues we use understand our requirements. Because of the depth of material we cover in the time we spend with the client, this venue is essentially our office. It's an extension of our company. This means that the client's experience in a conference centre or hotel at which we conduct our sessions can have a dramatic effect on their view or perspective about the quality of the outcome and, therefore, us.

Client satisfaction with the venue, being directly observable on client feedback forms, provides such connection to, and motivation for, the job our Workshop Coordinator is doing.

Knowing the score means keeping a scorecard in terms that are relevant to the individual. Knowing the score is about personally attaching or helping people understand the impact their role has on the outcomes of the organisation. That becomes their incentive to perform. It also defines accountability.

Now you could be thinking, for example, "That sounds fine, John. But I've told so-and-so a hundred times that we need to have that part in the warehouse by no later than the 15th of every month and they never get it right".

The key to ensuring that everyone knows the score is getting leaders to 'ask' rather than 'tell' and moving teams from responding to showing. If you ask the right questions and, therefore, engage the right thinking, the person will realise why it's so important to have the part in the warehouse by no later than the 15th of the month and will strive to achieve it.

Again, you don't tell people their importance by telling them how the company's going. A person can perform miserably and the company can still go well. Conversely, a person can perform exceptionally well and the company can still perform poorly. People are simply more motivated by some sort of measurement or benchmark to their own performance.

Now, what does that mean in terms of workgroup performance? Effective workgroups are managed by very clear and identifiable Key Performance Indicators (KPIs) that are measured and assessed against those measurements regularly, because that delivers a heightened sense of accountability and competitiveness.

It can never be negative for an individual to know and to receive *specific* feedback. People thrive on feedback yet, what we typically find, is that there is no performance appraisal process. There is no regular appraisal of staff. There are no written job descriptions. And, very often, it's because the business owner regards these as an *imposition* on his or her team.

People want to know where they stand. Business owners who interact a lot with their staff might think that, because they spend so much time with them, they are really 'appraising them all the time'. That is simply not true. Sidestepping the formality of measurement and appraisal is a very unproductive way to manage people. Working with someone is sharing *content*, appraising someone is applying *context*. Workgroup leaders can and need to do both.

Appraisal is a necessary and desired part of business life. How else can we grow and learn and become better? There is a saying, 'If it doesn't get measured, it doesn't get done'. I would change that around to say, 'If it gets measured regularly, it *will* get done'. Not measuring it doesn't necessarily mean it doesn't get done. But measuring it can guarantee it does get done.

I've come to realise – having coached, or done hundreds of job descriptions, in hundreds of businesses – that you discover certain human limitations. Generally speaking, an individual can be responsible for between 50 and 60 core tasks. And that will always boil down to about five or so Key Performance Indicators – five deliverables that can only happen if those 50 or 60 things are done well.

A person has to understand the five or so things by which they are going to be measured, the way they are going to be measured, and the frequency of measurement. There has to be some formality around the reporting against those measurements. That's the way to get the best out of people and get them to produce to their potential.

It's like driving a car. You have the dials on the dashboard to tell you how you are doing. There's the fuel gauge to tell you how much fuel is left, so you can work out if you have enough to reach your destination. You have your speedometer, so you can see how fast you are going to stay within the law. You have the oil light to ensure that your engine is healthy and happy. You have the revs indicator to monitor when you need to change gear. You have all your KPIs right in front of you, so you can monitor your progress, assess your likelihood of reaching your destination, and estimate your arrival time.

How difficult would it be if your car had none of these dials or indicators? You wouldn't know how much petrol you had left. You wouldn't know how fast you were going. Or whether the engine oil was adequate. You would have to guess, and hope you reached your destination in one piece without getting a speeding ticket. Imagine if each staff member had five 'KPI dials' in front of them so that they could track and monitor their performance every single day.

People's performance-KPIs will change, particularly in growing organisations, but that's no excuse to avoid having them. Reporting must be structured around the Key Performance Indicators, because KPIs then become an agenda for management and team meetings. Each person is here for those five things and that brings with it focus and clarity to move a business in the right direction.

As the workgroup leader, your desk would look like an aeroplane cockpit with a dial to represent everyone you supervise or employ. But, like a pilot, you just glance at most of them and only fiddle with a few when necessary. So it's not as daunting as it may at first appear.

It may sound long-winded and time-consuming but, once these things are set up, the advantages go way beyond a successful, happy, productive workgroup. The time savings are immense, too. If I know what your five KPIs are, I can have a brief but important discussion with you that doesn't necessarily involve the weather or what you did on the weekend. I can come up to you and say, "How's the marketing plan? What's the inquiry level like?" And when you ask your staff questions in that context, it continues to reinforce how their contribution is measured, and it also makes them continually aware of the correlation between their performance and the company's performance.

Be warned though: if you then stop measuring, people will notice and their performance will drop.

One of the key characteristics of an effective workgroup is that everybody has aligned with the fourth Business Law of Nature and everyone knows the score. And, if everybody in the business knows the score, based on a set of KPIs, this allows the business owner to know the score. And the business owner can then make whatever contribution *they* need to make to those KPIs by 'tweaking' the dials. If you're letting people know, on a regular basis, how they're going on the five things that matter, then you've got the basis for moving them past the historical contribution of 60 per cent of their potential.

The paradox of rules and procedures is that, contrary to popular opinion, they create freedom and expression not oppression and drudgery.

Imagine how easy your job would become if, as the workgroup leader, you could sit at your desk with your feet up with a mirror image of everybody's dashboard in front of you. Each dial would have a needle set at where productivity should be, with a floating needle telling you where it actually is. If the needle falls below the accepted productivity level, then a buzzer sounds and a light flashes on the desk of the staff member whose performance has dropped... If performance is not corrected within a certain period of time an electric current is sent to their chair.

While this is a tongue-in-cheek picture, it illustrates the role of effective KPIs. Your business could create such an environment. With rules and procedures, the paradox is that, contrary to popular opinion, they create freedom and expression, not oppression and drudgery. Your employees have the right to know the score. They have a right to feel ownership and pride for the role they play in the organisation. They also have the right to appropriate and fair feedback so they can develop and grow with the business.

Is everything measurable?

Every single thing is! People will often say you can't measure everything. Some important parts of an individual's job, particularly in customer service, can't be measured.

> I disagree.
>
> Everything can be benchmarked. No client has ever given a coach a key result area or Key Performance Indicator that we haven't been able to establish a measurement for. For example, a client will say, "Well, we want them to treat our customers well on the phone and have a great attitude on the phone – how do you measure that?"
>
> Very simple – you agree to survey your customers, and you set the benchmark that says, if we ring twenty customers at random, 80 per cent or more have to say that ringing us is a pleasant experience. And we're going to do that every three months – bingo!

Workshop Exercises

Technique 7 – My Top Five Exercise

For this exercise, the workgroup member has to imagine that s/he is being transferred overseas within the company, and that they can only reallocate five of their key responsibilities. What would those key responsibilities be? They have to make their selections then share with the group.

Note: this approach can also be used as a rudimentary way of devising what an individual's KPIs should be in the first place. You would assume that the workgroup member would pick the five most important parts of the job. However, this is often not the case, and this process can highlight those differences of perception.

The questions to ask are:

a) Are they really the five most important parts of your job?
b) If they are, how are they being measured and how can they be connected to the performance of the business?
c) If they are not, why does this person think that is?

Comprehension Check

Everybody Has A Right To Know The Score is about everybody understanding the contribution they make to the specific outcomes of the business. Surely if I understand that, in the context of *Knowing Every Other Player's Position*, I get a better picture of the contribution I make. I also get to understand the extent to which I can impede or enhance my colleagues' abilities to achieve their own outcomes.

Everybody Has A Right To Know The Score is also about understanding whether both you and the business are tracking toward the desired outcomes. It naturally motivates you to re-engineer your processes so you can better achieve the objectives that have been set and are regularly measured. That only enhances your understanding of *Every Player's Position* which makes you a better designer when it comes to designing your own pathway to success, which by now you understand you're empowered to do, because the business is behaving that way.

Plus, if everyone knows the score, then their respective elephants won't make assumptions about their contributions, fill in missing information and overreact. Remember, in the absence of regular feedback, the elephant will assume that its contribution is not sufficiently accepted or appreciated.

20
Business Laws of Nature 5: Business Is a Shortcut to an Outcome

Précis

A business must be a shortcut to an outcome. The rules of accountancy may value a business by stock and other tangibles at valuation time, or by the increasingly shaky commodity of 'goodwill'. But the real value of a business or workgroup is how much work it saves for its clients, not how much it generates. Some businesses are actually doing their business the long way. But, if a business like that doesn't find the shortest way in a hurry, its competitors will find it for them.

Once your business is a shortcut to generating an output, you don't even need to be unique. It's better to be unique but, even being the shortcut to something widely sought, gives you an advantage. Or, you can be unique by producing products that are themselves shortcuts to outcomes for clients. Either way, you can't lose if your business is the shortcut and everyone else is the long way around to the same result.

Behaviour

We know that businesses are strong and utilise more of their potential when they build their processes backward from the client or end-user, rather than from the product or service forward. They also tend not to take themselves too seriously. Most importantly, they take pride in their bottom line, at least as much as in their work. They build their strategy from an understanding of their clients' business that is often as acute as that of their own. They often have, or hire, expertise relevant to their clients' particular business challenges. They develop partnerships with clients and are always talking to them, whether by phone, conference call, or face-to-face. They may even be invited to participate in brainstorming sessions with them. They are always looking for easier and faster ways to get the job done.

Rationale

The fifth Business Law of Nature – *Business Is a Shortcut to an Outcome* means recognising that, at the end of the day, people use a product or service because it's quicker than making or doing it themselves.

> **Business Is a Shortcut to an Outcome means recognising that at the end of the day people use a product or service because it's quicker than making or doing it themselves.**

For all the professionals who are reading this book, the sobering reality is that the only reason your clients use you is because it's quicker than getting the qualifications themselves. It's reasonable to conclude that if you could get a legal qualification out of a cereal pack, most people would opt for that rather than retain a lawyer. It's no different from buying a loaf of bread. The reason people don't bake their own bread is that it is quicker to buy a loaf from the bakery. And, if through some miracle it was quicker to bake it than buy it, then they would.

When a brand is a unique invention, it may have some special advantage attached to it. If you totally pioneered something, people would buy only your product or service. But that's seldom the case. Commercial monogamy doesn't last long.

This fact does not, however, mean you should find shortcuts at the expense of the quality of your product or service. On the contrary, what it means is that once you've established and attained quality benchmarks in your business, you need to be dedicated to making it faster, to improving the process, simplifying the methodology and delivering your shortcuts in the quickest possible way – without lowering those quality benchmarks.

Obviously, if services are offered by two competing businesses, and the service quality and price are close, the client will ultimately prefer to deal with whichever organisation can deliver fastest.

One of the characteristics evident in effective workgroups is a constant attention and desire to speed up. It's almost like a game to see how things can be tweaked to make the product or service even better, using speed as the measure, rather than a 'new enhancement' or two. We've all heard the quip about complaints being a gift, but in these businesses, a complaint really is seen as a gift because it gives them a chance to improve.

> **The contradiction of Quality Benchmarks**
>
> In fact, the quality standards boom has been a major contributor to this reality. Unfortunately a system that was invented to raise the quality standards within an industry or profession has in fact meant that benchmarks for quality have become frozen.
>
> It meant that participating organisations going through a quality accreditation process to bring their own systems and procedures up to a particular standard, simply went on to focus on maintaining just that standard.
>
> Consequently we see that a process can meet ISO standards and yet be both second best and outdated because the imposition of quality standards has resulted in stagnation of innovation. This also has given people a license to be complacent.

Business Is a Shortcut to an Outcome is also an insight into the challenges we face in the technology race. Technological advances are often about one thing: speed. Once you can automate a process, that process naturally improves in terms of speed of delivery.

There is of course a happy medium. There is no point exceeding quality standards, if those improvements erode the profit margin. The only basis for exceeding the quality standards is that you can increase your margin as a result of the improved quality.

Businesses can make the mistake of assuming their quality standards are the quality standards their clients want. Then, when they try to sell or bill at that standard, they discover they're not going to be paid for it.

Visiting a client one day, I witnessed a classic example of this. This particular client was in the Printing industry and he had invented a 'Lighting Booth'. The clever thing about this contraption was that, if you put a brochure or any sort of coloured object underneath this lighting booth, it didn't matter what time of day or what climate, or what part of the hemisphere you were in, what you saw was its true appearance. For example, if you were in Brisbane, using this lighting booth, you could truly compare your print quality against a benchmark produced, say, in Germany.

It was an expensive piece of equipment. As the client pointed to a row of these beautiful cabinets, he proclaimed, "We can't sell them". The reason they were not selling was not because of the price. It was because the local industry standard was 'if it's as close as the naked eye will detect – it's good enough'.

There's a point beyond which customers will not pay for excellence. And, as a business owner, you need to know that point. It's like the staff member who delays something because they are trying to deliver to a quality standard that *they* are imposing. The output can become totally uncommercial.

It's such a frustrating experience when somebody goes beyond the brief you gave, then can't understand why you're totally unimpressed. They've taken it to an uncommercial level and, in many cases, they've delivered it beyond its use-by date. Good and on time is much better than perfect and late. Look at poor Augustine Le Prince. If he hadn't been so caught up in perfection, he might have lived longer and he, not Edison, would now be known as the father of the motion picture camera.

You may be thinking to yourself at this point, "That may be right but what about competitive advantage through improved customer service and relationships. After all, people do business with people they like".

> Good and on time is much better than perfect and late!

This is true. There is absolutely no question about that. But even the most likable person on the planet will eventually lose the business if they can't deliver on time, or if they fall behind their competitors in any measurable way.

Shortcuts improve relationships because the shorter the cut, the more time you have to *invest* in the relationship. And this is important for your elephant who is genetically designed for social interaction *not* business. If business is all about speed and efficiency, human beings are not – they want to build relationships and discuss what happened on the weekend. So, finding the best, fastest and most efficient way to do business pacifies the elephant by giving it time to do what it really loves – socialise and build alliances.

You can't build a relationship with anyone if you are consistently delivering things late, fighting fires, or your margins are being squeezed.

When we did home renovations some years back, a number of suppliers and tradesmen were involved. The guy who bid to make the kitchen arranged a meeting and came in to listen to what we wanted. He qualified our expectations. In other words, he talked us out of some of the things we were expecting, quite possibly because he was talking us into what he already had and already knew he could deliver. He set a date for delivery and delivered on that date. Only when he delivered, the cabinets didn't fit – the cavity was 30cm short. The mistake was clearly the cabinet builder's, not the kitchen manufacturer's. There was absolutely no discussion. He came out, assessed the situation, took one of the cabinets away and came back with a solution within three days and it was over and finished. He obviously assessed his margin and realised he still had some room to move to deliver a quality product while fixing someone else's mistake.

The kitchen was installed. Some of the whiz-bang things we had in mind weren't there, but we were totally satisfied because everything matched the expectations set by the provider. That's a precious experience in business. And we remember it.

The fact is most people are not hung up on perfection and an increasing level of quality. They just want what was promised. And they want consistency. Just look at McDonalds. It's not a 5-star gourmet experience but you could order a Big Mac in Vladivostok, Prague, Delhi or Sydney and they would all taste the same and look the same.

If you can give your customers a shortcut to what they want, when they want it, as quickly as they want it, then even if they could do it themselves – chances are they never will. (And if you can give them exactly what you promise, then you'll have them as clients next time, too.)

And, of course, this premise works from the other perspective too. The better I understand what my clients are trying to do, the better I can source the outcome. Interrogating clients about their intention is a way to find them shortcuts.

- It's about finding faster ways to do what you do.
- It's about better matching what you do to your clients' expectations.
- It's about finding ways to have the client pay you less – and you doing less while still delivering to the clients' requirements.
- It's about reverse-engineering your clients' outcomes and applying to them the same *thinking systems* that work on your team.

Workshop Exercises

Technique 8 – Time reduction Law

Each workgroup member must identify the five tasks they are responsible for that take the longest time to complete. Imagine that a law has been passed and you now have to reduce the time it takes to complete this task.

What sacrifices would you make to achieve the reductions?

Once each member has done this, the outcomes are to be shared with the group for discussion. The group will bring objectivity and the new knowledge learned from the previous workshops. So armed, the group is much more likely to discover new, faster ways – better shortcuts.

Technique 9 – Saving clients money
Conduct a brainstorming session around the question:

How can we save our top five clients money?

Comprehension Check

A Business Being a Shortcut to an Outcome requires people to be motivated to make their job less, not more.

Once they understand the score, and know how they're going to be measured, they no longer feel compelled to fill their day. Instead, they make more intelligent choices about what they should be focusing on. Once they make more intelligent decisions about what they should be focused on, they're more inclined to be more inventive about how to improve it for themselves and their clients because we've allowed them to be the *designers of their own outcomes*.

Plus the quality of the design improves because they *Know Every Other Player's Position*. This leads to an environment where, in time, things don't go wrong because they never have a chance to – they're changed well before they can go wrong.

Only the thinking brain – not the emotional one – can engage effectively in this level of commercial diagnosis.

21

Business Law of Nature 6: Only Do What Only You Should Do – *Lead*

Précis

The secret to making people brilliant is to keep them focused on what they do brilliantly. In other words, why try to train them to be something they're not. This is where I believe your old-fashioned spruiker-type motivation misses the point: it convinces people that 'anything is possible if you just believe'. I don't agree with the idea that anyone can do anything. I can't be anything, except in my dreams. But I can be brilliant at the few things I'm brilliant at.

However, there is one even more fundamental principle. There is only one job that no one in the workgroup can do but the leader. And that job is to lead. As leader, you have to learn how to manage elephants, otherwise the elephants of your workgroup will lead the group. In most businesses, the leader is identifiable by the fact that they sign off leave applications, maybe hire and fire people, occasionally tell people what to do. The rest of the time is spent bending, or breaking the rules in this book. For a workgroup to work, someone has to accept responsibility for getting the entity we call the team to work as one. And there is nothing commercial about that. It is all biology. So by understanding the biological

In a workgroup of twelve people, there can only be one leader. So if that person is you – then you need to act the leader.

hardwiring that you are constantly up against, you can learn how to pacify, tranquilise and distract the elephants in your workgroup and that's solely your *job.*

Behaviour

Leader behaviour is easy to spot in successful organisations. The leader knows the names of his or her staff members. They know what is important to them. A quick observation of them 'in the field' sees them acknowledge something special from a team member, or ask someone's advice on an issue. They say, "Good morning" and hear it boomerang back. More than anything, you can feel it in the air when you walk into the business. They know when to celebrate. They gauge the mood and do things to adjust it. They listen, listen, listen then talk. They also have a serious mood of their own that says 'do it – don't negotiate' and they get away with it because they so often listen, listen, listen. People stay and have loyalty to the workgroup and the leader. They don't need legislation to make them take interest in their teams' health and safety.

Rationale

The last Business Law of Nature – *Only Do What Only You Should Do* is specifically relevant to leadership of the workgroup. It means that in a workgroup of 12 people, there can only be one leader. So if that person is you – then you need to act the leader. For example, phoning key intermediaries to share with them some important piece of information. That's something anyone in the company can do, but it's something the leader *should* do.

Only Do What Only You Should Do is not about the task. It refers to the overall understanding that the one job that only you, the leader, can do is running the workgroup – and that means implementing the framework and behaviours outlined in this section so that the workgroup naturally aligns to the Six Business Laws of Nature and all the elephants in your team are successfully managed or placated. Don't have others do it; be in control. Choose the things to do that others *could* do but you believe you *should* do – leadership.

This aspect of behavior requires you to always be occupied with the thinking and productivity of the people in the workgroup. It's your job to understand them. It's your job to understand their strengths, adapt to their weaknesses and position people within the workgroup to allow for those differences so that you can manage the workgroup in your chosen direction.

This does not mean that being the boss is about delegating everything to everyone else while you sit at the desk with your feet up. There are plenty of people who can delegate well, but the fact that you're good at leaving things to other people doesn't necessarily make you a good delegator – it makes you a good sidestepper. And it doesn't necessarily make you a good boss.

Delegation and Leadership

If one of the keys to being a good leader is to delegate, consider how the application of these behaviours puts you in a position to be the 'perfect' delegator. The reason is simple: the resulting environment itself provides the necessary prerequisites for effective delegation. Those prerequisites are:

- You must suspect that the task will be done *'roughly' your way*
- You must have confidence that the person you delegate to can *actually do the task*
- You must have systems in place that will *tell* you if it is not done or not done well

But remember the critical rule of delegation: *the second-best way designed by the group beats the best way imposed by the boss.*

If your business were set up to support those three things, you would become a very good delegator. You don't have to change your personality to become one; you simply allow that behaviour to emerge from the implementation of this and the previous five Business Laws of Nature. They provide a framework that automatically pacifies the elephants and allows the very best of the workgroup to shine through. If everybody is designing their own success and you, the leader, have an opportunity to participate in that design and, if they're then telling you, the leader, how they are actually going to accomplish it, you *will* gain confidence in their ability. If they can explain to you how they're going to do it, they can do it. And, as their 'coach', you will ensure that every benchmark they set has some kind of measurement against it. So your 'delegatory' powers improve. This is a classic *virtuous circle*.

> Remember a critical rule of delegation: the second best way designed by the group beats the best way imposed by the boss!

Only Do What Only You Should Do is a concept specifically relevant to leadership of the workgroup, yet is still important at all levels within the workgroup. At a workgroup leader's level, it is to lead the workgroup. At a participant's level, it is to understand the part of the job that is uniquely yours, understand where you fit in and do your bit properly.

Imagine a Caterpillar grader operator sitting in his heavy machinery in that horribly uncomfortable plastic chair with 18 levers in front of him. Your workgroup is like that and *Only Do What Only You Should Do* is about getting everybody else's hands *off* the levers. Each one of those levers represents a staff member

> These protocols are not pills that you can swallow to make your business better. They are strategies for leadership behaviour that you can easily replicate, resulting in better outcomes and ultimately better business.

and your job, as workgroup leader, is to make sure that no one touches anyone else's lever.

Business can be hard. Successful business can be even harder, so don't make it harder still by worrying about whose hands are on what lever! The reason it's so difficult is that most people are bad at managing people because they've never been taught how to. People are bad at managing people because of the thinking challenges described in Parts One and Two.

By the time you've read this book, you'll understand the things you need to know about *managing thinking*. If you can manage the thinking, you can manage the people. And if you can do that, then much of what potentially makes business so hard in the first place, is removed. Follow the exercises. Behave like a leader and people will think you are a leader. Once they think you are a leader, you will behave even more like a leader and suddenly, one day, you'll wake up and realise that you are one. Another virtuous circle!

These Business Laws of Nature or operating protocols are not pills that you swallow to make your business better. They are strategies for leadership behaviour that you can easily replicate, resulting in better outcomes and ultimately better business.

Keys to Effective Leadership

Through our extensive research, we've found that there are a number of characteristics that great leaders display.

Accepting the Role

Being the leader of your business is your *first* and *primary* responsibility. What you do for a living, what product or service your company delivers, comes second (to you). Service and product are the number one responsibility for the team. The team is the number one responsibility for you.

That doesn't mean your team takes more of your time, but it does take more of your focus. Few people have the necessary 'people skills' to adequately manage a team unconsciously. Our research has proved conclusively that, for most of us, it is not a natural ability. However, our research has also proved that the characteristics of great leaders can be learned. The behaviour need only be duplicated and the result is great leadership. This requires a conscious effort – especially at the beginning – and it requires time and focus, but the results will astonish you. Focus is the key. I spend more time in front of audiences talking about business coaching than I do face-to-face with my staff. But the former is something I'm 'good' at and, therefore, it takes a lot of time but not a lot of 'focus'.

On the other hand, when it's appraisal time in the business, the activity of conducting the appraisals takes less time but a great deal more focus. The reason is that the activity of staff appraisals is still *not* something I do often enough for it to be automatic – even as a business coach.

Look at your diary and think about your 'Leadership Time'. Review your meeting schedule. Think of each staff member and ask the following questions:

> **Leadership in this context is not about leading teams, it is about knowing and understanding people, individuals, and developing them into a team with their co-operation.**

When is my regular time for getting to know each one?
When is my regular time for formally letting them know how they are going?
When is my regular time for introducing them to some other aspect of what we do?
When is their regular time for finding out how the business is going?

Leadership, in this context, is not about leading teams. It's about knowing and understanding people, individuals who, with their co-operation, you will develop into a team.

This, in turn, is less about psychology than it is about behaviour. Psychology is interesting dinner table conversation and people's innate characteristics are certainly a fascinating topic but, ultimately, it is by observing their behaviour that we can differentiate great teams from mediocre ones. Knowing what to do and doing what you know are, as mentioned previously, two entirely different things. It is behaviour, not knowledge, that draws the team around a good leader. When you start to get to know your people and they see you taking a direct interest in them – and this is a consistent behaviour you exhibit – then, over time, they will come to the conclusion that you are indeed the leader. We could write a psychology textbook on why this level of communication is important to people. Fortunately other people have written those books and, even more fortunately, we don't have to read them to be a good leader.

Rule Number One is to accept the job of leadership and be seen to do so.

Cautionary Note: If you feel you've been neglecting this responsibility, please don't announce to the team, "I've decided to take the leadership role seriously. I feel I've let you all down and have not taken enough interest in you as individuals or as a team . . . so I'm going to dedicate myself to accepting responsibility as leader of this team". This actually translates to, "The boss has been to another bloody seminar . . . s/he'll get over it soon. Nobody panic". Instead, say nothing. Just change your behaviour in line with the principles of this book. Don't broadcast what you intend to do. Demonstrate it through action and involvement. If you do that, they will not need to be told. They will see if for themselves and respond accordingly.

"*For things to change, I must change.*"
GHANDI

> ### The truth about Talent and Natural Ability
>
> Think about this . . .
>
> Suppose I was to hook up with Roger Federer – I hear he's a personable guy – and ask him if I can follow him around for three years. And in those three years I do exactly what he does. I eat when he eats and I eat what he eats. I play and practise when he plays and practises. I sleep when he sleeps. It won't matter because at the end of those three years I just won't be Roger Federer! I will be a better tennis player because I have learnt and improved my skill but I will not be a champion because tennis is neither my natural ability nor my talent; it's not what I'm built for.
>
> This whole premise that we can do anything we put our mind to is, in my view, the greatest lie perpetrated against humanity by the so-called motivational industry.
>
> It's simply not true!
>
> Talent is natural ability combined with a desire to repeat. For example, Karen has natural ability as a writer but she will only become a brilliant writer if she keeps writing. She will only keep writing if her desire to repeat and practise writing is high – each of which are natural abilities. Combined, they are the makings of a talent. By doing so her natural writing ability is combined with the increased level of skill, which moves her closer toward excellence.
>
> The talented sports person you knew at school, who 'never amounted to much because they didn't apply themselves' was not, in fact, talented at all. They had natural ability which, without the desire to repeat, is all it will ever be.
>
> So whilst there are certain things you can be if you put your mind to it, excellence in those areas is only possible by also having the natural gift and supplementing that gift with learnt skill and repetition.

Understand the things leaders do

Amongst the many things leaders do, there are five crucial points that we will focus on here. Demonstrate these characteristics and you will become a better leader, regardless of how good or bad you currently are in this role.

1. Great leaders care about their people

Caring about your people doesn't mean becoming everyone's best friend or the company confidant. We all know there's a fine line when it comes to staff/employer relationships. Many, unfortunately, err on the side of conservatism. You can be aloof and still lead, although that is a rare skill indeed. If, on the other hand, your staff believe you have even a passing interest in their life outside work, they'll be more likely to want to help you achieve your goals when it comes to the business itself.

This can be as simple as remembering their names. For extra brownie points, remember the names of their spouses and kids, and the milestones they face (weddings, birthdays, etc). Great leaders take an active and genuine interest in their people, not just as cogs in the wheel of their objective, but also as human beings. They will listen when their people are talking and they will easily and fluidly refer to milestones, or to upcoming occasions, or to previous conversations they've had with an individual. This does not mean they become the social conscience for your firm. That is best left to the party animals. But good leaders do make a personal connection at some level with each member of the team.

Never underestimate the power of a personal relationship. Contrary to popular belief, people do not just do their job because you pay them – they want to feel useful and needed too. Getting paid is *why* people work. Enjoyment in the team and ownership of the job is *how* they work. Payment alone is a poor motivator. At best, it creates a short-term increase in productivity but it is *no* substitute for feeling valued, liked, and respected. (The elephant will decide how long it lets you put up with neglect.)

2. Great leaders let the facts arrive before introducing emotion to the situation

How many times have you let your emotions affect an issue, only to find out later you were misinformed or wrong? Understand that if someone is enjoying an emotional moment, they are going to give you the 'facts' in a way that has the highest chance possible of leading you to the same emotional moment – so you can 'share'. Effective leaders don't play this game.

They will quickly identify the facts they need to know before they draw a conclusion based on those facts. If they can't get the facts straight away, they keep their emotions on hold until the facts arrive. This doesn't mean they are *not* emotional. Quite the contrary, because when you have all the facts and a particular conclusion is evident, you have confidence matched with the emotions, which is a powerful combination indeed.

3. Great leaders avoid being roadblocks for others

Leaders know when their team is relying on them for a contribution to a task so they can continue with their job. Think of the message it sends if *you* hold up the project. Whether you like it or not, it gives a very clear message about the importance not only of the job, but also of the person doing the job. Being quick to respond or deliver sets off a positive sequence of events through the business. If you respond slowly, your staff members have the right to continue slowly. In this sense, the leader is the pacesetter.

'Do what I say, not as I do' is a cliché created from this premise. However, at the end of the day, 'actions speak louder than words'. It's also as much about consistency and doing what you say you will, as it is about speed.

Great leaders keep their word and can be relied upon to deliver what they promise. Workshop to foster this skill. Task for each morning: write down in your diary the names of the people who are waiting for you. Don't write the task only: be sure to connect to the actual person who's waiting for you to complete something so they can earn their living. Also diarise every commitment you make, regardless of how trivial, and make sure you keep it. If you realise at any point you can't keep it, go to the person involved directly – either in person or on the telephone (email is a last resort) – and renegotiate the commitment as soon as you know you are not going to deliver on time.

4. Great leaders talk in Key Performance Indicators (KPIs)

Leaders have relevant and meaningful business discussions with their staff. Through this, they ensure that people know how they contribute individually to the business outcomes and also help their staff turn their key tasks into Key Performance Indicators (KPIs). As mentioned earlier, people are not necessarily interested in the performance of the company unless, and until, they can see a direct correlation between that performance and what they do as individuals each day. Every staff member has a right to know how he or she influences the business outcomes. Once made known, interaction between leaders and staff can touch on topics of personal interest, followed by a series of focused questions on KPIs. This sends several powerful messages about the level of awareness the leader has. Remember, if people think you are watching, they behave as if you are.

In your diary, next to the personal information, keep a record of each individual's KPIs so you can begin to make the connections between the person and the KPIs, in relation to who they are as people.

5. Great leaders invite innovation

It's more important to have it done to 'your standard' than it is to have it done 'your way'. The difference is subtle but very powerful. And leaders know it, often unconsciously. If you focus on the outcomes and work backward, you discover that there are many ways to proceed. However, the best way *sans* passion is not as good as the second-best way delivered with team commitment. Everything about a team members' contribution to the business improves when they are allowed to *suspect* that they are in control.

> Dedicate time to the challenge. Reach out to members of your team – you don't coach teams, you coach individuals into teams.

Final thoughts on Leadership

If you are an accomplished leader, then I hope these few observations have helped reinforce and validate your already powerful behaviour. If, on the other hand, like me, you are still developing those skills, I hope these observations help you on your journey.

Remember, take charge. It's the one job that sets you apart from the rest.

Dedicate time to the challenge. Reach out to members of your team – you don't coach teams, you coach individuals into teams. Let them know what's important. And keep reminding them, set the pace for the business and let the team have a stake in their job, if not the company. Oh, and be cool... better decisions are made when facts are collected first and emotions follow.

Workshop Exercise

Workshop to foster skill No. 1

List the names of your staff or team members in a journal or at the back of your diary. Next to each person, add as much information as you already know. You may be surprised by how much you actually do know about your team. Or you may be shocked by how little. Either way, you want to build up a profile of each person. Are they married, or in a relationship? If so, what is their partner's name? Do they have kids? If so, what are their names and ages? What about family pets? Hobbies? Passions? What do they enjoy doing when they're not at work? Do they have a favourite sport or team? The idea is not to build a file worthy of the KGB, but just some significant pieces of information to help you get to know your people.

Part of the exercise is to bring these factors into conscious awareness, so you can start to identify with your people as more than just 'staff'. They are human beings. They have lives, and things that make them happy and excited about life. This information is gold, so record it. You can't be expected to remember it all straight up, so write it down and soon, sometime in the future, you will find that you know that David's dog is called Brodie. It may not change your bottom line overnight, but it will over time.

People want to be recognised. They want to feel understood and valued and it is the little things that show that. It is the little considerations that bond a friendship or relationship. Hunting out an obscure book on wine making for a partner that loves the art of wine making, is far more valuable that an expensive box of chocolates or a ubiquitous piece of jewellery. But, in order to make that sort of impact, you have to get to know the person. And, if you're panicking that you couldn't possibly remember all that information – it is estimated that the human brain stores bits of information in the order of 2.8 x 10 to the power 20 in the course of an average lifetime.[57] That is 280,000,000,000,000,000,000 bits – equating to tens of billions of sets of Encyclopaedia Britannica.

So get scribbling. Oh, and don't cheat and go to the personnel files. Engage the person in conversation. Don't bombard them with 20 questions, just allow them to talk about themselves, even for a couple of minutes a day. Make a note of anything you discover in your diary then carry on with your day. Make it a game and have some fun with it. Try to find out one little piece of information about one of your team every day until you gain a clearer understanding of them as people.

Technique 10 – Past Five Days?
As the workgroup leader, review and list all the things that you have done in the past five days that are exclusively motivated by your responsibility to lead. Now think about how you intend to improve this situation.

Comprehension Check

When you have a team aligned to the previous five Business Laws of Nature, finally you have a platform to allow the business owner to *Only Do What You Should Do.*

You can't lead a team unless they invite you to. The extent to which they would invite you is largely driven by the degree of *'innovation'* you allow them. If everyone knows every other player's position, their elephant is likely to be much less moody and the tolerance and understanding between groups can be greatly improved. In addition, this brings a level of *binary thinking* to the business improvement process – often those uninvolved and, therefore, objective, can bring new ideas not previously considered. Defaults are less likely to be triggered as a result. If everyone in the business accepts that, in time, right will become wrong and, therefore, assumptions must be periodically challenged in order to stay ahead of the competition, then emotion and personal attachment to 'the way it's always been' is removed, silos are not so easy to maintain, and cooperation is much more possible.

As the leader, looking at the group from an aerial perspective rather than a detail perspective, you too will be able to see gaps in performance more easily. If people know the score and what is expected of them and how they'll be measured, they will be more secure in their position. This naturally tempers their *pessimistic and moody elephant* and allows them to self-correct along the way. Most people want to do a good job. They want to know that they've made a difference and are tracking well against their objectives. And if they are not, at least they, and you, have the information to hand to help rectify it before it becomes a problem. All of this helps you identify those things that remain for *you* to do, and allows you to step up, take the job and lead the people.

22

Overcoming the Elephant by Engineering Virtuous Circles

The foregoing six Business Laws of Nature, or operating protocols, are the characteristics of outstanding workgroups for the simple reason that they are antidotes to the challenges posed by your *elephant*. If I let you be the designer of your own process, that forces me to articulate exactly what my expectations are and allows you to confirm exactly what you perceive them to be. What's happened? Communication improved because we defined the meaning of the language we're using to explain what we want, what we will do and when we will do it. This establishes the same benchmarks or the same definitions for each of the bits of language. We have avoided the challenge to our thinking process brought on by the fact that our elephants are non-verbal and that language has no consistently, universally understood dictionary.

By using questions in this process, you are forcing the other person to describe exactly how they're going to accomplish the task at hand. You are both painting more of the picture together – making sure it is the same picture through the articulation of your wants and needs, thus raising your 'picture paints a thousand words' ratio from 70 to possibly 300 to 400, figuratively speaking, of course. Yet it has cost you no extra energy because it's the other person 'doing the doing' – they must explain how they anticipate doing it and then do it.

Making sure this process occurs not only ensures that you both understand the parameters and objectives of the project, but that you also have piece of mind knowing it will be done to your specification or at least to your standards. When someone specifically details how they will do something and are able to articulate that process to you, then chances are they really can do that task.

The second thing is that, as the business owner, if I don't have to do the job, I can have some objectivity about how it ought to be done. I'm also subjective, however, because when the business started, I probably was responsible for that task and therefore did it a certain way. For example, say I'm the business owner and you're the employee. There's a process that I want done and I have a certain point of view about how it should or could be done. I hire you do to the job because you have some experience in the area. What we now have is a mixture of subjectivity and objectivity in our respective minds. I'm subjective because there's a way I want it done, but I'm objective because I have the business's overriding responsibilities and profitability to deliver. So I'll have to be prepared to negotiate to some extent. You, on the other hand, have an objective view about the way my company does it because you weren't there when it was conceived. Then there are the subjective skills, knowledge and experience you bring to the role, based on your past experience. Often, when a new employee starts, they are so keen to make their mark that they want to introduce their own way before even testing the validity of the current way. However, if we bring those two points of view together in a constructive environment, we have a chance of negotiating the best possible way, rather than exclusively my way or your way.

This also means that default settings can be spotted more readily by the objective party, not left unchecked to circumvent accurate and productive thinking toward the ideal solution. This ensures that all the facts are gathered before emotion is added to the equation, if indeed it is ever added.

So when you align your behaviour to the Business Laws of Nature, you actually replicate the result normally reserved for smart thinking – you automatically bypass each and every one of the challenges you face due to your biological and genetic inheritance that stops or at least holds us back from our true potential.

Manage the beast and manage the questions

I remember going to see a client of mine whose company was about to go through an acquisition. He was excited and very animated about this new stage of his business. Not wanting to burst his bubble but also having an obligation to him as a client and friend, I asked if he had performed due diligence. Due diligence is nothing more than the process of checking to see that the business is what you think the business is.

My client, looking rather shocked at the question, told me they had done due diligence and, while he appreciated the question, the fact was the business he was about to buy belonged to a friend and colleague. My client, it turned out, had known the seller and his business for a long time. Apparently, he already had a fair degree of understanding about that company and a reasonable relationship with the owner.

My next question was, "Tell me, just out of interest, does that make the due diligence *more* important, or *less* important?"

I will never forget the look on his face when I asked that question. You could almost hear the cogs in his mind stopping dead in their tracks. I silently watched while the expression on his face changed as he realised the inescapable conclusion that, precisely because of his friendship and their history, due diligence became not just vital but imperative.

The really scary part was that, at that exact same moment, I realised I had made the exact same error of treating an acquisition in exactly the same way as my client six months prior to this very meeting. My company had acquired a business and our due diligence had been less than ruthless because we knew and trusted the business owner. I remember, to this day, the moment I realised my mistake. I felt physically sick at what I had done. That was the biggest, most expensive and most painful business mistake I ever made. If you get nothing else from this book, please get this: the right question is *everything*. I could have avoided my mistake. I should have avoided it. But I was in it and no one with an objective viewpoint was there to ask me the right questions.

My client was luckier. He had a coach and, prompted by the above dialogue, decided to go into extensive, impartial and thorough due diligence. Strangely enough, once the due diligence process started, the 'friend' who was the seller, elected not to sell the company to my client but sold it to somebody else who was left to later discover some of the hidden challenges in that company.

The right question saved a fortune. The right question saved agony. The right question avoided unnecessary energy being wasted.

One question can make or break a business. One question can make or break a relationship. One question can make or break an experiment. One question, at the right time, is everything.

The danger we face is presuming that finding the right question is some sort of liquid piece of creativity – that if we have the right experience in the right background at the right moment, the right question will indeed emerge.

That may indeed be the case, but finding the right question usually occurs six months, six weeks, six hours, or six minutes after you need it. Rarely do we find the right question at the right time unless we are trained to do so. The point is, if we think about the outcomes we hope to accomplish – and they are all definable and can reasonably be determined before the endeavour begins – then we can distil a right set of questions to ask before we even start the journey.

It shouldn't surprise people that businesses fail. It should surprise people that businesses succeed.

When someone originally goes into business, often the first service they will reach for to guide him or her through the process is an accountant. This is a logical decision, considering that accountants must have seen every conceivable mistake that business had or could or will ever make. Yet the reality is their clients keep making mistakes.

But there is a *formula*, a powerful tool, for avoiding those pitfalls. Learning to use that tool will help you avoid the errors others have made. Showing how to do so has been a major motivator for writing this book. There is a natural and obvious set of questions that needs to be attached to every decision that anyone ever makes, and those questions are business *thinking systems*.

> There really is no excuse for repeating errors, for making mistakes that others have already made, because there is a formula for avoiding pitfalls.

What we've been able to identify, working with thousands of workgroups, is that there is one best set of questions to apply to every situation or challenge. You can significantly reduce or eliminate errors in business and significantly improve the quality of business performance by the application of these *thinking systems*.

Accountants get paid, even when people make mistakes, so there's significant cover for them as they watch the accidents happen. Business coaches give you the map to help you avoid the mistake in the first place.

There will be a future, I promise you, when people will decide to go into business and the first ally they will search for will not be an accountant – it will be a business coach. Join the ranks of the smart business thinkers and get yourself a coach.

Good luck, and remember: life in business is a long journey, not an overnighter, so pack carefully . . .

About the Authors

John Vamos

Some time ago, John concluded that well-crafted questions were the key to closing the gap between an organisation's current performance and its full potential.

"The quality of the question determines the quality of the thought that it provokes and, as a result, the quality of the solution to the challenges facing business."

Over the past 15 years, the founder and Managing Director of Business Coaching Systems has crafted suites of purpose-designed and rigorously tested questions able to produce pure business solutions for clients, by clients. These questions now form the essence of John's *Thinking Systems*, which have effectively removed barriers to success for a wide range of firms.

"Unlike executive coaching, we do not borrow your business to train and improve your people," says John. "Instead, we borrow your people to help them transform your business." This is one of the many strategies that have contributed to the effective change management practices BCS clients are currently engaged in.

In short, John Vamos facilitates businesses to generate and manage change by providing them with the skills to work with stakeholders and ensure that everyone is working toward a common achievable vision and set of goals.

With absolute faith in his methodology and, more importantly, bottom line proof of its success, John recently established an Institute of Organisational Coaching. The Institute is providing others with the skills to deliver his unique approach to strategic planning, organisational change management, operational planning, performance management and executive coaching.

Recently, BCS partnered the University of Technology, Sydney in a groundbreaking research project about business coaching which provided qualitative and quantitative insights into the practice of coaching in organisations, leading to valuable information about much needed professional standards for the industry.

While his work with giant multinationals is recognised globally, he has long maintained a strong interest in SMEs, particularly family-run businesses that seek to reap the rewards of sometimes decades of hard work.

"Our thinking system methodology can ensure that SMEs enjoy the discipline and the benefits of a global company without sacrificing the character and the culture that makes an entrepreneurial family firm an appealing environment in which to succeed," John says.

In the foreword to this book, Professor Stewart Clegg of Sydney's University of Technology said, "What the book provides is a way of unlocking all the taken-for-granted and tacit knowledge, the constitutive grounds that we all already have but either don't recognise or know about, yet implicitly trade off in our everyday business life".

John is an active member of the International Coaching Federation and sits on the boards of companies in the financial services, management services, and hospitality industries. He is highly regarded for the courage and confidence that he readily instils in client companies and is best summed up in an end-of-year assessment prepared by one of those clients.

"Our business is celebrating an extraordinarily successful year. Our Leadership Team recognises that their first priority is the group. Key Performance Indicators (KPIs) ensure that responsibility for implementation is unmistakably clear. Our employees are motivated by the opportunity for success, not the fear of failure. They want to come to work tomorrow." The date on the report is 2012. With guidance from John, the client company has a clear grasp on where it is going, how it is going to get there, and of the rewards that lie at the end of the journey.

Karen McCreadie

Karen McCreadie is an author and professional ghost writer, specialising in non-fiction books. She has written more than 25 books, including an international bestseller and a TV tie-in for Channel Seven. She has also written a specialist e-publication called *How to Write a Book in 33 Days!* This book is aimed at those people who are seeking to create the ultimate business card – a book! Being an author creates powerful business development opportunities and can be an extremely efficient way to market a business.

As a ghost writer, Karen writes for CEOs, business leaders, international speakers, professional services personnel and entrepreneurs who have something worthwhile to share, but do not necessarily have the time to spend translating their ideas into a polished manuscript. After 10 years in Australia, Karen is now based in the UK but due to the wonders of modern technology, works with clients in the UK, the US, Canada and Australia and is very happy to count many of her past and present clients as friends – especially John Vamos. For more information, please visit www.wordarchitect.com

Bibliography and Notes

1. Clegg, S. R., Rhodes, C., Kornberger, M., Stilin, R. (2005) 'Business coaching: challenges for an emerging industry', *Industrial and Commercial Training*, 37(5): 218–223.
2. Clegg, S. R., Rhodes, C., and Kornberger, M. (2007) 'Desperately Seeking Legitimacy: Organizational Identity and Emerging Industries, *Organization Studies* 28, 4: 495–513.
3. Nicholas Carr, "*Is Google making us stupid?*", The Australian, June 2008.
4. The title of presentations – printed booklets by: J Vamos and K McCreadie, 2002.
5. Donald Hebb, "The organization of behavior", New York: Wiley, 1949.
6. Jonathan Haidt, Professor, Department of Psychology, University of Virginia.
7. Jonathan Haidt, "*The Happiness Hypothesis: Finding Modern Truth in Ancient Wisdom*", 2006.
8. The *rider*, or *jockey*, metaphorically represent your seeming dominance of your conscious thinking over the subconscious 'thoughts'.
9. *Subconscious* mind is *the elephant* in the metaphor.
10. *Conscious* mind is your conscious self.
11. Evan H Walker "*The Physics of Consciousness: The Quantum Mind and the Meaning of Life*", 2000.
12. Bruce H Lipton, "*Biology of Belief: Unleashing the Power of Consciousness, Matter and Miracles*", Elite Books, 2005, pg 97.
13. Norman Doidge, "*The Brain that Changed Itself*", Scribe Publications, 2007.
14. Joe Dispenza, "*Evolve your Brain – the Science of Changing Your Mind*", 2007.
15. Dispenza, op cit pg 41.
16. Dispenza, op cit pgs 106–107; John Ratey, "*A User's Guide to the Brain*", Little, Brown, 2001, pg 10.
17. Edward O. Wilson, "*Consilience*", Little, Brown 1998, pgs 280 and 211.

BIBLIOGRAPHY AND NOTES

18. Doidge, op cit pgs 293–294. Also see paper at website: http://www.sciencedaily.com/releases/2008/06/080608131209.htm
19. Robin Dunbar, Louise Barrett and John Lycett, "*Evolutionary Psychology*", 2007 pgs 113–114.
20. Dispenza, cp cit pg 68.
21. For a 'picture' of the brain see Dispenza, Op Cit pg 112.
22. Dispenza, op cit pgs 118–119.
23. E H. Walker, op cit. Also M Csikszentmihalyi "*Flow*" Sydney lecture, 17 March 1999.
24. Nigel Nicholson, London Business School: "*How Hardwired is Human Behaviour*", Harvard Business Review.
25. N Nicholson op cit.
26. Dispenza, op cit 258–259.
27. B Lipton, *op cit, Chapter 6*.
28. N Nicholson, op cit.
29. N Nicholson, op cit.
30. John Ratey, "*A User's Guide to the Brain*", Little, Brown, 2001 pg 30.
31. http://en.wikipedia.org/wiki/Gerald_Edelman
32. E O Wilson, op cit pg 173 and Chapter 7.
33. J LeDoux, "*The Emotional Brain – the Mysterious Underpinnings of Emotional Life*", Simon & Schuster, 1996.
34. D Goleman, "*Emotional Intelligence – Why it Can Matter More than IQ*", 1995 pgs 15–17.
35. Martin Lindstrom "*buy-OLOGY*", Random House 2008, p112.
36. B H Lipton, op cit p131.
37. Steven Pinker, "*The Stuff of Thought*", Penguin Books, 2008 pgs 77–83.
38. Bill Bryson "*Mother Tongue*" 1990, pg 3.
39. Ray L Birdwhistell: "*Kinesics and Context* – Essays on Body Motion Communication", Philadelphia, University of Pennsylvania Press, *1970*.
40. N Nicholson op cit.
41. N Nicholson op cit; Article also referencing Paul Ekman, "*Emotions Revealed: Recognizing Faces and Feelings to Improve Communication and Emotional Life*".
42. N Nicholson op cit.
43. N Nicholson op cit.
44. T Moore: "*Utopia*" ca. 1516.
45. Website: http://datasearch2.uts.edu.au/cmos/projects/detail.cfm?ProjectId=2003000451
46. Centre for Creative Leadership, Website http://www.ccl.org/leadership/pdf/publications/lia/lia24_6knowing.pdf
47. The explanations and examples in *Parts Three and Four* show how behaviours based on the *Thinking System* methodology are more effective and lead to more positive results.

48 Ratey, op cit pg 87.
49 B Bryson, "*A short history of just about everything*" 2005, pg 46.
50 Arthur Koestler, "The Act of Creation" (Google by author's name and work).
51 B Bryson, op cit pg 467.
52 Robert K Merton *"Social Theory and Social Structure"*, 1949, pg 185.
53 Marcus Buckingham & Curt Coffman: "*First Break all the Rules: What the World's Greatest Managers do Differently*", 1999. pg 11.
54 John R Searle, "*Minds, brains, and programs*", Behavioral and Brain Sciences 3 (3): 417–457, 1980.
55 Kurt Vonnegut Jr "*Hocus Pocus*", Jonathan Cape, 1990, also quoted on website *http://blogs.myspace.com/index.cfm?fuseaction=blog.view&friendID=54487172&blogID=349140536*
56 Ratey, op cit pgs 20–21.
57 John von Neumann quoted in "*Holographic Universe*" by Michael Talbot, 1996 pg 21.

Index

A
Action xi, 150
A simple thinking system 132, 133, 152, 156, 157
Australian Research Council 111
    Grant 111
    UTS Research Project 111

B
BCS iii, x, xi, 104, 111, 142, 149, 185, 186, 263, 264
BCS Coach xi
BCS Coaches iii, xi
BCS Eight Steps to Perfect Business Strategies 185
BCS Four Steps to Perfect Personal Performance 39
Binary thinking 121, 122, 123, 130, 131, 148
Biology 10, 31, 61, 266
Body language 89, 90, 91, 97
Brain 28, 31, 53, 256
    amygdala 69, 70, 78, 79, 81
    biology 114, 195
    elastic 28, 31, 53, 256
    hardwired 101, 102, 267
Brain science 109
Business
    core functions 39, 106, 116
    miracle of 116

Business Coaching viii, x, xi, 38, 111, 112, 185, 188, 263
Business Coaching Systems x, xi, 112, 185, 188, 263
Business impact 73
Business Laws of Nature i, ii, 11, 13, 14, 102, 193, 198, 199, 200, 201, 219, 237, 246, 247, 248, 256, 258, 260
Business Owners x
Business thinking systems 138, 148, 167, 178, 262

C
Carr, Nicholas xiv, 266
Chinese room 194, 195
Classification 53, 54, 58
Classification before calculus 58
Clegg, Stewart (Professor) vii, 112, 264
Coaches iii, xi, 142
Coaching ii, viii, x, xi, 38, 111, 112, 185, 188, 263, 264
    facilitation 186
Conclusions vs decisions 209
Conscious mind 9, 10, 11, 81

D
Darwinism
    modern 53, 58
    neural 53, 58

Default settings
   automatic 51, 52, 53, 57, 63
   genetic 51, 52, 53, 57, 63
Default settings 66
Delegation 246
Diagnosis thinking system 206
Dispenza, Joe (D.C.) 34, 266
Doidge, Norman 266

E
Edison, Thomas A. 74, 75, 76, 167, 241
Elephant 15, 27, 36, 46, 47, 59, 65, 80, 99, 104, 120, 258
   isn't verbal 80
   lazy 51, 52, 53, 55, 56, 57, 63
   metaphor ii, 12, 13, 15
   moody 77
   unqualified for business 99
Emotion 65, 66, 68, 70, 71, 74, 76, 78, 79, 143
Ethnomethodology vii, viii
Evolution 30
Evolutionary psychology 53, 58, 66, 78, 99, 100

F
Facilitation 186
Freud, Sigmund 66, 78
Frontal lobe ix, 10, 30, 31, 32, 33, 35, 63, 81, 89, 97, 155, 156, 161, 175, 190, 204, 212, 227

G
Gap problem 2, 13
Garfinkel, Harold vii
Gossip 62, 64, 100, 102
Gossiping 62, 64

H
Haidt, Jonathan (Professor) 8, 11, 266
Hebb's Model 7, 56
Hidden communication 81, 89

I
Ideas 129

J
Jung, Carl Gustav 66, 78

K
Knowledge Gap 18, 24, 25, 26

L
Language has no universal dictionary 81
Law of Association 7
Leader behaviour 245
Leadership 114, 246, 248, 249, 254, 265, 267
   effective 248
   things leaders do 251
Leaders, Workgroup ii, x, xi, 133, 134, 232
Lego 215, 216
Le Prince, Augustine 74, 75, 76, 167, 168, 241
Limbic system 30, 69, 70, 78, 81
Limbic System 30, 69, 78, 81
Limitations
   body language 89, 90, 91, 97
   language 80, 81, 83, 86, 95, 96, 98
Lipton, Bruce H. 10, 11, 61, 81, 266, 267

M
Managers x, 268
Managing thinking 204
Manipulating 72
McCreadie, Karen i, ii, x, 265
Metaphor 8, 15
Midbrain 29, 30, 34
Motivational
   industry 72
   speakers 72

N
Neo-cortex 29, 30, 34
Neuropsychology 53, 58
Nicholson, Nigel 101, 102, 267

O
Objectivity 145
Organisational Coaching ii, 264

P
Performance Gap 18, 23, 24, 26, 36, 109, 110, 115, 117
Personal Development 72, 79
Picture paints a thousand words 81, 87, 88, 97, 258
Protocol 82, 91, 200, 229

Q
Questioning
    Horizontal Sequential Questioning 170, 172, 173
    Vertical Sequential Questioning 170
Questions 160, 161, 162, 164, 165, 167, 168, 170, 173, 175, 176, 212
    build rapport 173
    drive our thinking 160, 161, 162, 164, 165, 167, 168, 170, 173, 175, 176, 212

R
Ratey, John 67, 122, 227, 266, 267, 268
reptilian
    Brain 30, 81

S
Staff Value Deficiency 37, 38, 43
Subconscious mind 266

Subjectivity 122, 123, 124, 130, 139, 144, 174, 259
SWOT 114, 115

T
Talent 251
Talking backwards 206
Template
    for diagnosing any problem 178, 184
The Australianzzz xiv, 266
The facilitation concept 186
The five stages of an idea 127, 128
The Thinking System xv, 121, 132, 142, 150, 153, 159
Thinking
    limitations 46, 195
    smart 6, 8, 46, 120, 121, 141, 178, 190, 200, 260
    structured 73, 79, 108, 201, 233
    systems iii, viii, 153, 156, 157, 159, 167, 178, 192, 210, 263

U
University of Technology, Sydney
    School of Management vii, viii, 112, 264

V
Vamos, John i, ii, vii, viii, x, 263, 265
Vicious circles 196
Virtuous circles 196, 198, 199, 203, 258

W
Workgroup ii, x, xi, 133, 134, 232
Workgroups xi, 37, 38, 39, 41, 105, 137, 179, 181, 190, 192, 194, 199, 201, 208, 216, 222, 224, 231, 239, 258, 262

www.ingramcontent.com/pod-product-compliance
Lightning Source LLC
Chambersburg PA
CBHW060113170426
43198CB00010B/872